# THE SPEYSIDE WAY
## WITH THE DAVA WAY AND MORAY COAST TRAIL

**About the Author**

Alan has trekked and cycled in over 30 countries within Europe, Asia, North and South America, Africa and Australasia, and for 17 years led organised walking holidays in several European countries. A member of the British Outdoor Writers and Photographers Guild, he has written 18 guidebooks, including the Cicerone guide to the Southern Upland Way. His longer solo walks include a Grand Traverse of the European Alps between Nice and Vienna (1510 miles), the E2 across Europe from Holland to the Mediterranean (1400 miles), the Pilgrim's Trail from Le Puy to Finisterre (960 miles), the Via de la Plata from Seville to Santiago de Compostela (620 miles) and a Coast-to-Coast across the French Pyrenees (540 miles). In Britain he has walked all of the National Trails, as well as many other long distance routes. Alan is also an enthusiastic hillwalker who has climbed many of the British hills, including all of the Munros in Scotland. An erstwhile National Secretary of the Long Distance Walkers Association, Alan lives at the foot of the Moffat Hills, in the heart of the Scottish Southern Uplands.

#### Other Cicerone guides by the author

*Walks In Volcano Country*
  *(Auvergne and Velay, France)*
*Walking the French Gorges*
  *(Provence and the Ardèche)*
*Walking the The River Rhine Trail*
*Walking in Bedfordshire*
*The John Muir Trail*
*The Southern Upland Way*
*The Robert Louis Stevenson Trail*
  *(Cévennes, France)*
*The Tour of the Queyras*
  *(French & Italian Alps)*
*The Grand Traverse of the Massif Central*
*Alan also wrote the first and second editions of The Corsican High Level Route and A Pyrenean Trail (GR10).*

# THE SPEYSIDE WAY
## WITH THE DAVA WAY AND MORAY COAST TRAIL
### by
### Alan Castle

2 POLICE SQUARE, MILNTHORPE, CUMBRIA LA7 7PY
www.cicerone.co.uk

© Alan Castle 2010
First edition 2010
ISBN: 978 185284 606 0
All photographs by the author, unless otherwise stated
A catalogue record for this book is available from the British Library.
Printed by KHL Printing, Singapore

*For Mum Cain*

'My heart's in the Highlands, wherever I go.'
'Freedom and whisky gang thegither!'
*Robert Burns (1759–1796)*

'May the road rise up to meet you,
may the wind be always at your back,
may the sun shine warm upon your face;
the rains fall soft upon your fields
and until we meet again,
may God hold you in the palm of his hand.'
*Traditional Gaelic blessing*

### Acknowledgements

My wife, Beryl, has always given freely of her advice, support and encouragement during the planning and writing of my guidebooks. For this book she has also carried out a considerable amount of research, without which it could not have been written, and I am ever grateful. My thanks to Jim Strachan, Speyside Way Manager, for his help and encouragement and for reading the book proofs. Norman Thomson, Chairman of the Moray Way Association, gave me much information on the Dava Way, Moray Coast Trail and Moray Way. Thanks also to Pete Mitchell and David Binney of the Dava Way Association and to Ian Douglas, Moray Access Manager. Finally, I thank Jonathan Williams and others at Cicerone Press for their professionalism in publishing this and all my guidebooks.

### Advice to Readers

While every effort is made by our authors to ensure the accuracy of guidebooks as they go to print, changes can occur during the lifetime of an edition. Please check this book's Updates page on our website (www.cicerone.co.uk) before planning your trip. It would be wise also to check information about transport, accommodation and facilities locally. We are always grateful for information about any changes you discover, sent by email to info@cicerone.co.uk or by post to Cicerone, 2 Police Square, Milnthorpe LA7 7PY, United Kingdom.

*Front cover:* General Wade's Military Road above the Spey near Newtonmore

# CONTENTS

**INTRODUCTION** . . . . . . . . . . . . . . . . . . . . . . . . . . . . . . . . . . . . . . . . . . . . . . . . 9
The official trails of Speyside and Moray. . . . . . . . . . . . . . . . . . . . . . . . . . 10
The routes in this guidebook. . . . . . . . . . . . . . . . . . . . . . . . . . . . . . . . . . . 15
The River Spey . . . . . . . . . . . . . . . . . . . . . . . . . . . . . . . . . . . . . . . . . . . . . . 18
When to walk. . . . . . . . . . . . . . . . . . . . . . . . . . . . . . . . . . . . . . . . . . . . . . . 22
Which direction to walk . . . . . . . . . . . . . . . . . . . . . . . . . . . . . . . . . . . . . . 26
Suggested longer routes . . . . . . . . . . . . . . . . . . . . . . . . . . . . . . . . . . . . . . 27
Suggested day walks. . . . . . . . . . . . . . . . . . . . . . . . . . . . . . . . . . . . . . . . . 28
Mountain biking and horse riding. . . . . . . . . . . . . . . . . . . . . . . . . . . . . . . 29
Getting there . . . . . . . . . . . . . . . . . . . . . . . . . . . . . . . . . . . . . . . . . . . . . . . 31
Public transport . . . . . . . . . . . . . . . . . . . . . . . . . . . . . . . . . . . . . . . . . . . . . 31
Accommodation. . . . . . . . . . . . . . . . . . . . . . . . . . . . . . . . . . . . . . . . . . . . . 32
Campsites and wild camping . . . . . . . . . . . . . . . . . . . . . . . . . . . . . . . . . . 33
Refreshments . . . . . . . . . . . . . . . . . . . . . . . . . . . . . . . . . . . . . . . . . . . . . . . 35
Tourist information . . . . . . . . . . . . . . . . . . . . . . . . . . . . . . . . . . . . . . . . . . 36
What to take. . . . . . . . . . . . . . . . . . . . . . . . . . . . . . . . . . . . . . . . . . . . . . . . 36
Maps . . . . . . . . . . . . . . . . . . . . . . . . . . . . . . . . . . . . . . . . . . . . . . . . . . . . . 38
Navigation and waymarking. . . . . . . . . . . . . . . . . . . . . . . . . . . . . . . . . . . 40
Walking in Scotland . . . . . . . . . . . . . . . . . . . . . . . . . . . . . . . . . . . . . . . . . 42
Using this guide . . . . . . . . . . . . . . . . . . . . . . . . . . . . . . . . . . . . . . . . . . . . 44

**THE SPEYSIDE WAY – SOURCE TO SEA**. . . . . . . . . . . . . . . . . . . . . . . . . 47
PROLOGUE. . . . . . . . . . . . . . . . . . . . . . . . . . . . . . . . . . . . . . . . . . . . . . . . 49
BADENOCH WAY AND LINKS . . . . . . . . . . . . . . . . . . . . . . . . . . . . . . . . 83

SPEYSIDE WAY. . . . . . . . . . . . . . . . . . . . . . . . . . . . . . . . . . . . . . . . . . . . . 99
Stage 1  Aviemore to Boat of Garten. . . . . . . . . . . . . . . . . . . . . . . . . . 104
Stage 2  Boat of Garten to Nethy Bridge . . . . . . . . . . . . . . . . . . . . . . . 107
Stage 3  Nethy Bridge to Grantown-on-Spey. . . . . . . . . . . . . . . . . . . . 111
Stage 4  Grantown-on-Spey to Cromdale . . . . . . . . . . . . . . . . . . . . . . 115
Stage 5  Cromdale to Ballindalloch station . . . . . . . . . . . . . . . . . . . . . 118
Stage 6  Ballindalloch station to Aberlour. . . . . . . . . . . . . . . . . . . . . . 123
Stage 7  Aberlour to Craigellachie . . . . . . . . . . . . . . . . . . . . . . . . . . . 127
Stage 8  Craigellachie to Fochabers . . . . . . . . . . . . . . . . . . . . . . . . . . 129
Stage 9  Fochabers to Spey Bay. . . . . . . . . . . . . . . . . . . . . . . . . . . . . . 134
Stage 10 Spey Bay to Buckie . . . . . . . . . . . . . . . . . . . . . . . . . . . . . . . . 137

| | | |
|---|---|---|
| TOMINTOUL SPUR | | 141 |
| DUFFTOWN LOOP | | 157 |
| **DAVA WAY** | | 165 |
| **MORAY COAST TRAIL** | | 181 |
| **APPENDIX A** | Route summary table | 215 |
| **APPENDIX B** | Useful contacts | 217 |
| **APPENDIX C** | Further reading | 219 |
| **APPENDIX D** | Whisky production and Speyside distilleries | 220 |

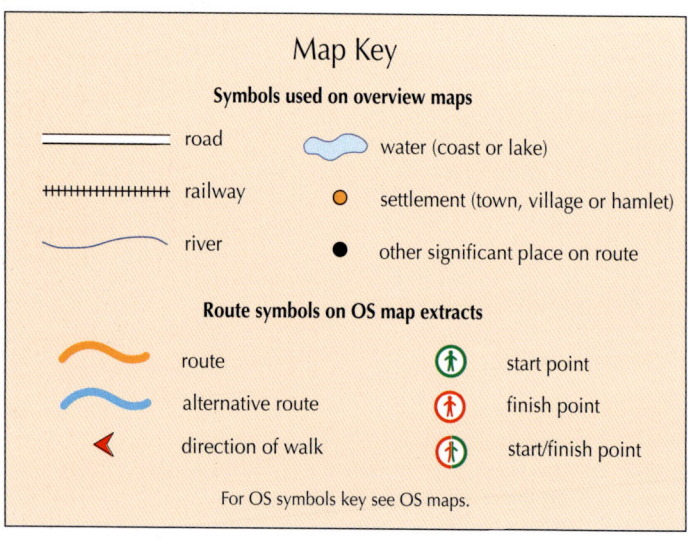

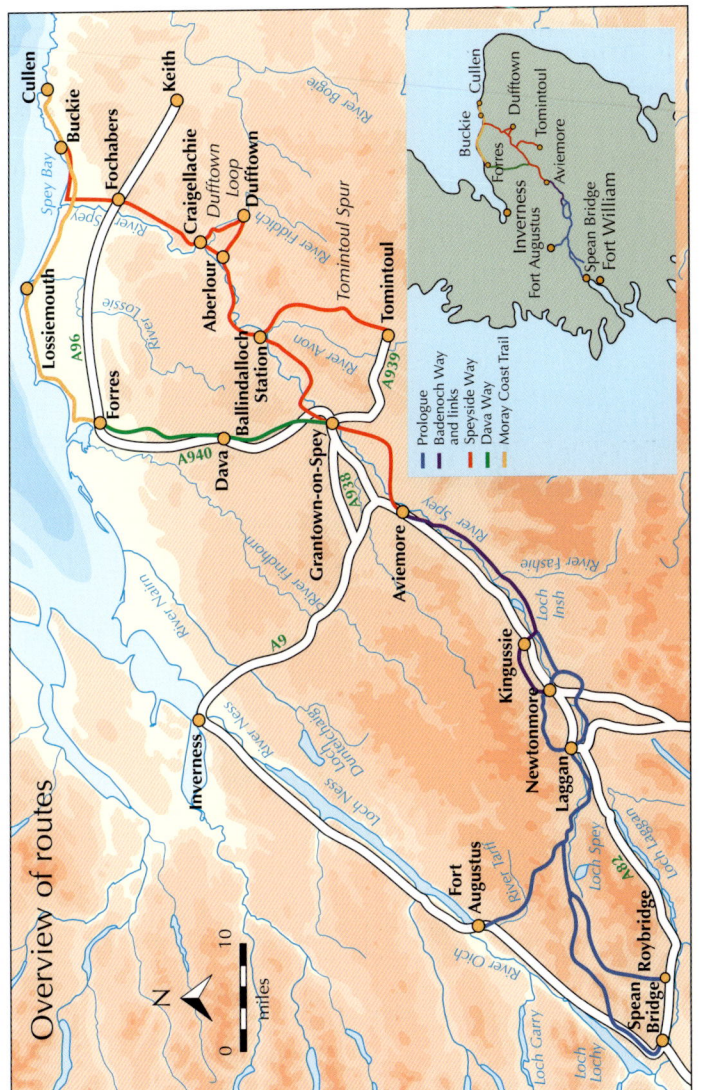

*A walker on the Speyside Way passing through Anagach Wood*

# INTRODUCTION

This guide focuses on the Speyside Way, one of Scotland's official Long Distance Routes, which follows the course of the beautiful River Spey from the edge of the mighty Cairngorm mountains at Aviemore, many miles downstream from its source, to Buckie on the Moray Firth. At only 66 miles in length, the main route of the Speyside Way is feasible for most walkers, even those of modest ability and ambition. But the guide also describes several other trails in Speyside and Moray that can be walked in their own right or linked to the Speyside Way to create longer and very varied routes through some of the region's best countryside.

Together, the trails take walkers from the rugged mountain landscape near the source of the Spey to Spey Bay, where the mighty river empties into the ocean, and the guide is unique in describing a route along the Spey from 'source to sea'.

The source of the Spey lies in the heart of a mountain and moorland wilderness in the huge upland range of the Monadhliath, to the west-south-west of Newtonmore. Wayfarers for centuries have been following routes through the remote upland glens of these mountains and over connecting passes. Although these documented trails, by their very nature and

The track winds through desolate Upper Glen Roy (Prologue)

*The Speyside Way*

location, are not part of the official Speyside Way, they do allow the experienced modern-day long distance hiker inroads into these hills and to the very source of the Spey itself.

The guide also includes the Dava Way and Moray Coast Trail, so describing all the major and linking long distance routes in this region of Scotland. The three trails are each quite different in character and complement each other well – a valley and riverside walk, a ramble along a famous disused railway line and finally a coastal walk on one of the finest stretches of coast in the UK.

The trails in Speyside and Moray have something for all types of rambler, from the seasoned long distance walker to the day stroller in the countryside, from the complete novice and those of limited walking ability to the experienced hillwalker and fit backpacker. Moreover, cyclists and horse riders can also use many sections of these trails, which provide safe, traffic-free routes. And this guide describes it all!

### THE OFFICIAL TRAILS OF SPEYSIDE AND MORAY

### The Speyside Way

The Speyside Way is one of the four official Long Distance Routes (LDRs) in Scotland, which are equivalent to the National Trails of England and Wales. Being so designated, it is waymarked throughout its length with a

*An official Speyside Way sign*

distinctive white Scottish thistle, as are the other three such trails in Scotland – the West Highland Way, Great Glen Way and the Southern Upland Way. Unlike many of the official long distance paths in Britain, the Speyside Way offers relatively easy walking, mainly on well-surfaced and easily graded tracks and paths, with relatively little total ascent and descent.

A couple of branch routes of the Speyside Way allow optional starting points for the trail, as well as providing walks of quite a different character to that of the main route along the Spey valley. Hillwalkers will enjoy the **Tomintoul Spur**, 15 miles on good paths across the hills from the highest village in the Highlands to join the main route of the Speyside Way at Ballindalloch station, a route that also allows a visit to the famous Glenlivet

Distillery along the way. Possibly the most well known of all the Speyside distilleries, Glenfiddich, is visited on the **Dufftown Loop**, a detour of the Speyside Way via Glen Fiddich and the whisky town of Dufftown.

Beautiful landscape, nature and wildlife, history both recent and ancient, and whisky combine to make The Speyside Way such a splendid trail. Speyside is undoubtedly one of the most beautiful areas of Scotland, a diverse landscape of mountain, heath and moorland, mixed deciduous woodland, conifer plantations, wide river valley and rich alluvial farmland. The neighbouring Moray coast, the southern boundary of the Moray Firth, exhibits a variety of coastal landscapes, from wide sandy beaches and extensive sand dunes backed by mixed coastal forest, to sandstone cliffs and dramatic rocky headlands, rock arches and sea stacks.

It is not surprising, therefore, that the region has a rich and varied wildlife. It is the place to come to see some of Britain's rarest but most endearing creatures, notably otters, pine martens, red squirrels and ospreys. Herds of red deer roam the mountains and glens, whilst the smaller roe deer make their home in the lowlands. Because the habitat is so mixed, so too is the birdlife. Raptors such as buzzards and falcons are common in the skies, and the lucky and observant may spot the iconic golden eagle, riding the high thermals above desolate moorland. Heron lift gracefully from burns and wetlands, dippers bob along on the waterways, and

*The meandering River Calder in Glen Banchor, north-west of Newtonmore (Prologue)*

songbirds aplenty are seen and heard in the many hedgerows that line the trails and in the abundant mixed woodlands. Along the Moray coast are found all manner of seabirds – fulmars, cormorants, shags, guillemots, gulls and more – and plenty of marine mammals, including large colonies of seals, and whale and dolphin pods.

Speyside and Moray are areas steeped in history, the land of the ancient Picts, a Celtic race that vanished in the ninth century AD, but who left behind evidence of their lives in a number of archaeological remains, from Pictish forts to elaborately decorated standing stones. The Jacobite campaigns of the 17th and 18th centuries have also left their mark on the landscape in the form of battlefields, old troop barracks and expertly constructed roads to aid military troop and supply movements.

In more recent times the great Victorian railway network penetrated the region, its lines connecting remote communities and bringing the first tourists from far afield to discover and delight in the beauties of this corner of Scotland. Today, the majority of these railways have closed, but fortunately many miles of trackbed have been rescued and converted into excellent pathways for walkers, cyclists and horse riders. There are probably few other areas of the UK where so many miles of disused railway tracks have been opened up for recreational use. Both the Speyside Way and Dava Way explore many miles of these old lines, and the Speyside Way even gives an opportunity to visit one of the country's most popular steam railways, the Strathspey Railway between Aviemore and Boat of Garten.

The peaty terrain over which the River Spey and its tributaries flow gives a character to their waters which is perfect for the production of whisky. The 'water of life' has been distilled in these valleys, often illicitly, for many centuries, long before the commercial distilleries made Speyside famous throughout the world for its single malt whisky. The Speyside distilleries are perhaps the best known of the Scottish whisky distilleries, with such household names as Glenfiddich and Glenlivet. Both of these celebrated distilleries and many others can be visited for their tours and tastings whilst walking the Speyside Way and its associated trails (see Appendix D).

It has long been the hope that the Speyside Way would be extended upriver from Aviemore back to Newtonmore. In 2009 the Scottish government approved such an extension in principle, but it will be several years before this becomes a reality. Monies have still to be committed and many processes undertaken, possibly including a public enquiry, before any work on the construction of the route can begin. The work was being progressed by the Cairngorms National Park, with a completion estimate of 2014. It is eagerly awaited not only by long distance walkers, but also by

*Ruthven Barracks complex near Kingussie (Badenoch Way)*

many in Newtonmore, where arrival of the official trail is likely to boost the local economy.

### The Badenoch Way
The Badenoch Way is an excellent 12½ mile trail that stretches along Strathspey from near Ruthven Barracks outside Kingussie, through the internationally renowned Insh Marshes National Nature Reserve, passing picturesque Loch Insh and following the River Spey for a short distance before crossing Dalraddy Moor to terminate on the B9152 just under 4 miles from Aviemore.

### The Dava Way
In recent years, the long distance path network in Scotland has developed considerably. Perhaps this is nowhere better seen than in the Moray region, where a couple of excellent initiatives have led to the establishment of two quite different medium-length trails, the Dava Way and the Moray Coast Trail (below), that perfectly complement the Speyside Way and allow a number of walking routes to be devised to suit walkers' differing interests and landscape preferences. The Dava Way (25 miles/40km) leaves the Speyside Way at Grantown-on-Spey to travel northwards on a disused railway line all the way to the elegant little Moray town of Forres. This trail is not only a mecca for railway buffs, but also offers a tranquil and easy walk through charming countryside and, for cyclists, offers the best and longest stretch of off-road biking in the district.

### The Moray Coast Trail
Forres, where the Dava Way ends, is also the starting point of the Moray Coast Trail (MCT). The MCT heads first along the huge bay at Findhorn, home to both massive colonies of seabirds and the latest military jets of

## THE SPEYSIDE WAY

*Coastal caves near Covesea (Moray Coast Trail)*

nearby RAF Kinloss. From Findhorn it heads eastwards along the southern coast of the Moray Firth, on a route that links all the coastal settlements of Moray district, through a rich variety of coastal landscapes to finish, after nearly 50 miles, at the village of Cullen. On this journey it crosses the Speyside Way near Spey Bay.

Thus it is possible to undertake a walking route of just under 100 miles on a 'triangular' route using parts of the Speyside Way, Dava Way and MCT, this route being known as the Moray Way.

### The Moray Way

The Moray Way (95 miles/153km) is a new circular, long distance route that uses sections of the three long distance trails in the Moray region – the Speyside Way, Dava Way and MCT. Signposting with a distinctive Moray Way waymark should be complete by 2011, and a good schematic map of the route was produced in 2010. Developed by the Moray Way Association, this circular trail can be started at the most convenient point and followed in either a clockwise or an anti-clockwise direction.

From Grantown-on-Spey the Moray Way follows the Dava Way in its entirety, northwards to Forres, and then the MCT eastwards along the southern shore of the Moray Firth until the Speyside Way is encountered at Garmouth Junction, just after the viaduct over the River Spey near Spey Bay. The main route of the Speyside Way is then followed south-westwards back to Grantown.

## THE ROUTES IN THIS GUIDEBOOK

| The official trails of Speyside and Moray | | |
|---|---|---|
| Badenoch Way | Kingussie to Dalraddy | 12½ miles/20km |
| Speyside Way: main route | Aviemore to Buckie | 66 miles/106km |
| Speyside Way: via Tomintoul Spur | Tomintoul to Buckie | 50 miles/80km |
| Dava Way | Grantown-on-Spey to Forres | 25 miles/40km |
| Moray Coast Trail | Forres to Cullen | 47 miles/76km |
| Moray Way | Grantown-on-Spey via Forres, Garmouth and Aberlour, using the DW and sections of the SW and MCT | 95 miles/153km |

### THE ROUTES IN THIS GUIDEBOOK

This guidebook features all the official trails in Speyside and Moray, as outlined above, and in addition describes other linking routes that together can be used to create a trail from the source of the River Spey to the sea on the Moray Firth. The major part of this trail is comprised of the Speyside Way from Aviemore to Buckie, but the sections further from the coast make use of a number of unofficial routes, many of which have been used for centuries by drovers, armies and others making their way through these Highland glens and over the region's remote and windswept mountain country. The major difference between these routes and the official trails is that the former are largely unwaymarked, so experience with a map and compass is essential for anyone using them. The source of the River Spey lies in the heart of a mountain wilderness, far from permanent habitation, and getting there requires considerable effort and some experience in trekking in such country.

Three alternative routes are described to the source in the **Prologue** – two from the west, from Roybridge (Stage 1) and from Spean Bridge (Stage 1A), and one from Fort Augustus in the north (Stage 1B). All of them are long and more suited to the hardy backpacker than to the inexperienced day rambler. But a short side trip, a 14-mile 'there and back' walk from the end of a public road at Garva Bridge, is also included in the Prologue for those who would like to visit the source but who don't wish to make a long trek across the mountains to reach it (transport may be required to Garva Bridge). All these

## THE SPEYSIDE WAY

*The footbridge over Conglass Water soon after leaving Tomintoul (Tomintoul Spur)*

upland trails converge at Garva Bridge and continue as one to the small village of Laggan in Upper Speyside, where accommodation is available. From Laggan two possible routes are described to Newtonmore – one to the north of the Spey valley (Stage 2) and the other to the south (Stage 2A). The latter requires no experience of mountain walking as it follows largely the line of one of General Wade's Military Roads, built in the 18th century to police the Highlands after the '45 Jacobite rebellion.

There is currently a gap between Newtonmore and the start of the Speyside Way at Aviemore. Plans are afoot to extend the official trail upriver from Aviemore back via Kingussie to Newtonmore, but it will be some considerable time before this route is finalised and opened. In the meantime the excellent waymarked **Badenoch Way** fills in much of the gap, running from near Kingussie to the B9152 road at Dalraddy, about 3½ miles short of Aviemore. At the south-western end, a link route from Newtonmore to Kingussie takes walkers to the start of the Badenoch Way, making use of a cycle trail. At the north-eastern end of the Way walkers have no alternative but to follow the B9152 into Aviemore. An alternative route for reaching Aviemore is also outlined, but as this is unwaymarked it is recommended mainly to more experienced walkers.

## The routes in this guidebook

From Aviemore walkers can take the main route of the **Speyside Way** (Stages 1–10) to complete a walk from source to sea. An alternative route is also described that runs along the Speyside Way to Grantown-on-Spey (Stage 3) then branches off on the **Dava Way** to Forres. From here taking the **Moray Coast Trail** to Cullen makes a fine end to a long trek over the hills, passing through the glens and along the rugged coastline of this exceptional part of Scotland.

Another option for those walking the Speyside Way is to take the **Dufftown Loop** at Aberlour (Stage 6), either as a day walk (round trip from Aberlour) or as an alternative to the official trail between Aberlour and Craigellachie.

Other walkers may prefer to start their route in the upland village of Tomintoul and follow the official **Tomintoul Spur** of the Speyside Way that joins the main Speyside Way route at Ballindalloch after 15 miles of delightful upland walking.

All these trails, described in the guide, allow numerous walking itineraries of varying length to be planned. Many walkers will be content to walk only the Speyside Way or one of the other official waymarked trails in one visit, so this book will offer inspiration and guidance for several walking excursions to Speyside and Moray.

| Summary of ascent on the Speyside Way and associated trails | | |
|---|---:|---:|
| Route/Stage | Feet | Metres |
| **Badenoch Way** | 490 | 150 |
| **Speyside Way** | | |
| **Stage 1** Aviemore to Boat of Garten | 130 | 40 |
| **Stages 2–4** Boat of Garten to Cromdale | 230 | 70 |
| **Stage 5** Cromdale to Ballindalloch station | 1050 | 320 |
| **Stage 6** Ballindalloch station to Aberlour | 0 | 0 |
| **Stages 7–8** Aberlour to Fochabers | 1150 | 350 |
| **Stages 9–10** Fochabers to Buckie | 0 | 0 |
| **Dufftown Loop** | 655 | 200 |
| **Tomintoul Spur** | 1800 | 550 |
| **TOTAL** Speyside Way – Aviemore to Buckie (main route) | 2560 | 780 |
| **TOTAL** Speyside Way – Tomintoul to Buckie | 2950 | 900 |

## *The Speyside Way*

### THE RIVER SPEY

Ptolemy tells us that the Romans called the Spey the 'Tuessis'. The river's modern name is Celtic in origin, possibly meaning 'hawthorn stream' or describing its frothing swiftness. The 12th-century manuscript *De Situ Albaniae* describes it as 'Magnum et miserabile flumen, quod vocatur Spe' ('the large and dangerous river, which is called Spey'). In the early period of Scottish history it provided the boundary between the provinces of Moray and Scotia. FH Groome, in his *Ordnance Gazetteer of Scotland* published in the 1880s, stated that the Spey had little commercial significance – very different from the Spey of today with its important tourist, fly-fishing and whisky industries, not to mention the importance of walking to the present economy.

At 98 miles long the Spey is the second longest river in Scotland and has three main tributaries, the Fiddich, the Avon and the Feshie. It is the fastest flowing river in Britain, dropping around 600ft (180m) in its last 35 miles to the sea, its force constantly changing the layout of its estuary. Over 400 million years ago the Grampian mountains were formed, but erosion over aeons of time has resulted in the rounded shapes of the Monadhliath, where the very first waters of the Spey flow into Loch Spey, 1150ft (457m) above sea level. During the past couple of million years the great strath ('broad valley' in Gaelic) of the Spey was formed by massive glaciers scraping away rock and leaving gravel and sand in its place. The middle section of the valley between Newtonmore and Grantown is today known as

*The River Spey seen from Speybank Walk near Kincraig (Badenoch Way)*

*A fisherman in the River Spey on the approach to Tugnet (Beryl Castle) (Speyside Way)*

Strathspey. Finally, near the sea the Spey passes over sandstone and terminates on the coastal shingle ridges of the wide Spey Bay.

Until the 18th and 19th centuries the river was either forded or crossed by ferry at various points along its length. Then the great bridge builders took over. Craigellachie Bridge over the Spey, the oldest surviving bridge in Scotland, was designed by Thomas Telford and built between 1812 and 1814. The longest bridge over the river is the large Garmouth viaduct built in 1886 – the force and changing course of the Spey being the reasons for its great width. Timber-floating began on the river in the middle of the 16th century, but during the 18th and 19th centuries there was massive log-floating activity from Strathspey to service the extensive shipbuilding industry at Kingston, with Speymouth becoming one of the major exporters of timber in Britain. Today most craft on the river are recreational canoes.

The Spey is one of the most important rivers for Atlantic salmon and sea trout in Western Europe. On average over 7500 salmon and 3500 sea trout are rod-caught each year, generating over £8 million per annum for the local economy. The Spey Fishery Board was established in the 1860s under Salmon Fisheries legislation and is still today responsible for the management, protection, enhancement and conservation of salmon and sea trout stocks in the river. A team of bailiffs patrols the river and coastline, as poaching is a serious problem, and the bailiffs are also responsible for the Board's hatchery, where up to a million River Spey salmon are hatched and distributed to rebuild stocks in depleted areas. The Spey Research Trust is another responsibility of the Board; it both monitors stocks and promotes awareness of the Board's work to locals and tourists. Sea lamprey, freshwater pearl and otter, which are endangered or rare, also survive in the clean waters of the Spey. This has resulted in the river being designated both as a Site of Special Scientific Interest (SSSI) and a Special Area of Conservation (SAC).

### Fishing

Fly-fishing, the premier sport on the Spey, has been practised for thousands of years. One of the earliest descriptions of fly-fishing appeared over 2000 years ago in *De Animalium Natura*, where Claudius Aelianus reported that 'fishermen wind red wool around their hooks and fasten to the wool two feathers that grow under a cock's wattles'. The first British book on fly-fishing was written by Dame Juliana Berners in 1496: *Treatise of Fishing with an Angle*.

The young salmon spend a few years in the river in which they were born before swimming out to the saltwater feeding ground of the Atlantic. Only a tiny percentage of those hatched survive to return up-stream to the waters of their birth to breed, but it is these that provide the sport for fly-fishing. Keen fishermen and women will spend many hours in waders, standing in the deep waters of the Spey and hoping that the salmon will rise to take the fly at the end of their rod and line. The season on the Spey opens on 11th February and closes on 30th September. The cost of fishing on the Spey varies from moderately reasonable to extremely expensive, depending on the time in the season and the location of the beat.

### Whisky production

Speyside has been inextricably linked with whisky production, both illicit and legal, for several hundred years. The first written reference to its production in Scotland appears in the 1494 Exchequer Rolls, which record the granting 'To Friar John Cor, by order of the King to make aqua vitae, VIII bols of malt'. Friar John was based at Lindores Abbey in north-west Fife; as eight bols is equivalent to over 94 stone in weight, it would suggest that the abbey was involved in large-scale distilling. *Aqua vitae* in Latin translates as 'water of life', which became *uisge beatha* in the Gaelic, which was eventually anglicised to 'whisky'. The raw spirit produced from early stills was probably very rough, and so would have been flavoured with berries and herbs. The earliest records show that malt has always been a key ingredient in Scottish whisky.

In 1644 the first duty on whisky was introduced by an act of the Scottish Parliament, and this drove 'underground' much whisky production which, at that time, was predominantly a cottage industry. In 1823 the licensing of distilleries was introduced, which ensured both the quality and safety of the whisky produced; much of the illegally produced spirit may well have been poisonous! George Smith, founder of the Glenlivet Distillery, was the first to take out a licence under the 1823 act of Parliament, and so started the legal production of whisky on Speyside, where today nearly half of the distilleries in Scotland are located. The export of whisky is an important source of revenue for the Scottish economy, contributing over £2.5 billion per annum and providing over 40,000 jobs.

Many whisky distilleries are passed on, or are within walking distance of, the Speyside Way and the other trails (see Appendix D). The principal ones from south to north are: Tormore*, Cragganmore, Tamdhu*, Knockando*, Cardhu (off-route), Dailuaine*, Aberlour, Glenallachie* (off-route), Craigellachie, Macallan (off-route), Speyside cooperage (off-route – not a distillery), Glen Grant (off-route in Rothes, but visible from the Speyside Way), Glenfiddich (Dufftown Loop), The Glenlivet (Tomintoul Spur), Dallas Dhu (Dava Way) and Benromach (MCT). Those marked with an asterisk* are closed to the public, but all the others offer tours to visitors, most only between Easter and October.

Several of the Speyside distilleries offer tours to visitors in which the production process (see Appendix D) is explained in detail, and there are also many books available on the subject.

## The old railways

The disused railway lines of the region provide routes for considerable sections of the Speyside Way (for example from Ballindalloch to Craigellachie) and most of the Dava Way. Steam-rail enthusiasts flock to travel on the Strathspey Steam Railway from Aviemore to Broomhill, on the longest heritage railway in Scotland, and tourists can also enjoy weekend trips on the Keith and Dufftown Heritage Railway (see 'Dufftown Loop'). However, the economic importance of the railways in Speyside and Moray predates the current tourism industry by over 150 years.

During the Highland railway-building boom of the mid-1800s several small railway companies were involved in building sections of railway to link Perth to Inverness. The original line followed a long route around the Moray coast, as the shorter cross-country route was deemed too difficult to construct economically. However, such a route was eventually opened up by the Inverness and Perth Junction Railway. The first turf was cut in 1861 for the 103-mile section from Dunkeld to Forres, and after less than two years the 36 miles from Forres to Aviemore opened. It had required 8 viaducts, 126 bridges and 119 road bridges!

*Ticket office at the former Cromdale station (Speyside Way)*

The railway allowed local farmers much easier access to their markets. Cattle and sheep that had taken six weeks to reach the south could make the journey now in one or two days. Dunphail Sidings (now on the Dava Way) reputedly had the longest platform in the country, so that sheep could be loaded speedily into awaiting railway trucks. The whisky industry on the River Spey benefited both from large quantities of coal being delivered by rail and by its finished product being moved to distributors by the railways. Cragganmore on Speyside was the first distillery to be built to take advantage of the adjacent railway. The railways brought tourists into the Speyside and Moray regions in ever greater numbers. Large Victorian hotels in towns such as Aviemore bear witness to the facilities that were developed to service these new visitors.

## WHEN TO WALK

The three trails can be walked at any time of the year, as they are predominantly in low-lying country, with the exception of the Tomintoul Spur. However, the region is one of the coldest in Britain, and severe, cold weather is not unusual in wintertime, making a walk along the trails at best very unpleasant, but a dangerous venture for the ill-prepared. If it is planned to walk the routes during the winter months then the best option is to do them as a series of day walks, preferably in good weather, and walking only short sections at a time in

## WHEN TO WALK

order to reduce the risk of becoming benighted on the trail. This option, of course, is really feasible only for those living in or close to the area. Others would need to organise accommodation in B&Bs or hotels, but bear in mind that many of these are not open during the winter months. Similarly, public transport services operate reduced winter timetables, and many of the tourist attractions of the area, such as Distillery Tours, are closed until the spring.

It hardly needs stating that good quality waterproof, windproof and warm winter clothing, including hats and gloves, must be worn. The Tomintoul Spur reaches a height of nearly 2000ft (610m), and consequently the temperatures on these hills in winter is much lower than in the valley, and the amount of snow often significant. The possibility of severe winter weather, coupled with short daylight hours from the end of October until the beginning of March at these northerly latitudes, makes winter walking along these trails only suitable for the well equipped and well prepared.

Flooding of the Spey and other rivers, particularly during the wet autumn months and in the springtime, when the winter snows melt from the surrounding mountains, is not uncommon and can make the trails extremely wet underfoot in some areas, if not actually impassable or dangerous (heavy rains and flooding at Fochabers in the autumn of 2009 caused a major diversion to the Speyside Way in the area).

*Daffodils line the Spey by the old bridge at Nethy Bridge (Beryl Castle) (Speyside Way)*

*The trail in springtime north of Glenfiddich Distillery (Dufftown Loop)*

Violent storms with heavy rain and gale-force winds can occur at any time of the year, but are more common in the late autumn and winter months. The Moray Coast is particularly prone to very strong winds, often blustering.

Walking the Speyside Way, Dava Way and MCT is best reserved for the spring, summer and early autumn months, when weather conditions are generally more suitable. Daylight hours are long at these high latitudes, 16–18 hours from May to July, so there is plenty of time for the longest or the slowest of walks. Summer has the advantage of generally warmer days, but as this is the period when the majority of people take their holidays, there will be more competition for the available bed space in the area.

Spring and autumn are therefore the best seasons. High pressure is perhaps more common during the spring in Scotland, and days during May and June often (but not always!) present ideal walking conditions – bright, sunny and not overly warm. The general freshness and rebirth of life is stimulating during springtime, birds can be heard singing everywhere and wild flower displays are a particular joy. The bright yellow flowers of the many broom bushes in the area are especially striking. Autumn is a charming time of the year in northern Scotland, with its mellow colours and general feeling of seasonal contentment. The abundance of deciduous trees in Speyside and Moray means that the displays of autumn tints are among the finest in the UK. The

## When to walk

heather moorland is a blaze of purple, and the landscape is at its driest of the year after the warmth of the summer sun before the winter rains arrive. The romantic roar of stags can sometimes be heard during the annual rutting season in October. Accommodation tends to be less fully booked than in July and August, and days in early autumn are still of an adequate length for walking relatively long distances.

The wilderness mountain areas near the source of the Spey suffer from much more severe weather conditions than the valleys, even though the walks in these areas (see Prologue section) do not go much over 1000ft (300m) in altitude. Winter comes earlier in these regions and spring later, and their very inaccessibility and remoteness mean that the walker cannot easily vacate the area if weather conditions suddenly and rapidly deteriorate. The long nature of the walks, with little possibility of finding shelter apart from the occasional bothy, mean that a walk that could easily be completed in two days during the period between spring to early autumn would require at least an extra day in wintertime, with its very limited amount of daylight. Very long, dark and bitterly cold nights would have to be tolerated in tent or bothy, and more food, equipment and warm clothing carried. Hence these traverses during the wintertime are only for the very experienced and very well equipped.

Snow, torrential or persistent rain, very high winds and low temperatures can occur in this environment at any time of the year, so all who venture there must be prepared for the worst. Never attempt these sections in periods of very unsettled weather; always check the weather forecast before venturing out. If rain has been heavy in the preceding days then the necessary river crossings may be dangerous or impassable.

The late summer and early autumn months, from August to October, are not ideal for the Stage 1 or 1A walks of the Prologue, nor the Glen Banchor route in Stage 2. This is the period when deer stalking takes place in the Highland estates, and not only can it be dangerous to walk in areas where a stalk is taking place, but the presence of walkers can disrupt the sport, which is a vital part of the Highland economy. Be sure to first contact the relevant estate if considering walking these routes during this period (the 'Hillphones' service, see Appendix B, is the easiest way to make contact with the keepers and learn the whereabouts and dates of the stalking activities in the area).

A pest in these mountain areas is the notorious Highland midge, whose frenzied biting has to be experienced to be fully appreciated! Fortunately, they are less of a problem in the eastern Highlands than in western areas; and far fewer will be encountered in the valley and low-lying areas through which the three main trails pass than in the mountain country of the Prologue walks. It is a good idea to carry a midge

## THE SPEYSIDE WAY

Sueno's Stone (Beryl Castle) (Moray Coast Trail)

repellent. The first frosts of autumn kill off this pest until the following spring. They are most active between early June and late September and on overcast, calm days.

### WHICH DIRECTION TO WALK

The trails in this guidebook start from the west and follow a generally north-eastern direction, but can, of course, be walked the opposite way. The **Speyside Way** has been described from Buckie to Aviemore in other guides, but strangely never before in the more natural and obvious direction, downriver from source to sea. This downstream direction is the better one, as it gives a definite goal or end-point of the walk, at the coast, and is the direction that most walkers travel when following long distance river trails. The other advantage of walking in a north-easterly direction, towards the sea, is that you should have the wind at your back, rather than directly blowing into your face. If nothing else, by walking downriver there is less ascent than walking up from the coast, even if this is quite small over such a distance!

In 1990 a major **official spur** of the Speyside Way was opened from the upland village of **Tomintoul** to Ballindalloch. Many may wish to start their Speyside Way journey at **Tomintoul**, and in the author's opinion the walk from Tomintoul to Ballindalloch is better than that from Aviemore. The main description in this book of the Spur is from south to north, heading towards the Moray coast. Some may wish to follow a 'horseshoe walk' north-easterly from Newtonmore/Aviemore to Ballindalloch and then southwards up to Tomintoul; so the Spur is also described in the opposite direction, from Ballindalloch to Tomintoul.

An option for those walking northwards from Aviemore is to leave the Speyside Way at Grantown-on-Spey and instead follow the other main trail towards the Moray Coast, the **Dava Way**, which is also described from south to north in this book. The Dava Way terminates at Forres where the **MCT** starts. This is described from west to east, Forres to Cullen, the reason again being that when walking in this direction the predominant westerly winds will be at the rear.

## SUGGESTED LONGER ROUTES

The three official trails constitute a considerable network of long-distance pathways in the north-central and north-eastern areas of Scotland and can be used to devise a variety of multi-stage walks of varying length, type and grade. The following are the main options to consider:

1. The **standard route of the Speyside Way**, starting from either Aviemore or from Newtonmore and walking to the Moray coast at Buckie, a walk of either 66 miles (from Aviemore) or 85 miles (from Newtonmore).

2. The **Tomintoul route** of the Speyside Way, starting from Tomintoul and walking the hill route over to Ballindalloch, from where the standard way is followed to Buckie. This is a shorter trek (50 miles) than that along the standard route, but the first 15 miles are of a somewhat more strenuous nature. Options 1 and 2 can both be extended, and indeed improved, by following the **Dufftown Loop** from Aberlour to Dufftown and on to Craigellachie, adding about 7 miles to the length of the walk.

3. A walk along the Speyside Way, starting at **Dufftown** and finishing at **Buckie** (27½ miles or 30 miles if via Aberlour).

4. The **Speyside Way** from Aviemore or Newtonmore to Ballindalloch and then from there northwards along the **Tomintoul Spur** to finish in the village of Tomintoul. 46 miles from Aviemore or 65 miles from Newtonmore.

5. The **Dava Way** from Grantown-on-Spey to Forres (25 miles).

6. The **Moray Coast Trail** from Forres to Cullen (47 miles).

7. From Grantown-on-Spey to Cullen on the Moray Coast by following the full length of the **Dava Way** to Forres and then continuing along the **Moray Coast Trail** all the way to its termination at Cullen. This combined Dava Way and MCT trek is 72 miles in length.

8. Commencing at either Newtonmore or Aviemore and following the **Badenoch Way** and **Speyside Way** to Grantown, and then taking **Option No. 7** to Forres and on to Cullen. This would make a walking route of either 88½ miles (from Aviemore) or 107½ miles (from Newtonmore).

9. Experienced hillwalkers can make a self-supported trek from Lochaber to Speyside across mountains and moorland, either from **Roybridge** or from **Spean Bridge** to **Laggan** and then on via Glen Banchor to **Newtonmore** (39 miles from Roybridge or 44½ miles from Spean Bridge). Alternatively, the walk could be commenced at **Fort Augustus** (41 miles to Newtonmore).

10. Less experienced walkers who wish to include a visit to the source of the Spey at Loch Spey can commence at **Garva Bridge**, provided

## THE SPEYSIDE WAY

transport can be arranged, visit Loch Spey (Prologue, Side trip), walking to Laggan and then to **Newtonmore** via General Wade's Military Road, a total distance of 36 miles.

11. As **Option No. 9 or 10** but continuing along the Badenoch Way and the Speyside Way to **Buckie** or from **Grantown** to **Forres** and **Cullen** on the Dava Way and MCT. Distances for the various main long distance options are listed in the box below.

12. The **Moray Way** (see page 14). The total distance is about 95 miles.

Therefore, this marvellous network of long distance routes in this part of Scotland can be used to create walking trails from 25 to 146 miles in length – from a weekend break to a full fortnight's holiday – and from walks on a flat railway line to wilderness treks over mountain passes.

### SUGGESTED DAY WALKS

The Speyside Way and the other trails are not the sole preserve of the long distance walker, and not everyone will have the ambition to walk every foot of the Way. For walkers living or staying in the area, who can travel to the routes either by car or by public transport, the Speyside Way and the other trails may be used for just part of a day walk or longer expedition across the region. Simply walk the stages in any order as takes your fancy or is most convenient, until all the route has been covered. There are three main variations of the 'day walks method' – use just one or a mixture of all three.

1. Walk one section at a time in a 'there and back' manner. Drive or take public transport to the start of the trail. Walk along the Way to a village, town or point on a road where a car can be safely and responsibly parked, or public

---

Roybridge > Laggan > Glen Banchor > Newtonmore > Aviemore > Buckie = **124 miles**

Spean Bridge > Laggan > Glen Banchor > Newtonmore > Aviemore > Buckie = **130 miles**

Fort Augustus > Loch Spey > Laggan > Glen Banchor > Newtonmore > Aviemore > Buckie = **126 miles**

Roybridge > Laggan > Glen Banchor > Newtonmore > Aviemore > Grantown-on-Spey > Forres > Cullen = **146 miles**

Obviously by 'mixing and matching' various route options, even more combinations are possible. These can all be walked with the aid of this guidebook.

## MOUNTAIN BIKING AND HORSE RIDING

*Railway station in Aviemore (Speyside Way)*

transport taken at a later date. Walk back along the trail to your starting point. On your second visit drive or take public transport to the point you reached at the end of the first day of the trail. Repeat this technique for as long as it takes to walk the whole of the Speyside Way or one of the other routes.

2. Plan to walk sections of the route with friends taking two cars. Park one car at the end of the section you intend to walk, and drive together to the start of your day walk, leaving the second car there. On reaching the end of your walk, drive back to your starting point in the second car. A variation of this is to split the group into two, one parking a car at one end of the section and the other at the other end, and each group walking in opposite directions. Swap car keys on meeting halfway through your day. This can only go wrong if one or both groups stray from the line of the Way! Bear in mind that reception for mobile phones can be unreliable in some of the areas through which these trails pass. A safer option is for each driver to carry keys for the other car.

3. Use the Speyside Way or other trail as part of a large number of circular walks. Continue these, 'filling in the blanks' in the Way until eventually an entire trail has been covered.

### MOUNTAIN BIKING AND HORSE RIDING

This book is primarily intended as a guide for walkers, but many sections of these three trails are also suitable

## THE SPEYSIDE WAY

The most suitable and appropriate areas for cycling or mountain biking on the three official trails are as follows:

**Speyside Way**
Aviemore to Boat of Garten
Ballindalloch to Fochabers
Do not cycle on the sections between Cromdale and Ballindalloch or on the Tomintoul Spur.*

**Dava Way**
The whole of the trail between Grantown and Forres, although in some small areas cyclists must avoid paths designated only for walkers; alternative trails suitable for cyclists and mountain bikers are signposted.

**Moray Coast Trail**
Forres to Findhorn
Portgordon to Portessie
Findochty to Portknockie

\* Cyclists who want to cycle a modified Speyside Way from Aviemore to Buckie can do so by linking the rideable sections of the official Way with a number of public roads, most of which carry only light traffic: the B970 between Boat of Garten, Nethy Bridge and Grantown, the B9102 followed by a minor road to Cromdale, another minor road via Wester and Easter Rynaballoch to Millton and the Mains of Dalvey, the A95 (take care) and the B9137 to Ballindalloch station, the B9104 from Fochabers to Spey Bay and a minor road via Nether Dallachy to Portgordon. Cyclists starting at Tomintoul can make use of either the B9008 via Tomnavoulin or the B9136 down Glen Avon, which meets with the B9008 about 3½ miles before the latter reaches the A95 near the Bridge of Avon, and hence to Ballindalloch and the railway line heading north along the Spey valley.

for cyclists. Gradients are generally gentle ones, with no long strenuous stages. Mountain bikes or at least 'on-road/off-road' hybrids are recommended, and road bikes with thin tyres are not advised. The Dava Way, which follows the course of an old railway line for most of its 25 miles, is the most suitable of the three routes for cycling and makes an ideal day out for cyclists; fit riders could even ride from Grantown to Forres and back in one day. There are few hazards other than the sharp needles from gorse and hawthorn bushes that line several sections of the trails, which are ideal for acquiring punctures (the author writes from experience!). Cyclists must take special care when close to pedestrians – always be considerate and give way to them.

Horse riders are welcomed on some sections of the Speyside Way, notably the railway line between Ballindalloch station and Aberlour (contact the Ranger Service at Aberlour for the current situation). The Dava Way railway line is also suitable for horse riders and is described in a leaflet entitled 'Horse Riding Routes in Moray', produced by the Moray Equestrian Access Group and available at local tourist offices.

## GETTING THERE

Aviemore, Newtonmore and Kingussie can be reached easily by **train**, using either the direct service from Glasgow and Inverness or that from Edinburgh (change at Perth). Apart from the five or so Glasgow trains a day, there is also the daily overnight sleeper direct from London.

Fort William, Spean Bridge and Roybridge are all on the Glasgow to Mallaig line, which has about four trains a day. From Edinburgh there is only one direct slow train a day.

Forres and Elgin can be reached by train from Edinburgh via Inverness. These stations are both on the Inverness to Aberdeen line.

There are also direct **coaches** (Citylink) from both Glasgow and Edinburgh to Newtonmore, Kingussie and Aviemore en route to Inverness. Grantown-on-Spey can be reached by a frequent local **bus** service from either Aviemore or Inverness, or alternatively the **Strathspey Steam Railway** can be used from Aviemore to Boat of Garten and on to Broomhill, where a bus connects to Grantown-on-Spey. Citylink also operates the services from Glasgow and Edinburgh to Fort William, from where the Fort William to Inverness service, which stops at Spean Bridge and Fort Augustus, can be taken.

Dufftown can be reached from Forres on the very frequent **Whisky Trail bus service** operated by Stagecoach Bluebird, which travels through Findhorn, Craigellachie and Aberlour.

Reaching Tomintoul by public transport is more difficult. There is a once-a-day, school days only **bus** service from Aberlour, and a service three times a week from Dufftown. When funding is available, a Heather Hooper bus service is operated daily in the tourist season between Newtonmore and Ballater.

The frequent **bus** service between Inverness and Aberdeen stops at Cullen, Buckie and Elgin. From Elgin, a bus or train can be used to return to Aviemore.

Many of the transport providers have websites (see Appendix B).

If a **car** is used for reaching the area then arrangements for safe parking will have to be made for the duration of the walk. One option is to ask the proprietors of your B&B or hotel at the start of the walk whether it is possible to park there (it would be polite to offer to stay there for a second night before picking up your car for the drive home). Two cars are useful for small groups planning to walk the trails as a series of day walks (see 'Suggested Day Walks' above).

## PUBLIC TRANSPORT

The official Speyside Way website (see Appendix B) has a Guide to Public Transport which provides an excellent

## THE SPEYSIDE WAY

*Luib-chonnal Bothy in Upper Glen Roy (Prologue)*

map and contact details for all the relevant services in the area covered by the Speyside Way, Dava Way and MCT. Also very useful is 'Cairngorms Explorer, Travel without a Car', published annually by the Cairngorms National Park Authority and available at local Tourist Information Centres (TICs) and National Park offices. This booklet contains timetables and other information on the bus and train services within an area from Grantown-on-Spey in the north to Dalwhinnie in the south, and from Laggan in the west to Ballater in the east. Using these two sources of information it is possible to plan public transport along the three official trails.

### ACCOMMODATION

There is little shortage of **B&B** and **hotel** accommodation in the Spey valley, from Newtonmore downriver to Fochabers. Similarly on the Moray coast from Forres to Cullen, there are plenty of places to stay. Booking accommodation in advance is advisable, particularly during the main summer season and on bank holiday weekends. The internet is ideal for finding and booking accommodation, otherwise local TICs have lists of accommodation and will be pleased to recommend and, if necessary, book B&Bs or hotels on your behalf.

An annual leaflet of accommodation along the Speyside Way

is available from the Ranger Service in Aberlour (see Appendix B), and a searchable database of accommodation is maintained on the official Speyside Way website (Appendix B). The MCT website (Appendix B) does not contain a list of accommodation along the trail, but there are links to all relevant community websites, which contain details of local accommodation. Note that there is no accommodation along or even close to the Dava Way (see advice on this potential problem under 'Refreshments' below). However, the Dava Way website contains an extensive list of accommodation options in both Grantown and Forres, the start and end points of the Way.

There are Scottish Youth Hostel Association **hostels** at Aviemore (Speyside Way) and at Tomintoul (Tomintoul Spur). There are also **independent hostels** or **bunkhouses** at Laggan and two at Newtonmore (Prologue); on the Badenoch Way at Kingussie and Kincraig; on the Speyside Way at Aviemore, Boat of Garten, Nethy Bridge and Grantown-on-Spey, and on the MCT at Cullen.

There are no places of accommodation in the wilderness areas that the walks in the Prologue pass through, other than at the starting locations of Roybridge, Spean Bridge and Fort Augustus and at the end of Stages 1 and 1A at, and near, Laggan. Walkers will need to carry a tent and/or make use of the bothies passed en route (see Prologue for full details).

## CAMPSITES AND WILD CAMPING

The Speyside Way, Dava Way and the MCT are all suitable for backpacking, using campsites along the trails for overnight accommodation.

Most **campsites** cater primarily for caravans, campervans and large family tents, but all will take small backpacking tents. On most occasions a place will be found for you for one overnight stay, without prior reservation, but it is nevertheless worth checking for availability by phone before arriving. Reservations are advisable during the main summer season and particularly over bank holiday periods. It is always worth asking for a discount for a small tent and for the fact that you are not bringing a car onto the site. Most commercial campsites are closed during the winter months. Campsites come and go, like other types of accommodation, so do check at the planning stage of your trip that the sites that you intend to use are still open, and check for possible new sites along the trails by contacting a local Tourist Information Centre.

The three main trails are generally not suitable for **wild camping**, as they are for the most part in lowland areas where farming and other commercial interests make such activity inappropriate, the possible exception being on the more upland sections of the Tomintoul Spur. However, the walks described in the Prologue, in the wild mountain and moorland areas of the Monadhliath mountains of the Central

Highlands, offer ideal opportunity for wild camping. Campers must act responsibly, follow the Scottish Outdoor Access Code, locate their tent well away from any habitation, stay in each location for one night only (unless the situation is an emergency), not pollute water sources in any way and leave no evidence whatsoever of their passing. Even if a tent is carried it is a good idea to make full use of the bothies that are passed on these walks (see Prologue and Appendix B).

### Speyside Way

Backpackers are particularly well provided for along the Speyside Way with a number of simple, basic but free sites along the trail, intended solely for use by Speyside Way walkers and cyclists. There are three of these camping areas situated on the main Aviemore–Buckie trail at the following locations:

- **Ballindalloch station** – toilet facilities April to October only
- **Blacksboat station** – water tap only
- **Fiddich Park** in Craigellachie – toilet facilities April to October only.

Unfortunately these are not well spaced along the Way, all being in the central section of the route, so it is not possible to use them exclusively when walking the trail.

In addition there is a free Speyside Way campsite at **Tomintoul**. This is provided courtesy of the Glenlivet Estate, and is situated by the Estate Visitor Centre at the south-east end of the village, with toilet facilities in the village car park. These four free Speyside Way campsites cannot be reserved in advance – simply arrive and pitch your tent. If you are not walking the Speyside Way, then please do not use these free campsites, which are reserved solely for Speyside Way backpackers.

At the time of research there were commercial campsites at **Aviemore** (tel. 01479 810636), **Boat of Garten** (tel. 01479 831652), **Nethy Bridge** (tel. 01479 821642), **Grantown-on-Spey** (tel. 01479 872474), **Aberlour** (tel. 01340 871586) and **Fochabers** (tel. 01343 820511). Note that the campsite shown on some maps at Spey Bay is now closed. There is also a large campsite in **Newtonmore** (at Spey Bridge, south of the village, tel. 01540 673275). On the Prologue walks there are campsites only at the start points of **Roybridge** (2 sites: tel. 01397 712332 and 01397 712275) and **Fort Augustus** (tel. 01320 366618).

### Dava Way

There is a campsite at **Grantown-on-Spey** (tel. 01479 872474) at the southern terminus of the trail, but no other on or near the Way.

### Moray Coast Trail

There are several campsites along the Moray coastline which are of use to the walker, but note that there is a large gap with no sites between Lossiemouth and Portessie, east of Buckie. There are campsites at **Kinloss** (tel. 01309 690218), **Findhorn Bay** (2 sites: tel. 01309 690203 and 01309 690324), **Burghead** (tel. 01343 830084), **Hopeman** (tel. 01343 830880), **Lossiemouth** (tel. 01343 813262), **Portessie** (tel. 01224 696679), **Findochty** (tel. 01542 835303) and **Cullen** (tel. 01542 840766). Note that there is no longer a campsite at Spey Bay.

## REFRESHMENTS

Both the **Speyside Way** and the **MCT** pass through many villages and small towns, and consequently are well served with grocery shops, small supermarkets, pubs offering meals, cafés, teashops and restaurants. In some areas the distances between facilities are much longer than in others (for example there is no shop between Grantown and Aberlour on the Speyside Way), but careful planning should avoid lengthy detours to find refreshment. The facilities that you can expect to find in the villages and towns along these trails are given in this guidebook. Apart from Co-op stores, most food shops tend to close on Sundays. If you intend to walk the trails during the winter months, then remember that some establishments, particularly cafés and teashops, close during this period, or have more limited opening hours.

Those walking the **Dava Way** should be aware that there are no facilities of any sort after leaving Grantown,

*The Fiddichside Inn on outskirts of Craigellachie (Speyside Way)*

until the town of Forres is reached at the very end of the trail. Very fit and fast walkers would be able to complete the trail in one day during the spring and summer months, when the days are long, and all but the slowest and inexperienced of cyclists should be able to cover this modest cycling distance within one day. Slower or less fit ramblers will have to carry adequate food and drink and (as wild camping is not appropriate) arrange for a vehicle to meet them at the end of the day to drive them to overnight accommodation and refreshment.

The only places of refreshment on the **wilderness walks** in the Prologue are at the starting points of Roybridge, Spean Bridge and Fort Augustus, and at Laggan at the end of Stages 1 and 1A. All food and drink must be carried for the duration of these walks, although there is abundant water to drink in the many burns (you may wish to treat this water with a purifying agent before drinking).

## TOURIST INFORMATION

The Spey valley is well served with Tourist Information Centres (TICs), with offices at Newtonmore, Kingussie, Aviemore and Grantown-on-Spey. There is a TIC at Tomintoul on the Spur route and another at Dufftown in Glen Fiddich on the Dufftown Loop. Only those at Aviemore and Newtonmore are open all year, the others being closed from October to Easter. There is a seasonal TIC at Forres, where the Dava Way ends and the MCT begins, and elsewhere in Moray there is a tourist office open all year at Elgin. Two of the starting locations for the treks described in the Prologue, Spean Bridge and Fort Augustus, both have seasonal TICs. Scotland's Tourist Board, known as Visit Scotland, has an informative website at www.visitscotland.com.

One of the joys of walking the Speyside Way and the trails of Moray is that there are so many interesting things to do and places to visit either on route or with a short detour from the trail. The most obvious attractions are the numerous whisky distilleries, many of which offer free guided tours during the spring and summer months (see Appendix D). But there are also castles to visit, archaeological sites to examine, steam railways to ride, wildlife reserves to enjoy and many more places of interest along the way. The area is a magnet for birdwatchers. Golfers and anglers can even stop walking for a half-day or more to enjoy their sport before continuing on the Way. Further details of the various visitor attractions will be found in the relevant sections of this guide.

## WHAT TO TAKE

The amount and type of equipment to take depends on whether you intend to hike these trails over a number of consecutive days, staying at accommodation each night, or as a series of day walks. The day walker needs only

*Crossing a footbridge in the rain just before Aberlour (Speyside Way)*

a very light pack, containing map, guidebook, food and drink for the day, and perhaps a camera. But you should always take waterproof, windproof and warm clothing, even in summertime, as weather conditions can change rapidly in these northern latitudes, even at relatively low altitudes.

The quantity of equipment needed by the walker using B&B, hotel or hostel accommodation is much less that that of the backpacker camping out each night. The most important consideration, always, is to ensure that the pack is as light as possible; do not take unnecessary items. Nothing spoils a walking holiday more than having to endure the excessive weight of an overloaded rucksack. Assemble your equipment and then go through it carefully to see what may safely be left behind.

If staying at a B&B, hotel or hostel it should not be necessary to carry more than 15–20lbs (6.5–9kg), even including food and drink. Take clothing made from lightweight wicking material and do not carry large amounts of spare clothes (follow the 'wear one/wash one' philosophy). Backpackers should aim for under 30lbs (13.5kg) and certainly never more than 35lbs (16kg) on a route of this nature, where food can be bought from shops, cafés and pubs at regular intervals along the trails (except on the Dava Way). People who want to take a heavy rucksack, but not to carry it, should contact a taxi company in the region that will transport baggage from place to place along these trails on a daily basis (see Appendix B).

The **rucksack**, the size of which will depend on whether or not camping equipment is to be carried, is possibly the most important item of gear. Make sure that it offers a comfortable carry before you set out on your holiday. A dustbin liner for the rucksack and a supply of plastic bags should keep the contents dry in heavy rain. Make sure you pack:

- a good pair of lightweight boots – heavier mountaineering boots are not necessary on the main trails in the summer months – and sufficient clothing to keep you warm, dry and safe
- maps, guidebook, compass
- a basic first-aid kit plus any personal medicines
- a small washing kit (no towel needed if using B&B or hotel accommodation)
- sufficient food and drink
- a mobile phone, but be aware that you may not always get a signal in the areas covered by these trails.

Most other items will be superfluous. My luxuries consist only of a camera and a small exercise book to be used as a travel journal.

Backpackers will also need a good lightweight **tent**, **sleeping bag** (not a heavy five-season one if walking during the summer months), a lightweight insulating **mat/air bed** and a lightweight **travel towel**. If you intend to cook your own food then obviously a **cooking stove**, **utensils** and **fuel** will be required. As food shops, pubs, restaurants, and fish and chip shops are frequently encountered on the main trails, the backpacker should decide before setting out whether to make use of these and leave the stove at home. Only backpackers can sensibly consider the walks described in the Prologue through the remote mountain and moorland areas of the Grampians. If venturing into these regions then it is necessary to think more carefully about what is taken on the trek and what left behind – certainly take extra emergency food, a torch and an emergency blanket.

Remember that, with the exceptions of the treks outlined in the Prologue and the Tomintoul Spur of the Speyside Way, most sections of the trails described in this book offer easy-grade, relatively low-level walking on good paths and tracks, rarely far from most modern facilities. Therefore for these trips it is not necessary to spend large sums of money on the sort of high-tech mountain equipment that is more appropriate to remote and high mountain areas of the world. The mantra 'think safe, think sensible, think warm and dry, think light, think economical' is not a bad one.

## MAPS

This guidebook contains Ordnance Survey mapping of the entire Speyside Way, the Dava Way, the Moray Coast Trail and the other described trails, with the route of each clearly overlaid. Provided no serious navigational errors are made en route, or long detours from the Way are envisaged, then this is the only mapping that is required to

*Cyclist on Dava Way alongside Dallas Dhu Distillery (Beryl Castle)*

walk the trails. However, many walkers will want to carry some general maps of the area in order to identify interesting landscape features along the way and to locate off-route places of interest. They will also be useful if you have to divert from the line of the trail to secure a night's accommodation.

### Speyside Way

For the Speyside Way the best **strip map** (showing at least a mile either side of the route) is the excellent one published by Footprint (see Appendix C). The whole route of the Speyside Way, from Aviemore to Buckie, as well as the spur from Tomintoul, the Dufftown routes and the Badenoch Way, are all included on one sheet at a scale of 1:45,000. An alternative strip map is published by Harvey Maps at a scale of 1:40,000. This is a metric map printed on tough waterproof material and is GPS compatible (but does not mark the Dufftown routes or the Badenoch Way).

If more area either side of the trail is required, then the relevant **OS maps** are the ones to acquire, either at 1:50,000 scale (the Landranger series) or at 1:25,000 scale (Explorer maps).

- **Landranger** (covers all the official Speyside Way route, including the Tomintoul Spur): sheets 36 (Grantown & Aviemore) and 28 (Elgin & Dufftown)
- **Explorer** (whole route): sheets 403 (Cairn Gorm & Aviemore), 419 (Grantown-on-Spey & Hills of Cromdale) and 424 (Buckie & Keith). **Note**: all but the first ½ mile from Tomintoul village of the Tomintoul Spur is covered by Explorer sheet 419.

*The Speyside Way*

For those who wish to follow an **unofficial route** from the source of the Spey to the official start of the Speyside Way at Aviemore, additional maps will be required, either Landranger 34 (Fort Augustus) and 35 (Kingussie & Monadhliath Mountains) (the latter map also covers the Badenoch Way), or Explorer maps 401 (Loch Laggan & Creag Meagaidh) and 402 (Badenoch & Upper Strathspey), and possibly, depending on exact route, Explorer sheet 400 (Loch Lochy & Glen Roy).

## Dava Way

**Landranger** maps 36 (Grantown & Aviemore) and 27 (Nairn & Forres) are required to cover the entire length of the Dava Way, but all but the first mile of the route from Grantown-on-Spey is covered by sheet 27. The corresponding **Explorer** maps for the Dava Way are sheets 419 (Grantown-on-Spey & Hills of Cromdale) and 423 (Elgin, Forres & Lossiemouth). (An appreciable length of the Way is also shown on Explorer sheet 418 (Lochindorb, Grantown-on-Spey & Carrbridge), although there is no part of it that is not also covered by sheet 419.)

## Moray Coast Trail

The Moray Coast Trail laps over three **Landranger** maps, 27 (Nairn & Forres), 28 (Elgin & Dufftown) and 29 (Banff & Huntly). Over three quarters of the trail is covered by Sheet 28, which overlaps Sheet 29, such that the latter is only necessary for the last ½ mile into Cullen at the eastern end of the route. The **Explorer** alternatives are 423 (Elgin, Forres & Lossiemouth), 424 (Buckie & Keith) and 425 (Huntly & Cullen).

## The Moray Way

The Moray Way requires either **Landranger** maps 36 (Grantown & Aviemore), 27 (Nairn & Forres) and 28 (Elgin & Dufftown) or Explorer maps 419 (Grantown-on-Spey & Hills of Cromdale), 423 (Elgin, Forres & Lossiemouth) and 424 (Buckie & Keith). The Moray Way Association has produced a comprehensive map at 1:70,000 scale that covers the entire Moray Way in significant detail (see Appendix C).

## NAVIGATION AND WAYMARKING

No special navigational skills are required to walk the official routes of the Speyside Way, Dava Way and MCT. The trails are generally well waymarked, and by following the routes and maps in this guidebook you should have few problems in finding your way along them. The landscape through which most of these routes pass is relatively low lying, and the walker is rarely very far from public roads, villages or towns where help could be sought in cases of emergency. So even if the walker or cyclist does mislay the route, he or she is unlikely to come to any serious grief. The one exception to this is on the Tomintoul Spur, which

## NAVIGATION AND WAYMARKING

heads into the hills for several miles, to a height just a little below 2000ft (610m), and where getting lost could have more serious consequences, so a familiarity with map and compass work is strongly advisable. However, the route is well waymarked in this section too, and in normal weather conditions and good visibility most people would be able to negotiate the section safely. The walks described in the Prologue require a much higher level of navigational skill and experience (see below).

The Speyside Way is waymarked with a white Scottish thistle, identical to that used on all the other official Long Distance Routes in Scotland (West Highland Way, Great Glen Way and Southern Upland Way). These waymarks appear most often on wooden posts. The Tomintoul Spur is similarly waymarked, but the trails of the Dufftown Loop between Aberlour, Dufftown and Craigellachie do not carry the thistle waymarking. Where the Way crosses public roads and at other important junctions along the route, special Speyside Way signposts have been erected, often indicating the distance to the next village along the route. The Speyside Way has its official logo, and this appears on Speyside Way waymarks, signposts and information boards.

The Dava Way, MCT and Moray Way are all waymarked with distinctive logos (see above). The Dava Way carries a triangular logo, depicting a railway viaduct and a bootprint, and the MCT has a distinctive fulmar logo. The sections of the Speyside Way, Dava Way and the MCT that make up the circular Moray Way carry, in addition to their individual trail waymarks and signposts, a special Moray Way logo, which consists of an inverted triangle, with a hiking man symbol, plus a wheel and horseshoe design, within it. The Badenoch Way has simple circular waymarks showing a directional arrow with the words 'Badenoch Way' around the perimeter. There are also numerous signposts or fingerposts on all four trails carrying the trail name and/or logo, reassuring the walker or cyclist that he or she is on the line of the named Way, and usually indicating a distance to the next village, town or amenity.

Other waymarks and signposts will from time to time be encountered. Local signposts indicating paths to nearby villages or sites of interest, waterfalls, distilleries, detours from the specific trails, occur occasionally, as do yellow or blue arrow waymarks, depicting footpath or bridleway. Scottish Rights of Way & Access Society (SROW Society) signposts will be seen in some areas, particularly on the Badenoch Way and Dufftown Loop, and also on some of the trails described in the Prologue. This organisation, founded in 1845, is dedicated to improving countryside access in Scotland, and many of their signposts, often green ones, can be seen all over Scotland indicating ancient rights of way.

The routes in the Prologue require navigational skills of a reasonably high level, and the ability to use map and compass in wilderness mountain and moorland areas, where population density is extremely low and the chances of obtaining assistance in case of difficulty are slim. Getting lost in such a landscape is not an option if a safe traverse of these hills is to be made. Hill fog frequently occurs in these mountains, and an ability to navigate safely in these conditions is essential; the weather can change rapidly, and a warm, clear and fine day can soon become a very wet, cold and foggy one.

In particular the routes from Roybridge/Spean Bridge to Garva Bridge are very long, with no settlements and very few farms en route. Considerable sections are over pathless terrain, in the heart of a wilderness mountain area, although the majority of the routes do follow good tracks and narrow metalled roads. Apart from the occasional SROW Society signposts, no other waymarking or signposting will be found and very few or no other people encountered. The route descriptions in the guidebook are to be used in conjunction with the relevant map. Six-figure grid references are given in the Prologue sections as an aid to navigation. The use of a GPS is recommended, but walkers are strongly advised not to rely on this method of navigation alone.

## WALKING IN SCOTLAND

### Rights of access

The Land Reform (Scotland) Act became law in 2005. This gives the public considerable statutory rights of access to the outdoors, and is one of the most enlightened laws of its kind in Europe. But never forget that these rights of access come with important

*A Badenoch Way waymark*

*The Dava Way follows the disused railway line, heading towards the Bridge of Divie*

responsibilities. The main points of the Scottish Access Code are – take responsibility for your own actions, respect people's privacy and peace of mind, help those who work in the countryside to do so safely and effectively, care for the environment and keep your dog under proper control. It is a good idea, if unfamiliar with walking in Scotland, to acquaint yourself with the new access code by visiting www.outdooraccess-scotland.com or phoning Scottish Natural Heritage on 01738 458545.

The only access problems likely to arise on the Speyside Way, Dava Way and MCT are if a landslip or something similar caused the closure of a section of path for safety reasons, or if tree felling or other forestry operations caused the temporary closure of routes through forestry plantations. Those contemplating the Prologue walks to the source of the River Spey and beyond to Newtonmore should also note that some Highland mountain and moorland estates restrict access to certain areas during the stalking season, from August to October (to check this use the 'Hillphones' service, see Appendix B), and sometimes for the culling of hinds in the winter months.

### Ticks

Tick populations appear to be on the increase in the upland areas of Britain. The usual hosts of the tick are sheep and deer, but care should be exercised to avoid humans being bitten, as ticks are carriers of Lyme's Disease, a serious condition. It should not be cause for great concern, nor spoil your walk, but do be aware of the problem. Long trousers rather than shorts are advisable as ticks are most commonly picked up from vegetation along the route. Check the skin frequently for ticks, and if found remove them at once, taking care not to leave the mouthparts still attached (a special small tool can be purchased for this purpose). Those walking the upland areas described in the Prologue are at a greater risk of encountering these pests than those who keep to the standard trails. Visit www.tickalert.org for further information.

## USING THIS GUIDE

The guide is divided into three main sections:
- the **Speyside Way** – source to sea, which includes:
  - **Prologue** – details of routes to the source of the River Spey and from there to Newtonmore, which will eventually be the official starting point of the Speyside Way
  - the **Badenoch Way** and links – a route from Newtonmore to Aviemore
  - the **Speyside Way**, including the Tomintoul Spur and Dufftown Loop
- the **Dava Way**
- the **Moray Coast Trail**.

Each section has an introduction outlining the main features of the trails, their history and various points of special interest. A sketch map of each of the trails is also given, for easy reference. Then comes the practical guide to the trail, with details of the route in black type and notes on places of interest in brown type, so that each is easily identified when using the guide in the field. The 'places of interest' notes will help you to make the most of your walking holiday and not miss a visit to those places that convert a walk in the countryside into a full and satisfying holiday break.

At the start of each stage of the route is an information box giving details of the relevant trail distance and maps.

In other boxes is information on the various towns and villages along the trails, and brief notes on the facilities likely to be found there (hotels, hostels, B&Bs, campsites, grocery shops, cafés, restaurants, pharmacies, banks, post offices, and bus and train services). Be sure to check these 'Facilities' sections before you set out on a particular stage, so that you will not be caught unawares when arriving in a location with few or no places to eat or stay for the night.

Particular attention has been taken with the route description in areas where special care in navigation is required. If the route description is read in conjunction with the maps in this guidebook there should be, it is hoped, no possibility of mislaying the trail.

Appendix A contains a Route Summary Table, giving distances for the main stages of the described

*A Highland cow in a field on the edge of Arndilly wood (Speyside Way)*

routes and for the entire trails. If you are concerned about the amount of ascent involved in a section of the trail, then this can easily be checked in the table on page 17.

Distances are generally given in this guidebook in miles and yards, and heights in feet (followed by metres), as this is the system used on the Footprint strip maps to the Speyside Way and on the Speyside Way information boards along the official trail. Distances are given in miles and kilometres in the boxes at the start of each stage of the trail and in the Route Summary Table.

Note that references to 'right' and 'left' banks of rivers in the route descriptions refer to the 'true' right or left bank (ie looking downstream).

Although this guide should be all that is required to walk these routes successfully, it is always advisable to check the websites to the various trails before you leave home to confirm that there are no recent changes that will affect your walk or holiday. Usually there are no problems, but just occasionally severe weather conditions can cause flooding, landslips and erosion problems that can make the trail impassable or unsafe in places, leading to necessary diversions. These will all be posted on the trail websites, which are given under Appendix B, along with other websites and addresses of organisations and associations of interest to those walking in Speyside and Moray. Included in the appendix is the Speyside Way Ranger Service in Aberlour; it is also a good idea to contact them for an up-to-date information pack and a list of accommodation, as well as to check for any possible alterations or diversions in operation that may affect your trip.

## LDWA REGISTER OF NATIONAL TRAIL WALKERS

The Long Distance Walkers Association (LDWA) operates a scheme to encourage more walkers to enjoy the National Trails of England and Wales and the official Long Distance Routes of Scotland. After completing a minimum of five trails, the walker qualifies for a Bronze Award and a certificate and their name appears on the Register of National Trail Walkers maintained on the LDWA's website (www.ldwa.org.uk). As an official Long Distance Route, the Speyside Way is one of the trails that counts towards this award, but the Dava Way and Moray Coast Trail do not. There are three higher awards, for walking a minimum of 10 trails (Silver Award), 15 trails (Gold) and the total 18 trails (Diamond).

*Setting sun from Portgordon beach (Moray Coast Trail and Speyside Way)*

# THE SPEYSIDE WAY – SOURCE TO SEA

*Creag Dubh and the River Spey in Upper Speyside*

## THE SPEYSIDE WAY

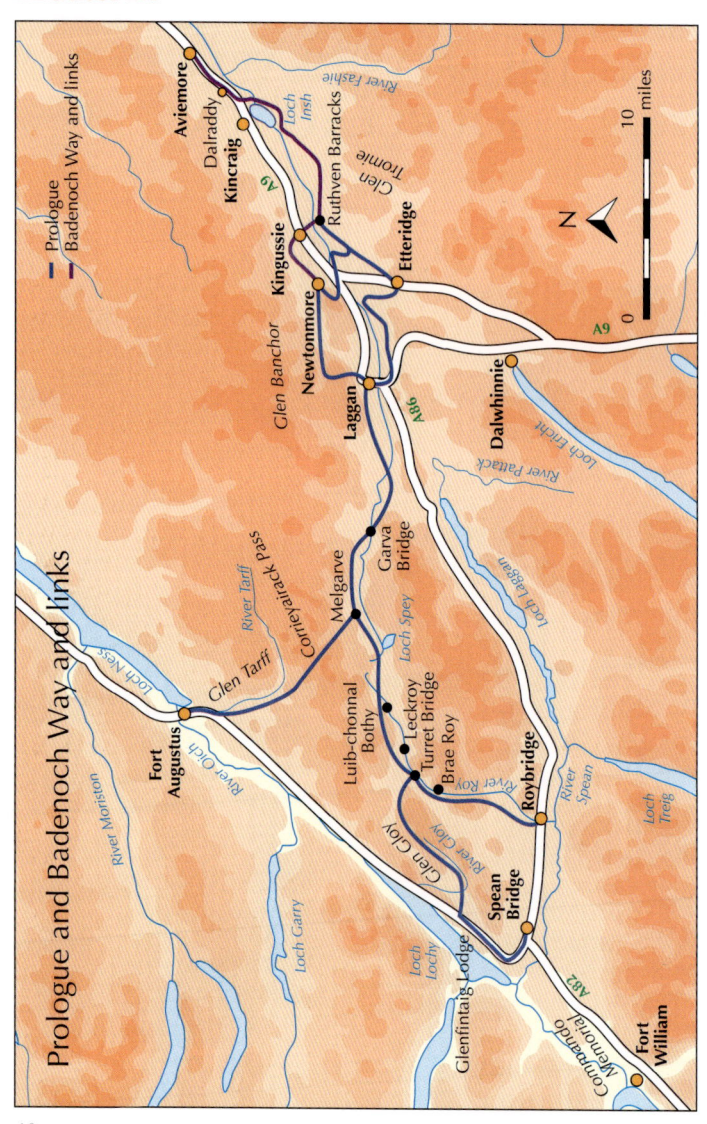

# PROLOGUE

## ROYBRIDGE, SPEAN BRIDGE OR FORT AUGUSTUS TO NEWTONMORE

The official Speyside Way does not follow the River Spey from source to sea, unlike many of the other major river trails in the UK, such as the Thames Path, the Severn Way and the Annandale Way. The main reason for this is that the source of the Spey is in a remote location in the southern region of the huge range of the Monadhliath mountains in the Central Highlands. The very inaccessibility of the source, over 7 miles from the nearest public road and deep in remote mountain country, precludes any possibility of including it in an official Scottish Long Distance Route. Furthermore, any route to the source involves negotiating pathless terrain and fording at least one bridgeless river. Nonetheless, walkers experienced in wilderness hill walking would have no problems in reaching the source in reasonable weather conditions. Although long, the most feasible routes to the source follow fairly well-established Highland routes and for most of their length are on good tracks, paths or minor roads. The remote location of the source of the River Spey adds to the romance of Scotland's most famous Highland river, and for many the fascination of visiting the source will make a visit irresistible.

First, there is the question of where that source is. It is generally considered to be the small body of water known as Loch Spey, which is about ⅓ mile long and 200 yards across at it widest, in a remote spot at NN 420 938, 1150ft (350m) above sea level. From the nearest settlements of any note the loch lies very approximately, as the crow flies, 10 miles south-south-east of Fort Augustus, 12½ miles north-east of Roybridge in Glen Spean and 19 miles west-south-west of Newtonmore. Remote indeed!

However, because a number of burns lead into Loch Spey from the surrounding mountains, the actual source of the River Spey may be elsewhere. Groome's 19th-century *Ordnance Gazetteer of Scotland* (1885) gives the source of the River Spey as 'a small stream which rises about 1500ft above sea level on the south-east side of Creag a' Chail, close to the watershed between the east and west coasts of Scotland ... about one mile from the source this stream enters Loch Spey'. From this description, given before the days of a grid system for the UK, and by study of the relevant OS map, it can be assumed that the main source of the Spey is at or about NN 413 949. The source of the River Spey in this

*The river near Dalnashallag Bothy*

guidebook is considered to be the traditional source, namely Loch Spey. Only very experienced hill walkers should attempt to locate the actual source.

But how to reach the source at Loch Spey? The easiest and shortest route is from the end of the public road at Garva Bridge to the east. This involves a walk of about 7 miles to Loch Spey, on good narrow roads and tracks until the last 1¼ miles, which is over pathless terrain and involves one river crossing, which in normal conditions should present little problem. The return from the source is by the reverse of the outward route.

The experienced hill walker may wish to reach the source by crossing over the watershed from Lochaber in the west. This makes for a fine expedition, which although very long is within the capabilities of most seasoned mountain walkers in good conditions.

Routes from **Roybridge** (Stage 1) and from **Spean Bridge** (Stage 1A) are described below; these meet in upper Glen Roy and follow the same route from there to the end of the trek at Laggan in Speyside. Another approach is the Great Glen to the north, and a route is described from **Fort Augustus** (Stage 1B) over the Corrieyairack Pass.

Walkers wishing to visit Loch Spey, but who do not want to follow any of the long cross-country routes in this section, can reach to source of the river by means of a modest 14-mile 'there-and-back' **side trip** from Garva Bridge (see below), which can be reached by road from Laggan.

From Laggan there are very feasible and pleasant routes to

## PROLOGUE

**Newtonmore** following either the northern or southern side of the Spey valley, which can be conveniently walked as part of a source-to-sea Speyside Walk. The northern route via **Glen Banchor** (Stage 2) and the southern trail along part of General Wade's **Military Road** (Stage 2A) are both described below.

> It is important for the inexperienced to realise that the trails described in this Prologue are not waymarked, except for very occasional SROW Society signposts. Use of map and compass is essential.

The only form of accommodation (B&B/hotel) on these routes is at the three starting points of Roybridge, Spean Bridge and Fort Augustus and at the end of Stage 1, in or near the small village of Laggan. The only form of shelter between these points is at a number of mountain bothies. These are very basic, watertight (usually!), unmanned buildings open to all wayfarers in the hills. Some of them are maintained by the Mountain Bothies Association (MBA – see Appendix B), whilst others are provided by the Highland estates on whose land they are situated.

In the bothies there are seldom toilets (a shovel is usually provided for burying human waste at a sensible distance away from the bothy) and no cookers/stoves. Sometimes there is a fireplace, but fuel for this has to be collected from the vicinity, if available. There are no taps or sinks,

*Palatial living inside Luib-chonnal Bothy, Upper Glen Roy*

although there is usually a source of water (burn or spring) nearby. Sleeping is on the floor or on wooden sleeping platforms (no mattresses – take your own sleeping bag and sleeping mat). The only furniture consists of some chairs and a table. The building will have no electricity or gas supply, with no form of lighting, so bring your own candles.

Despite being very basic, bothies are often a welcome haven for mountain travellers, particularly during inclement weather. They are intended for individuals or groups of two or three friends, never more than six people to a group. Take all your rubbish away with you and leave the bothy clean and tidy. Four bothies are passed on the described trails between Lochaber/Great Glen and Newtonmore, as follows.

### Luib Chonnal (MBA)
In upper Glen Roy at NN 394 937. Stage 1/1A: on the route from Roybridge/Spean Bridge to Laggan.

### Blackburn (MBA)
Below the Corrieyairack Pass at NH 382 029. Stage 1B: on the route between Fort Augustus and Laggan.

### Dalnashallag
In upper Glen Banchor at NN 648 984. Stage 2: on the route between Laggan and Newtonmore via Glen Banchor.

### Luibleathann
Near Lochan Odhar, south of Strathspey and south-east of Newtonmore at NN 738 971. Maintained by the Ralia Estates, on whose land it is situated. Stage 2A: on the route between Laggan and Newtonmore via General Wade's Military Road.

*Backpackers in Newtonmore (Beryl Castle)*

Before departing for these expeditions, it is important to check the weather forecast before leaving the safety of your valley base, and do not set out in very poor and worsening conditions.

## STAGE 1
*Roybridge to Laggan*

| **Distance** | 28½ miles/46km |
|---|---|
| **Maps** | OS Landranger 34 (Fort Augustus) and 35 (Kingussie) |

Although the trail follows minor roads and very good tracks for most of its distance, it traverses very remote mountainous country. It cannot be accomplished in one day except by the very fittest of hill walkers who make an exceptionally early start. All food necessary for a two-day expedition must be carried, plus tent and sleeping bag, although the bothy of Luib Chonnal, 12½ miles from Roybridge, would provide convenient overnight shelter.

The Allt Chonnal must be crossed immediately after the bothy, and if in spate would be very difficult and dangerous to cross. Likewise the Allt Shesgnan could also present problems when the water is running high and

*Falls of Roy in Upper Glen Roy*

## THE SPEYSIDE WAY

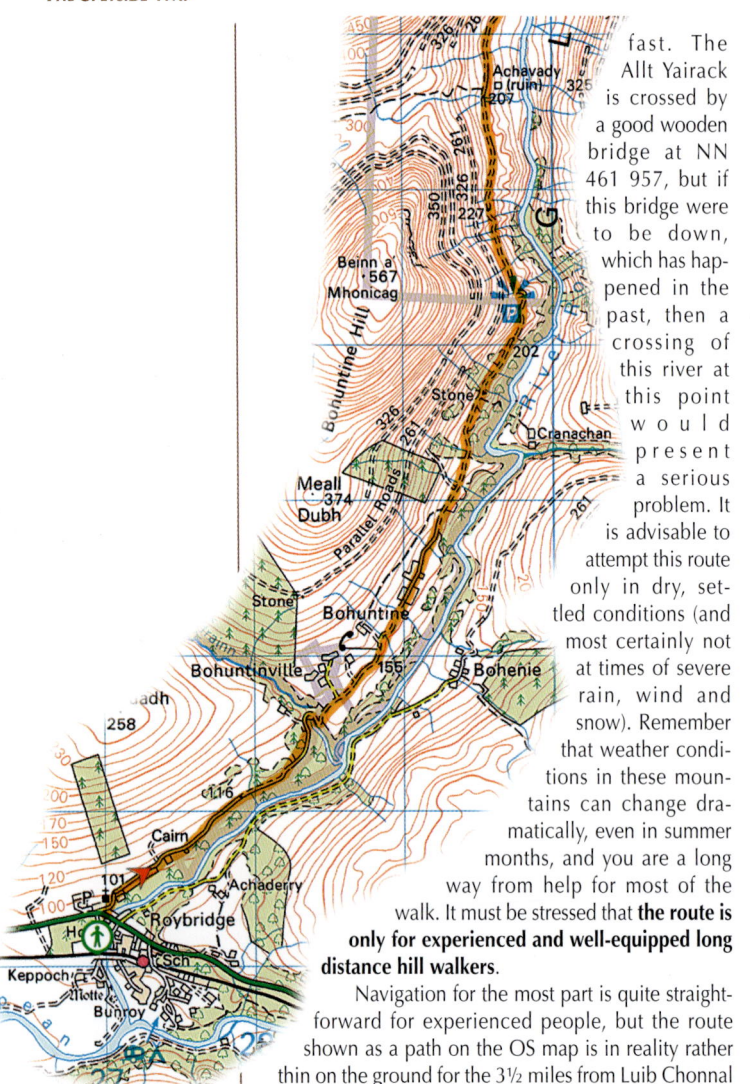

fast. The Allt Yairack is crossed by a good wooden bridge at NN 461 957, but if this bridge were to be down, which has happened in the past, then a crossing of this river at this point would present a serious problem. It is advisable to attempt this route only in dry, settled conditions (and most certainly not at times of severe rain, wind and snow). Remember that weather conditions in these mountains can change dramatically, even in summer months, and you are a long way from help for most of the walk. It must be stressed that **the route is only for experienced and well-equipped long distance hill walkers**.

Navigation for the most part is quite straightforward for experienced people, but the route shown as a path on the OS map is in reality rather thin on the ground for the 3½ miles from Luib Chonnal to Shesgnan over the watershed. In hill fog it may well be

## Prologue Stage 1 – Roybridge to Laggan

confusing, and a compass and map, and the ability to use them, are essential. The highest point reached is 1150ft (350m). The walk is a very fine one indeed, crossing some of the best country in the Central Highlands. Herds of red deer will almost certainly be seen on the crossing.

There is narrow public road for several miles at either end of the route, and if transport is arranged for a drop-off at the end of the public road just before Brae Lodge in Glen Roy, then it would be possible for strong walkers to walk over in one day to Garva Bridge, where a waiting car could be parked in the parking area at the end of the public road.

The stag-stalking season is from 15 August to 20 October, and the hind cull runs from 21 October to 15 February on the Braeroy Estate. During these periods please contact the estate (tel 01397 712587) or use the Hillphones system (see Appendix B) to find out where deer control is taking place before setting out.

*Map continued on page 56*

*The Speyside Way*

## ROYBRIDGE

When the West Highland Railway built a station by the River Roy in 1894 it needed a name and Roybridge was chosen. The village around the station expanded in the late 1920s to house the workers of the Lochaber Project, a massive building project of dams and tunnels.

**Facilities**: independent hostel, hotels, inn, B&B, campsite, village shop with post office

Starting from **Roybridge** walk up Glen Roy along the narrow public road (traffic will be very light) that follows the right bank of the River Roy on the western side of the glen. There are good views of the famous Parallel Roads from the glen road, and a viewpoint and car park with information board will be passed just under a mile south of Achavady.

The remarkable **Parallel Roads** are not man-made roads, but landscape features created thousands of years ago by glacial action. During the last Ice Age advancing glaciers dammed a succession of large lakes in Glen Roy. As these retreated a series of deposits from these shorelines were left, and it is these 'roads' that can still be seen in the glen today. The Parallel Roads

## Prologue Stage 1 – Roybridge to Laggan

and associated landforms are protected as a Site of Special Scientific Interest (SSSI).

From the end of the public road pass **Brae Roy Lodge** and continue on the track along the right bank of the river for about 400 yards to **Turret Bridge** (NN 338 918).

Head north-eastwards on a good track towards the upper reaches of Glen Roy, bearing east after a little over ½ mile, passing **Leckroy** and noting the isolated cottage of Amat south of Leckroy, on the opposite side of the River Roy.

*Map continued on page 58*

About 3 miles after Leckroy take great care to locate an indistinct path which leaves the main track a little before the latter comes to an end and heads for **Luib Chonnal Bothy**, the roof of which can be seen from the track. The bothy is located at NN 394 937, and from it there is a good view to the south-east of White Falls, which is at its most impressive when the river is in spate.

From the bothy to Shesgnan, a distance of almost 3½ miles, the way is over rough, boggy, pathless terrain. Leave the bothy and cross the Allt Chonnal. There is no bridge, so it will be necessary to wade across. Do not attempt a crossing if the river is in spate. Head over very wet and boggy ground aiming for the point at 350m marked 'Col' on the OS Landranger map at NN 410 943.

## THE SPEYSIDE WAY

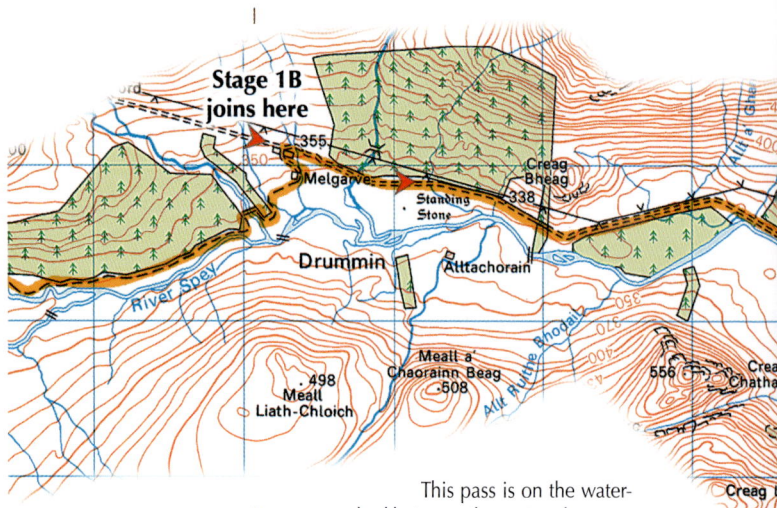

This pass is on the watershed between the east and west coast of Scotland. Pass over the col leaving Glen Roy behind and entering, at long last, the upper reaches of the Spey valley. Head in an east-south-easterly direction until the water of **Loch Spey** comes into view. Head for this and dip your toes in the water, the traditional source of the River Spey. The actual source of the river lies at approximately NN 413 949. Only experienced hill walkers should attempt to reach this point, which involves a tramp over rough ground to the north (a GPS is of considerable use).

Walk east along the northern shore of Loch Spey to its outlet stream, the nascent River Spey. Follow this on its northern bank, heading eastwards. Head towards the large plantation seen ahead, and when the solitary building of Shesgnan comes into view, head directly for it. On the way it is necessary to cross Shesgnan Burn, which is normally a fairly easy crossing, but do not cross in spate conditions. The ground from here onwards tends to be firm and grassy. At **Shesgnan** (private) take the earthen path. All is easy underfoot from now on. Follow the wide path, eventually crossing a wooden bridge over the

## PROLOGUE STAGE 1 – ROYBRIDGE TO LAGGAN

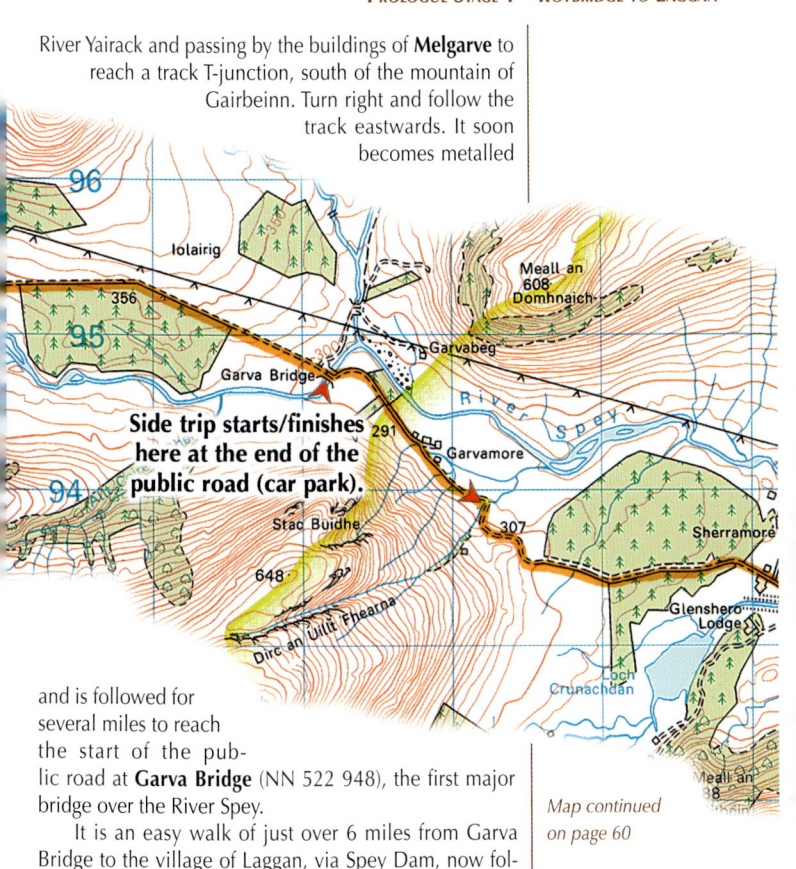

River Yairack and passing by the buildings of **Melgarve** to reach a track T-junction, south of the mountain of Gairbeinn. Turn right and follow the track eastwards. It soon becomes metalled and is followed for several miles to reach the start of the public road at **Garva Bridge** (NN 522 948), the first major bridge over the River Spey.

It is an easy walk of just over 6 miles from Garva Bridge to the village of Laggan, via Spey Dam, now following the young Spey valley out of the mountains. The walk follows a narrow tarmac road, which carries very little traffic. There are opportunities to spot red deer en route, and often several oystercatchers can be seen in the vicinity of the loch to the west of Spey Dam. You will encounter your first street lights since leaving Roybridge in **Laggan**, where there are seats and picnic tables at the pleasant Pond and Picnic Area, located by a parking area to the right of the road.

*Map continued on page 60*

*The Speyside Way*

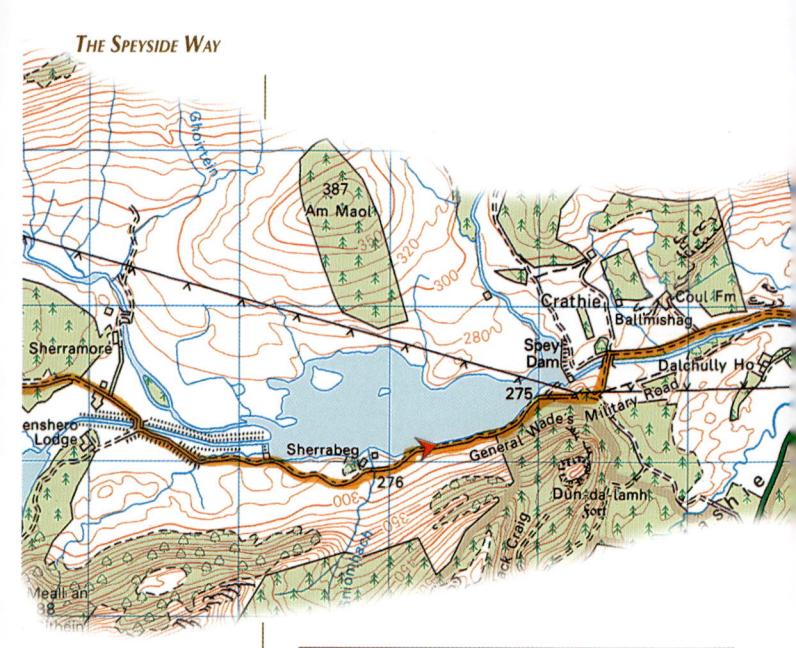

## LAGGAN

Thomas Telford was active here, designing the church in 1785 and the original bridge over the Spey. On the prominent hill of Carn Dearg to the south stands a monument to Cluny McPherson, an old clan chief who once owned all the land visible from the hill. The monument is seen to good advantage from the village, as is 'Copes Turn', the point where in 1745 General Cope, who was commanding Government forces, retreated to Inverness on hearing of the Jacobite advance. Drumgask Farm, south of the Spey, was once a famous coaching inn. In more recent memory the shop at Laggan will be familiar as 'Glenbogle Stores' to viewers of the TV series 'Monarch of the Glen'.

**Facilities**: 2 nearby hotels (one passed on the Glen Banchor route and another on General Wade's Military Road route – see below) and some B&Bs. The village shop, open 7 days a week, sells hot drinks; there is

## PROLOGUE STAGE 1 – ROYBRIDGE TO LAGGAN

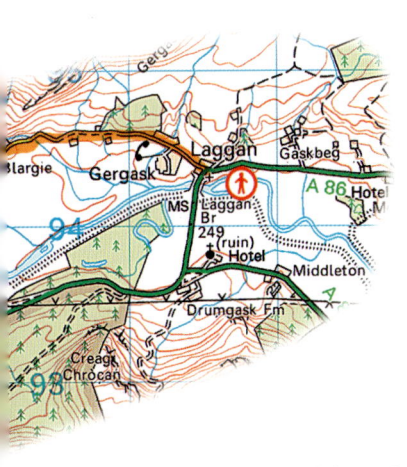

a limited bus service on school days only (bus from Newtonmore at 7.40am and return from Laggan Bridge at 4.30pm). A café and a bunkhouse are situated just outside the village.

*The infant River Spey near Shesgnan, Upper Speyside*

## STAGE 1A
### Spean Bridge to Laggan

| | |
|---|---|
| **Distance** | 34½ miles/55.4km |
| **Maps** | OS Landranger 34 (Fort Augustus) and 35 (Kingussie) |

This route via Glen Gloy is longer and more difficult than the trail from Roybridge for three reasons.

- The first 3½ miles follow the busy A82 trunk road to Glenfintaig Lodge (NN 223 864). This road carries fast and often heavy traffic, and so it is unsafe to walk from the Commando's Monument to Glenfintaig Lodge, a section on which there is no pavement, unless a very early start in the morning is made from Spean Bridge when traffic is usually very light (but this should only be done at the time of year when there is daylight in the very early morning). The only sensible and safe option is to arrange transport to Glenfintaig Lodge (if travelling by bus ask the driver if he will drop you here).
- Navigational skills are required to negotiate the pathless trail from Auchivarie to Turret Bridge. The terrain is very rough, steep at times and very remote. **This walk is for experienced, well-equipped wilderness mountain walkers only, who are capable of navigating considerable distances over featureless and pathless terrain.** The route rises to a maximum height of 1170ft (357m).
- It is considerably longer than the trail from Roybridge. Two or even three days are required, and the only shelter, as with the Glen Roy route, is at the Bothy of Luib Chonnal, 18 miles from Spean Bridge.

It meets the route from Roybridge at Turret Bridge and from thereon the two routes run together.

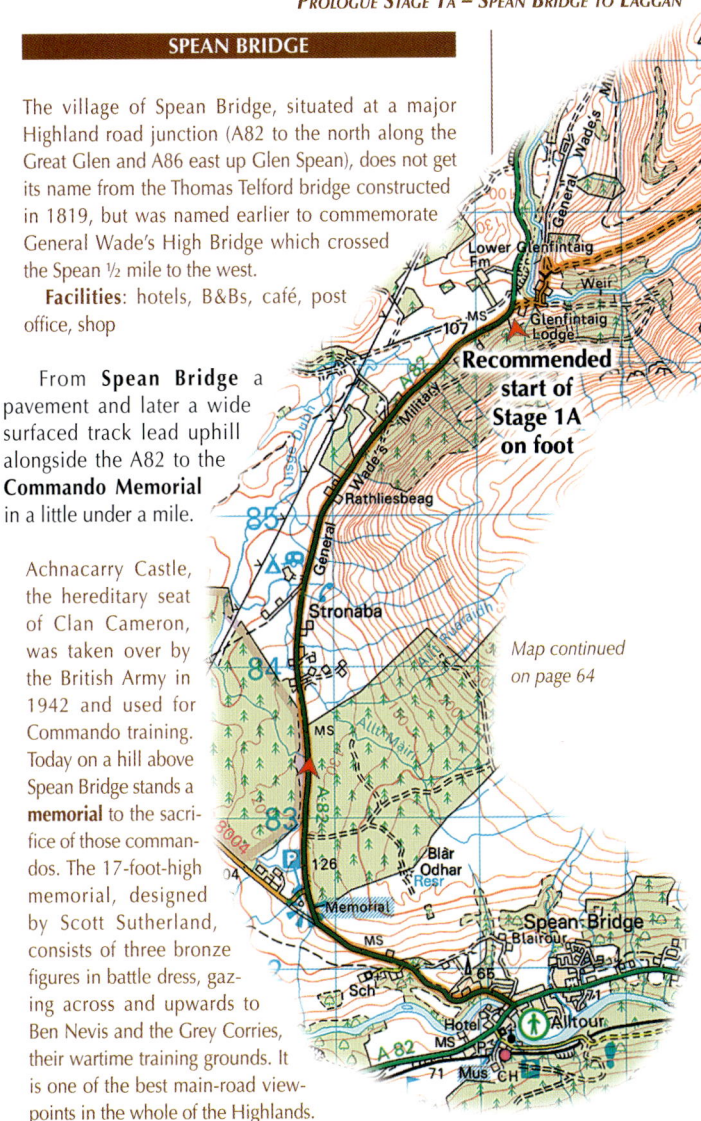

## PROLOGUE STAGE 1A – SPEAN BRIDGE TO LAGGAN

### SPEAN BRIDGE

The village of Spean Bridge, situated at a major Highland road junction (A82 to the north along the Great Glen and A86 east up Glen Spean), does not get its name from the Thomas Telford bridge constructed in 1819, but was named earlier to commemorate General Wade's High Bridge which crossed the Spean ½ mile to the west.

**Facilities**: hotels, B&Bs, café, post office, shop

From **Spean Bridge** a pavement and later a wide surfaced track lead uphill alongside the A82 to the **Commando Memorial** in a little under a mile.

Achnacarry Castle, the hereditary seat of Clan Cameron, was taken over by the British Army in 1942 and used for Commando training. Today on a hill above Spean Bridge stands a **memorial** to the sacrifice of those commandos. The 17-foot-high memorial, designed by Scott Sutherland, consists of three bronze figures in battle dress, gazing across and upwards to Ben Nevis and the Grey Corries, their wartime training grounds. It is one of the best main-road viewpoints in the whole of the Highlands.

*Map continued on page 64*

Recommended start of Stage 1A on foot

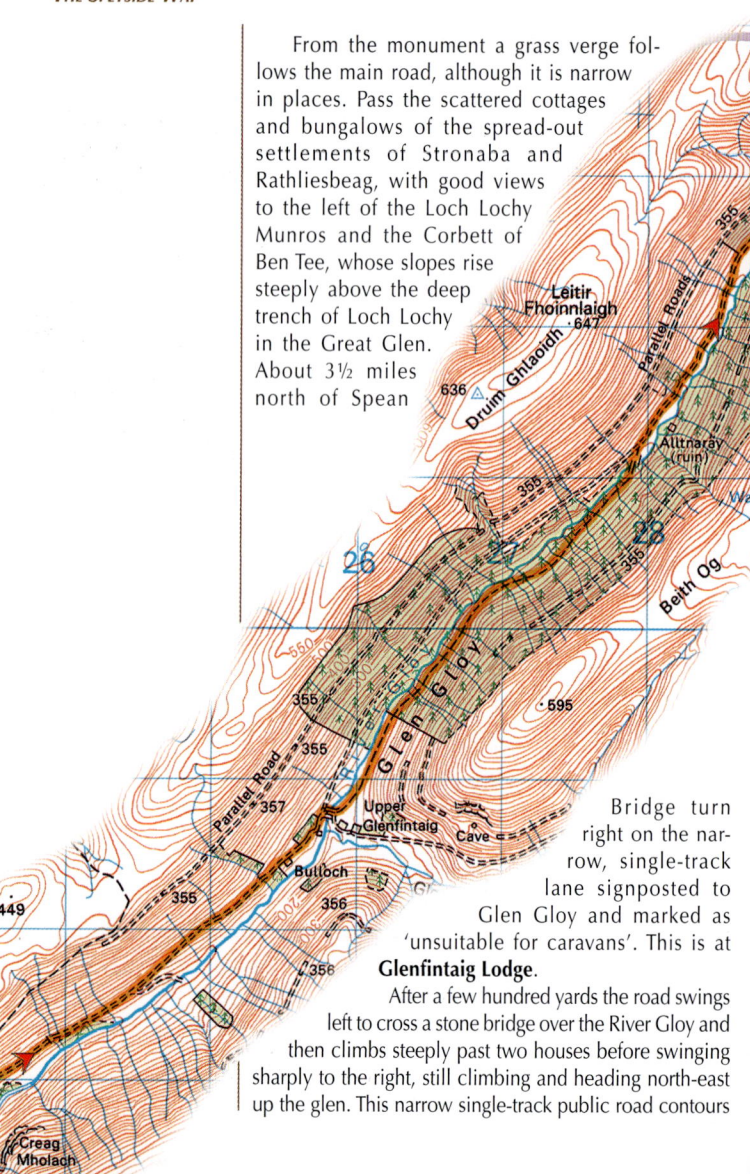

## THE SPEYSIDE WAY

From the monument a grass verge follows the main road, although it is narrow in places. Pass the scattered cottages and bungalows of the spread-out settlements of Stronaba and Rathliesbeag, with good views to the left of the Loch Lochy Munros and the Corbett of Ben Tee, whose slopes rise steeply above the deep trench of Loch Lochy in the Great Glen. About 3½ miles north of Spean Bridge turn right on the narrow, single-track lane signposted to Glen Gloy and marked as 'unsuitable for caravans'. This is at **Glenfintaig Lodge**.

After a few hundred yards the road swings left to cross a stone bridge over the River Gloy and then climbs steeply past two houses before swinging sharply to the right, still climbing and heading north-east up the glen. This narrow single-track public road contours

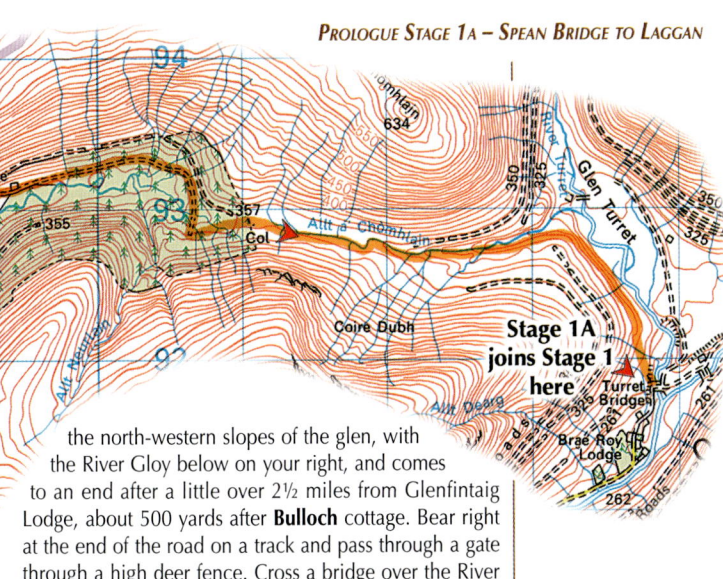

## PROLOGUE STAGE 1A – SPEAN BRIDGE TO LAGGAN

the north-western slopes of the glen, with the River Gloy below on your right, and comes to an end after a little over 2½ miles from Glenfintaig Lodge, about 500 yards after **Bulloch** cottage. Bear right at the end of the road on a track and pass through a gate through a high deer fence. Cross a bridge over the River Gloy and in about 40 yards, before the large house ahead, turn left through another gate (be sure to fasten both gates securely).

Take the grassy track heading up the valley, now with the river below on your left. Follow this often wet and ill-defined track through a large plantation, eventually descending to cross a wooden bridge at NN 279 911. Continue now with the River Gloy on your right, soon joining a more substantial track, heading up the glen and now in open country. Soon afterwards note the sparse ruins of **Alltnaray** on the opposite bank of the river. After a further 1½ miles the track passes the two solitary buildings of **Auchivarie** and then enters woodland, soon climbing, before coming to an abrupt end at NN 306 928.

From here to Turret Bridge the route requires very careful navigation, and to proceed from here requires experience in such terrain; a GPS would be a considerable asset. Leave the track heading slightly north of east through the trees. Progress will require ducking and weaving under trees and over very rough ground. After little more than 5 minutes you should reach a boggy clearing in the trees as you begin to reach the edge of the forest plantation, where the density of the trees thins out. It is essential to locate a large stile in the deer fence that signifies the limit of the plantation; this is at NN 311 929.

Climb over the stile and head eastwards over this wide col (1170ft, 357m) on boggy, pathless grassland. Keep over to the right, so that when the deeply cut valley begins to appear, the river is over to your left. The aim is to reach Turret Bridge at NN 338 918. This requires careful navigation over rough and often steep ground. Beware the final approach to the bridge, as it is quite steep. Eventually descend to a track and cross the stone **Turret Bridge**, which is about 400 yards north of **Brae Roy Lodge**. From here follow the route described in Stage 1 to **Garva Bridge** and **Laggan**.

## SIDE TRIP
*Garva Bridge to Loch Spey and back*

| | |
|---|---|
| **Distance** | 14 miles/22km return |
| **Maps** | OS Landranger 35 (Kingussie) and 34 (Fort Augustus) |

The shortest and easiest way to reach the source of the River Spey at Loch Spey is from the end of the public Road at **Garva Bridge**, NN 522 948. (Note that Garva Bridge is not served by public transport, so it will be necessary to either walk from Laggan (a 13-mile round trip) or else use private transport or taxi.)

The walk is an easy one on a metalled track until just before **Melgarve**, and then on good tracks and wide, clear paths to the building of **Shesgnan**. The final 1¼ miles to Loch Spey is, however, over featureless and pathless terrain where care should be exercised. From Shesgnan head south-westwards. It is necessary to cross the bridgeless Allt Shesgnan in order to reach the northern shore of **Loch Spey**, a fairly easy crossing in normal conditions,

## PROLOGUE SIDE TRIP – GARVA BRIDGE TO LOCH SPEY AND BACK

but do not attempt a crossing if the burn is high and fast flowing. Return by the reverse of the outward route.

Although this walk is not of the severity of the routes from Roybridge and Spean Bridge, Loch Spey is nevertheless in remote country, and the last section is over trackless and rough terrain. Do not attempt the walk in bad weather conditions. It is important to carry and use both map and compass.

*Track near Shesgnan, Upper Speyside*

Garva Bridge over the infant River Spey at the end of the public road west of Laggan is the important changeover point (from foot to cycles/mountain bikes) in the **Corrieyairack Challenge**, a fellrunning/walking–mountain biking duathlon event held every year in July (43 miles from Fort Augustus to Kincraig). On that day the narrow road will be bustling with traffic and the small car park at Garva Bridge packed with vehicles and waiting bicycles.

## STAGE 1B
*Fort Augustus to Laggan*

| | |
|---|---|
| **Distance** | 31 miles/50km |
| **Maps** | OS Landranger 34 (Fort Augustus) and 35 (Kingussie) |

A third possible approach to Loch Spey is from Fort Augustus in the north. This is a long, but in good conditions relatively easy walk on a good track, one of General Wade's Military Roads, over the famous Corrieyairack Pass, used by Bonny Prince Charlie on his march south from Glenfinnan in 1745.

Head south from **Fort Augustus** on minor public roads to **Culachy**, from where Wade's road climbs by numerous sharp bends to the summit of the **Corrieyairack Pass**. The small bothy of Blackburn (MBA) is passed en route for the summit of the pass at NH 382 029. More hairpin bends lead down into Speyside. At **Melgarve** make the 3-mile detour to **Loch Spey**, returning by the same route and then continuing to **Garva Bridge** and **Laggan** (see Stage 1 above).

Although somewhat less serious than the routes from Roybridge and Spean Bridge, the Corrieyairack Pass does reach a height of 2540ft (775m), far higher than on either of the other two trails. Do not attempt the route in bad weather conditions.

## PROLOGUE STAGE 1B – FORT AUGUSTUS TO LAGGAN

*Map continued on page 70*

*THE SPEYSIDE WAY*

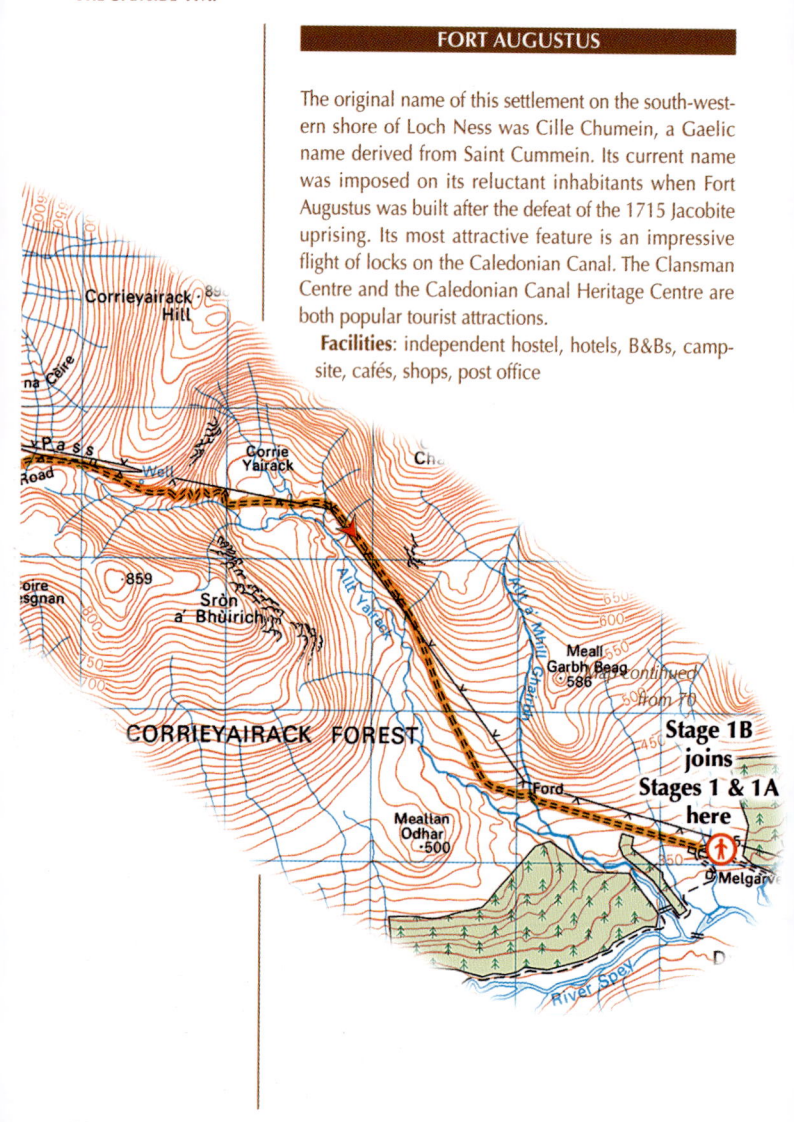

## FORT AUGUSTUS

The original name of this settlement on the south-western shore of Loch Ness was Cille Chumein, a Gaelic name derived from Saint Cummein. Its current name was imposed on its reluctant inhabitants when Fort Augustus was built after the defeat of the 1715 Jacobite uprising. Its most attractive feature is an impressive flight of locks on the Caledonian Canal. The Clansman Centre and the Caledonian Canal Heritage Centre are both popular tourist attractions.

**Facilities**: independent hostel, hotels, B&Bs, campsite, cafés, shops, post office

## STAGE 2
*Laggan to Newtonmore via Glen Banchor*

| Distance | 10 miles/16.2km |
|---|---|
| Map | OS Landranger 35 (Kingussie) |

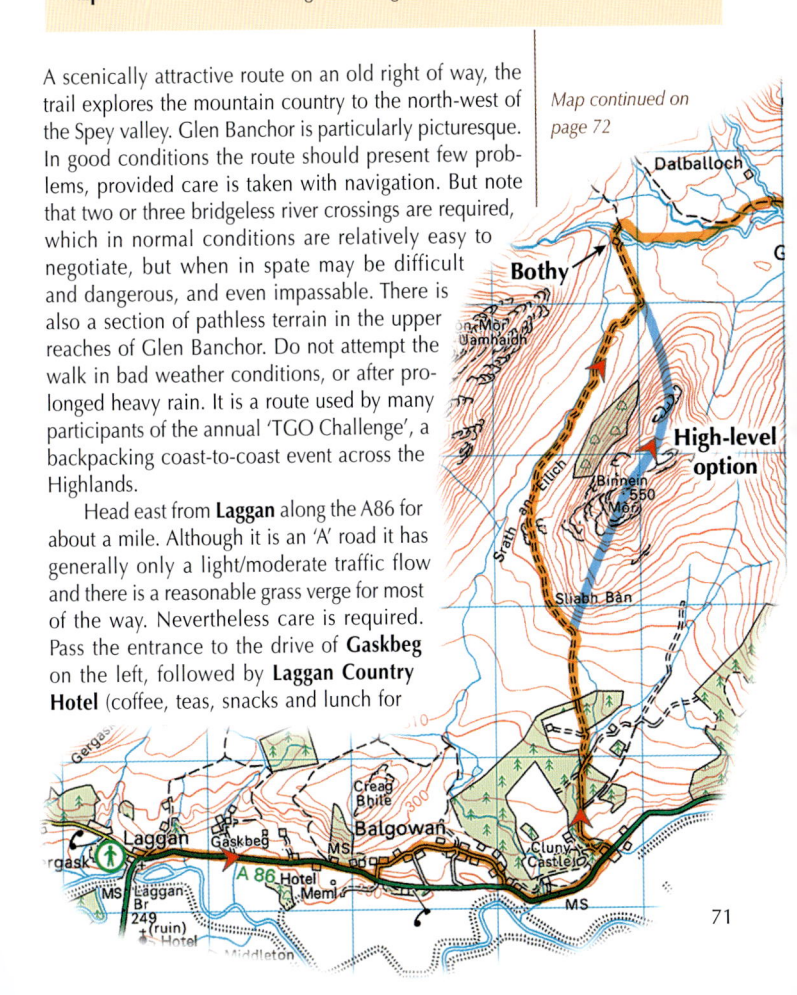

A scenically attractive route on an old right of way, the trail explores the mountain country to the north-west of the Spey valley. Glen Banchor is particularly picturesque. In good conditions the route should present few problems, provided care is taken with navigation. But note that two or three bridgeless river crossings are required, which in normal conditions are relatively easy to negotiate, but when in spate may be difficult and dangerous, and even impassable. There is also a section of pathless terrain in the upper reaches of Glen Banchor. Do not attempt the walk in bad weather conditions, or after prolonged heavy rain. It is a route used by many participants of the annual 'TGO Challenge', a backpacking coast-to-coast event across the Highlands.

Head east from **Laggan** along the A86 for about a mile. Although it is an 'A' road it has generally only a light/moderate traffic flow and there is a reasonable grass verge for most of the way. Nevertheless care is required. Pass the entrance to the drive of **Gaskbeg** on the left, followed by **Laggan Country Hotel** (coffee, teas, snacks and lunch for

*Map continued on page 72*

*The Speyside Way*

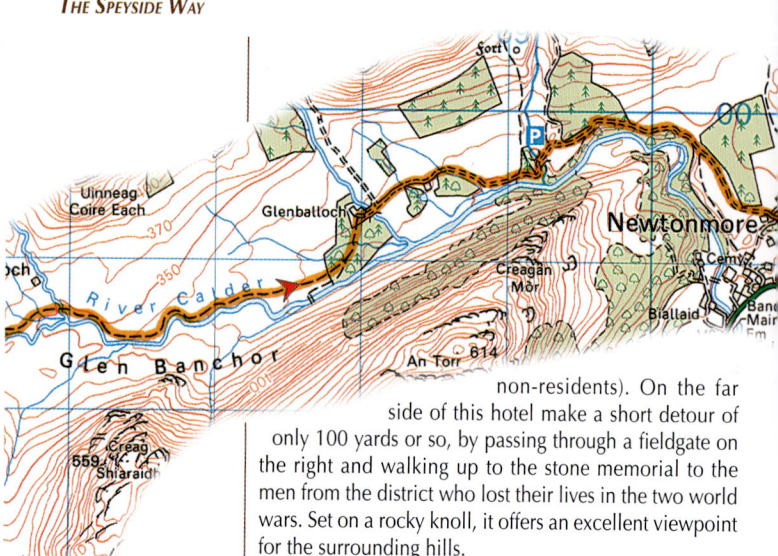

non-residents). On the far side of this hotel make a short detour of only 100 yards or so, by passing through a fieldgate on the right and walking up to the stone memorial to the men from the district who lost their lives in the two world wars. Set on a rocky knoll, it offers an excellent viewpoint for the surrounding hills.

Return to the road and continue along it for another 350 yards to the minor road on the left signposted to **Balgowan**. Follow this tranquil lane as it passes several farms and house, then rejoins the A86 after a little over ½ mile at the entrance gates to **Cluny Castle**. Follow the A86 for a further ½ mile to the green SROW Society's signpost indicating the public footpath to Newtonmore via Glen Banchor. Turn left on the track here, continuing to a gate where another SROW waymark points the way north up Srath an Eilich. On reaching a pair of fieldgates on the edge of woodland, be sure to pass through the one on the left and then follow the track ahead. Next pass through a gate in a deer fence, and then take the right hand of two tracks. A final bridlegate to the right of a fieldgate takes you out onto open moorland.

### High-level option
The heather-covered hill ahead, slightly to the right, is **Binnein Mor** (1804ft, 550m). Enthusiastic

## Prologue Stage 2 – Laggan to Newtonmore via Glen Banchor

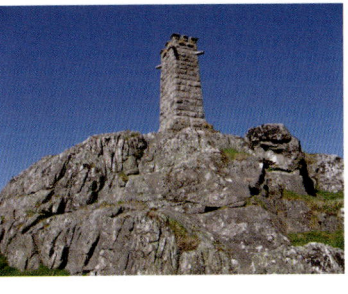

*Memorial to the fallen of both world wars on hill top near Balgowan*

> hillwalkers have the opportunity to climb this en route to Dalnashallag Bothy, although do bear in mind that there is no path to the summit. To bag the hill leave the track at NN 645 959 and climb the south-south-west ridge over a series of false summits to the rarely visited summit cairn, from where a fine all-round view is ample reward for the effort. The prominent hill of Creag Dhubh lies to the east, and the high mountains that were passed on the previous day's jaunt to Laggan can be seen on a clear day to the south-west. Descend the north-north-east ridge, curving off to the left on the lower slopes to rejoin the track at NN 650 980.

The easy alternative to the high-level option is to follow the track all the way up Srath an Eilich to the non-MBA **bothy** of Dalnashallag at NN 648 984 in upper Glen Banchor. The bothy, run by the estate, is a cosy little place, with a fireplace and a comfy settee.

The **bridge** shown on the OS map over the Allt Madagain was, in May 2009, very unsafe. If it has not been replaced or strengthened then it will be necessary to ford this burn. Follow this mountain stream downstream. There is little evidence of a path on the ground. Next, cross Allt an Lochain Duibh followed by Allt Ballach, two further burns. All three streams have now joined to form

*Summit cairn of Binnein Mor, looking towards Glen Banchor*

the River Calder. Note the isolated building of **Dalballoch** a few hundred yards to the north as you continue down Glen Banchor, following the River Calder downstream, eastwards along its northern bank.

A path will soon be encountered, although it is easily lost from time to time in boggy ground. The path becomes clearer the further east one travels. Eventually a gate is reached in a deer fence. Pass through this and then follow a grassy path through trees, soon crossing a small stream before swinging north to meet the gate, a trio of buildings and a bridge over the Allt Fionndrigh at **Glenballoch**. After the bridge, walk ahead on the track for ¾ mile to cross the bridge over the Allt Chaorainn, where a narrow metalled public road is reached, near a small car park and public footpath sign.

Follow this quiet lane for almost 1½ miles to Newtonmore. This road offers a very scenic route and there are several benches along it on which to relax and enjoy the extensive views. The lane eventually descends to pass the town car park and meet the high street in the heart of **Newtonmore**.

## NEWTONMORE

Prior to the early 19th century there was no recorded village at Newtonmore, but following the construction of a new Spey bridge in 1756 a new road joining the drove road from Laggan to Fort William developed, and alongside this a few houses were built. A plan of the village in 1828 shows these houses and refers to the settlement as Newtown-more (the 'new town on the moor', not the 'large new town', as might be expected from the Gaelic 'mor' meaning 'big' or 'great'). Traffic along the drove road aided the development of the settlement, and the opening of the Highland Railway in 1863 made the village accessible to tourists from the south, following in the footsteps of Queen Victoria.

**Attractions**: excellent **Clan MacPherson Museum**, open April to October, 7 days a week, free but donation requested; **Wild Cat Information Centre** (open most mornings) with information on a 10km walk encircling the village; **Waltzing Waters**, an elaborate 40-minute water, light and music show, open 7 days a week, gift shop and small café; **Highland Folk Museum** (see under Badenoch Way, Stage 1). **Shinty** is a very popular sport in this region, and matches can be watched most Saturdays between April and September at the Newtonmore Shinty ground.

**Facilities**: 2 independent hostels on Main Street, two hotels, several B&Bs. A Camping & Caravanning Club listed site is on the outskirts of village. Several cafés. Newtonmore Grill on outskirts of village on Old Perth Road can be recommended (open 7 days a week from early until late with good food, popular with lorry drivers). Co-op food shop open 7 days a week. Bookshop. Post office and bank with ATM. Mainline railway station and bus services. Tourist Information Centre and internet in Newtonmore Craft Centre and Garden Café.

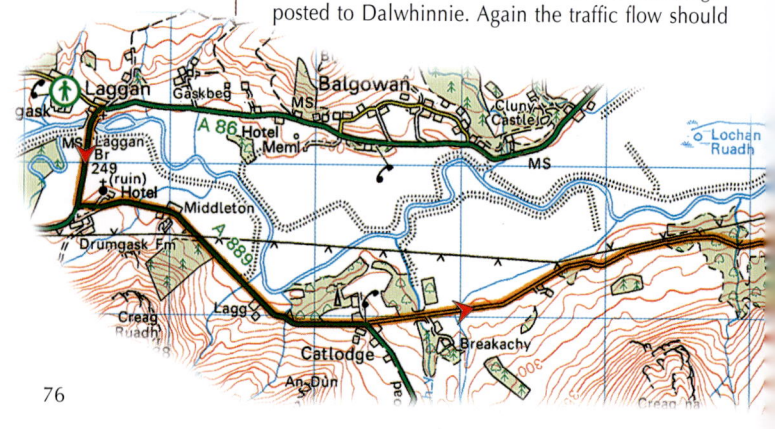

*THE SPEYSIDE WAY*

## STAGE 2A
*Laggan to Newtonmore via the Military Road*

| | |
|---|---|
| **Distance** | 15 miles/24.4km |
| **Map** | OS Landranger 35 (Kingussie) |

A longer alternative to the Glen Banchor route, but safe to walk in wet weather conditions, as there are no bridge-less river crossings to negotiate. This route follows the line of General Wade's 18th-century military road on good grassy tracks, straight as a die for several miles, on the edge of moorland to the south-east of the Spey valley. There is some road walking, at the beginning and end of the trail, but the views to the surrounding mountains are often excellent, and for most of the trail the walker can enjoy tranquil and picturesque Highland surroundings. It is a walk through a variety of landscapes, from native deciduous woodland to open hillsides and moorland.

Cross the bridge over the River Spey at **Laggan** and walk south on the A86. There is a narrow grass verge, but generally the numbers of vehicles is only moderate/light, as the bulk of the traffic uses the nearby A9 trunk road. After about ⅓ mile turn left onto the A889, signposted to Dalwhinnie. Again the traffic flow should

## PROLOGUE STAGE 2A – LAGGAN TO NEWTONMORE VIA THE MILITARY ROAD

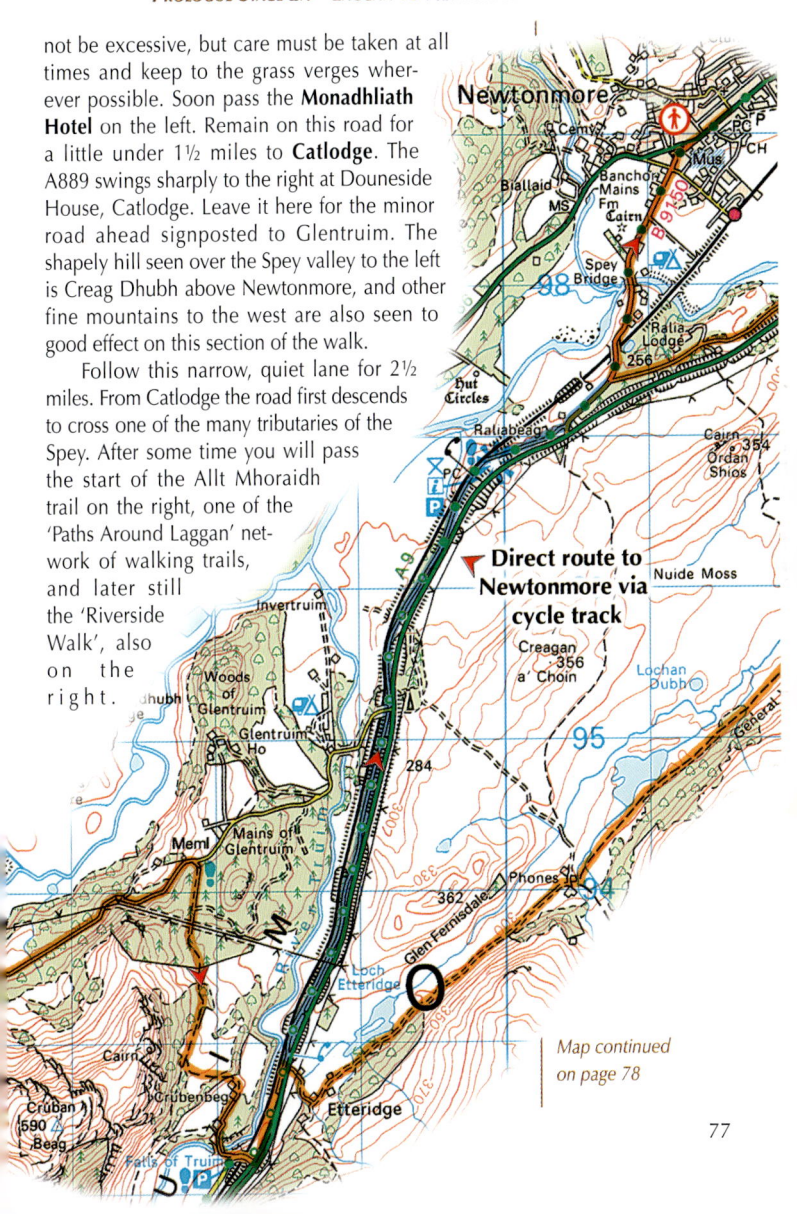

not be excessive, but care must be taken at all times and keep to the grass verges wherever possible. Soon pass the **Monadhliath Hotel** on the left. Remain on this road for a little under 1½ miles to **Catlodge**. The A889 swings sharply to the right at Douneside House, Catlodge. Leave it here for the minor road ahead signposted to Glentruim. The shapely hill seen over the Spey valley to the left is Creag Dhubh above Newtonmore, and other fine mountains to the west are also seen to good effect on this section of the walk.

Follow this narrow, quiet lane for 2½ miles. From Catlodge the road first descends to cross one of the many tributaries of the Spey. After some time you will pass the start of the Allt Mhoraidh trail on the right, one of the 'Paths Around Laggan' network of walking trails, and later still the 'Riverside Walk', also on the right.

*Map continued on page 78*

## THE SPEYSIDE WAY

About 750 yards after passing under high-tension electricity cables reach, on your left, a large **memorial cairn** to Clan McPherson. Some 50 yards later see a third 'Paths Around Laggan' signpost on the right, this one for the Glen Truim Trail. Turn right on the earthen track here, leaving the metalled lane at this point.

The **Clan McPherson memorial cairn** is dedicated by the chief of the McPherson Clan to Ewan McPherson of Cluny (1706–1764), a loyal Jacobite who was strongly involved in the '45 rebellion of the 18th century before escaping to France in 1755. The memorial was unveiled just over 250 years after the Jacobite uprising, in a ceremony in 1996. The McPherson Clan has the enigmatic motto: 'Touch not the Cat But a Glove'. Benches surround the cairn, from where a fine view of Craig Dhubh, which towers above Newtonmore, can be enjoyed.

Head south through delightful Truim Woods, ignoring signed paths to right and left. The trail emerges into

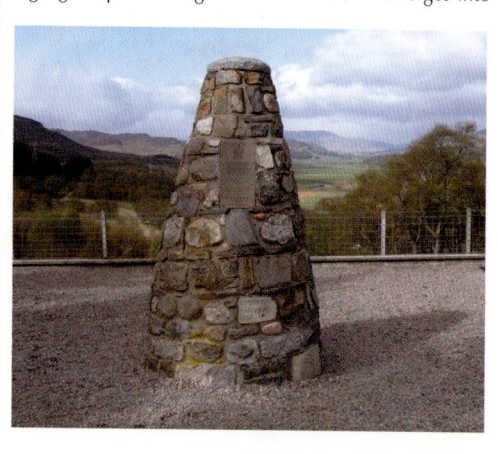

*The Clan McPherson monument, south-west of the Mains of Glentruim*

## Prologue Stage 2a – Laggan to Newtonmore via the Military Road

open country, soon following a dry stone wall on the left and again offering good views of the distant high mountains. Soon a prominent green metal signpost is reached, indicating the right of way to the Perth Road. Take this, following wooden waymarker posts. Keep a wire fence over to your left as you first descend a grassy field and then follow a path through sparse woodland to a gate. Pass through this and cross the grassy field ahead before descending, following waymarkers around the perimeter of the buildings of **Crubenbeg** Farm and emerging onto a narrow metalled lane. Follow this road to cross a bridge over the River Truim, a tributary of the Spey, and then follow the lane as it swings to the left to cross over the mainline railway line and meet the A9 trunk road.

The quickest and easiest (but certainly not the most pleasant) way to Newtonmore from here is along the **cycle path** (part of National Cycle Route 7); turn left and follow it alongside the busy A9. This cycleway is completely free of vehicular traffic, but do beware of occasional approaching cyclists. The cycleway is wedged between the mainline railway and the A9 and follows the route of the old A9, built before the modern trunk road was constructed.

To continue with Wade's route carefully cross the A9, which is busy with very-fast moving traffic. Then take the wide grass verge northwards along the A9 for about ⅓ mile to reach a green SROW Society's signpost at Etteridge. This indicates the 'Public Footpath to Ruthven Barracks by Wade's Military Road'. Turn right here onto the track to pass through the tiny community of **Etteridge** and reach a track T-junction on the far side of Etteridge Farm. Turn left to leave Etteridge on General Wade's Military Road, a well-surfaced track, passing Loch Etteridge to arrive at **Phones** Lodge. Here, bear to the right, with the large buildings of the lodge on your right, then swing left across a wooden bridge over a burn and continue ahead on a grassy track. Wade's Road continues more or less in a straight line, heading north-east. The trail offers first-rate walking on a very pleasant track, with expansive views of distant mountains.

*Stone bridge on General Wade's Road north of Phones*

## GENERAL WADE'S MILITARY ROADS

In 1724, an era of Jacobite rebellion, General Wade identified that a lack of roads and bridges in the Highlands made it difficult for British troops to effectively respond to uprisings. The building of these roads was undertaken by British troops, who were paid double wages whilst working on the roads. The roads often followed the lines of previous routes, particularly drove roads. They were built at a standard 16 feet width, and wherever possible were constructed as straight lines. Camps for soldiers were situated at 10-mile intervals alongside the roads, and inns ('kinghouses') were also built. By 1740, when Wade left Scotland on being promoted to Field Marshall, over 300 miles had been constructed. His successor, Major Caulfeild, oversaw construction of a further 800 miles of road.

After an area of mature silver birch woodland, pass through a gate in a deer fence to follow a path over heather moorland. On the way to **Lochan Odhar** a stone memorial to a local gamekeeper is passed. Eventually reach a cross-tracks (NN 736 973) on the far side of this

## Prologue Stage 2a – Laggan to Newtonmore via the Military Road

lochan. Some 300 yards to the right (south-east) lies the bothy of **Luibleathann** (at NN 738 971), whereas the continuing route to Newtonmore turns to the left here. Luibleathann Bothy, open to all, is maintained by the Ralia Estates on whose land it stands. ▶ It is quite a large building with a fireplace and wood store, the latter in the porch. There is a bothy book inside, which makes interesting reading, with accounts from the many different people who have stayed there.

> The bothy is worth a stop, maybe for a snack or for shelter from inclement weather.

After visiting the bothy, return to the cross-tracks by **Lochan Odhar** at NN 736 973 (* see below) and take the path heading north-west. After about 250 yards go ahead at an oblique cross-tracks. There is a superb view ahead of the mountain ranges north and west of the Spey valley. Descend on this track to the **A9**. Cross this trunk road with great care, turn right and walk with caution along the grass verge of the road for about 400 yards to a minor road on the left. Take this narrow lane and follow it for a little over 1½ miles to a road T-junction, south of Newtonmore. This is the road leading from the A9 to Newtonmore and is part of National Cycle Route 7. Turn right along it, keeping to the roadside verges, taking special care of traffic over the narrow bridge across the railway line. Cross the Spey Bridge, noting that the river is now considerably wider that it was near its source. Pass the Spey Bridge Caravan and Camp Site and keep straight on to enter **Newtonmore** High Street.

### Route avoiding Newtonmore

It is possible to short cut the route and head straight to Kingussie or to the Badenoch Way from the cross-tracks at NN 736 973 (see above), saving several miles of walking. (It is 2½ miles to Ruthven Barracks, near Kingussie and the Badenoch Way, by this direct route.) To do this pass through a metal gate at the **cross-tracks** and continue ahead, still heading north-east. Kingussie is now in view ahead left in the Spey valley below. Walk ahead at the next (oblique) cross-tracks. Soon cross a wide, fast-flowing river by means of a wooden bridge over to the right, and then rejoin the main track, maintaining

*View of the Mondahliath Mountains from Luibleathann Bothy*

direction. On reaching a deer fence at a path Y-junction, pass through the gate and continue ahead, with the deer fence on your left. Pass over a stile and a gate at a second deer fence and pass a narrow strip of conifer plantation. Continue ahead to meet the **A9** at a SROW Society signpost. Cross the busy A9 with extreme care and then turn right along its wide grassy verge for about 300 yards to a track on the left. Take this track, which in 40 yards meets an old metalled lane. Turn right along this minor road, now directly above the River Spey. In around 400 yards this lane takes an **underpass** below the A9. Remain on the lane through tiny **Knappach** to reach the B970 at a right-angled bend in the latter, 500 yards to the south-west of Ruthven Barracks. Keep ahead on the B970 to join the route of the Badenoch Way a little after **Ruthven Barracks**, or turn left to walk over the Spey Bridge into **Kingussie**.

# BADENOCH WAY AND LINKS

## NEWTONMORE TO AVIEMORE

The Badenoch Way (12½ miles/20km), developed by local authorities, runs on the south-eastern side of the Spey valley, from Ruthven, just outside Kingussie, and a few miles from Newtonmore, to Loch Insh, and then continues above the north-western bank of the river to end at Dalraddy on the B9152, a little over 3 miles short of Aviemore. The route from Newtonmore to Aviemore (19 miles/30.6km), as described in this guide, mainly follows the Badenoch Way, though there are sections at the start and finish not covered by the Way, and other routes are followed (see below).

The Badenoch Way is a splendid trail and not to be missed in any complete exploration of the Spey valley. The

*Looking over the waterlogged Insh Marshes*

major highlight of the route, which is well waymarked, very picturesque and varied in scenery, is the Insh Marshes National Nature Reserve, a habitat of national and international importance for wildlife. The first section in particular, north of the B970, is a delight for nature lovers, particularly in springtime. There are several sheltered hides from which to observe the varied and numerous birds that inhabit the marshes, the banks of the Spey and Loch Insh. After the village of Kincraig the trail follows an undulating path above the valley, offering what many feel are the best views down to the River Spey to be had along its entire length. The giants of the Cairngorm mountains, now quite close at hand to the east, are also seen to good effect whilst walking the trail. The Badenoch Way and links, from Newtonmore to Aviemore, has approximately 500ft (152m) of ascent, about 100ft (30m) more if walking from Aviemore to Newtonmore, and so, like the main trail of the Speyside Way, is not a strenuous trek.

## Linking up the route

The Badenoch Way does not completely cover the route between Newtonmore and Aviemore, and there are a few miles at both ends to be negotiated. This is an easy task at the south-western end, as there is a good cycleway, part of the National Cycle Network, leading directly from Newtonmore to Kingussie. Pedestrians may also use this trail, which is fenced off from the main highway, so safe to walk, although walkers must keep a wary eye on any approaching cyclists. Badenoch Way signposts start from Kingussie and lead along a minor road past Ruthven Barracks to the official start of the Way at the entrance to Insh Marshes NNR.

The north-eastern end of the trail presents a much more difficult and potentially dangerous problem. The Badenoch Way comes to an abrupt end on the B9152 by Dalraddy caravan site, several miles short of Aviemore. From here there is no footpath route to avoid the sometimes busy road into Aviemore. A new route will eventually be constructed to take the extended Speyside Way into Aviemore, but in the meantime the recommended option is to arrange for transport to meet you at the end of the Badenoch Way to drive into Aviemore and continue walking the trail northwards from there. If continuing on foot from Dalraddy into Aviemore then proceed with extreme care.

## Joining Newtonmore to the Speyside Way

When the Speyside Way was first conceived it was always the intention for the trail to wend its way along and above the Spey valley from the first major town on Speyside, Newtonmore, to the North Sea on the Moray Firth. When first opened in 1982 the Way started at Ballindalloch, and it was not until the beginning of the new millennium, on 8th April 2000, that the way was officially extended back to Aviemore. A continuation back to Newtonmore was still sought, but was hampered by land access agreements and other problems. Eventually, in 2009, the Scottish Government gave official approval for a Newtonmore extension, but it will probably be several more years before this is implemented and the new trail developed, waymarked and officially opened.

The route of the Speyside Way, when it is finally extended and opened, will follow to a large extent the Badenoch Way. There will be some relatively short sections of the Way, on newly constructed paths, that are not co-incident with the Badenoch Way, but walkers will be guided through these by the usual 'thistle' waymarks.

## Alternative route

Experienced walkers have an alternative route between Tromie Bridge on the B970, reached after the first mile on the Badenoch Way, and Aviemore. This avoids all but very remote and quiet roads, being mainly on forest tracks and paths. Although it avoids the problem of the link between the end of the Badenoch Way and Aviemore, it is, however, much longer than the Badenoch Way route (about 17 miles from Tromie Bridge to Aviemore) and for the large part is unwaymarked. Use of an OS map is essential.

The route from Tromie Bridge is at first eastwards through forest to cross the Allt Chomhraig on a footbridge, and then on a track through further forest to reach Glen

Feshie near Stronetoper (NN 849 971). Follow the unfrequented private glen road northwards, and then paths and tracks up the west bank of the River Feshie to Feshiebridge. From here forest roads and tracks are followed north-eastwards, then eastwards, and finally there is a path to Loch an Eilein. Follow the south-eastern side of this loch and then a track to reach a car park to the east of Ord Ban at NH 897 087. From here tracks and minor roads lead to Inverdruie, just over ½ mile south-east of Aviemore. The route is described in detail in *Scottish Hill Tracks* (5th edn, rev., 2011), published by the SROW Society (see Appendix C), part of route numbers 180 and 182X.

## STAGE 1
*Newtonmore to Kingussie*

| | |
|---|---|
| **Distance** | 2¾ miles/4.5km |
| **Map** | OS Landranger 35 (Kingussie & Monadhliath Mountains) |

*For details of Newtonmore, see under Prologue (Stage 2).*

Leave **Newtonmore** by heading east to the end of the village where a cycle path will be found, starting immediately after the Highland Museum. This is part of National Cycle Route 7.

### HIGHLAND FOLK MUSEUM

Dr Isabel F. Grant, the founder of the Highland Folk Museum, opened her first site on Speyside at Kingussie in June 1944, at Pitmain Lodge; this houses over 10,000 items but is opened only by appointment for research in the library or archives. To allow the development of a larger open-air site, 80 acres of land was acquired on the outskirts of Newtonmore in the late 1980s. The museum opened in 1996, and the site continues to develop as additional traditional buildings under threat are moved to the museum site.

## BADENOCH WAY AND LINKS STAGE 1 – NEWTONMORE TO KINGUSSIE

The site is divided into four main areas: Aultlarie, a traditional working farm displayed as it would have been in the 1930s; a range of buildings including a school, church, post office, clockmaker's workshop and tailor's shop from the 1930s; the Pinewoods; and Baile Gean, a unique reconstruction of an early 18th-century Highland township. Knowledgeable, costumed staff provide information to visitors. There is an audio-visual display, café and gift shop. The museum is open 7 days a week, April to October. Admission is currently free, but visitors are requested to make a donation to help fund the site. Highly recommended.

*Display boards and traveller's camp at Highland Folk Museum, Newtonmore (Beryl Castle)*

*Map continued on page 88*

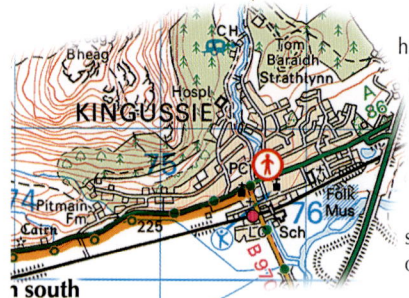

The cycle path runs along the right-hand side of the main road that connects Newtonmore with Kingussie. Watch out for cyclists using the track, though most are considerate of pedestrians. The track forms a relatively safe and quite scenic route for walkers all the way to **Kingussie**. Walk along Kingussie high street until you reach the Ruthven Road on your right.

## KINGUSSIE

For many centuries the major settlement on this section of the Spey was on the south side of the river at Ruthven next to the imposing barracks. This changed in 1799 when the Duke of Gordon decided that the parish needed a village, and the planned settlement of Kingussie was laid out. It grew only slowly at first, but the village expanded when the River Spey and River Laggan were bridged in 1808 and 1815 respectively, placing Kingussie on the new or improved main road from Inverness to Fort William. Tenants cleared from their lands in surrounding areas to make room for sheep were resettled here, and Kingussie had grown considerably by the time the railway arrived in 1863. Kingussie's planned development has resulted in fine stone villas and hotels laid out in a regular pattern. Golf came to the village in 1890 with the development of an 18-hole moorland course above Glen Gynack to the north of the town. Shinty is a major sport in Kingussie, which is the location of the governing body of the game.

**Facilities**: independent hostel, hotels, B&Bs. Cafés (all closed on Sunday), fish and chip shop with café, open 7 days a week. Co-op food shop open 7 days a week. Range of other shops including pharmacy, most closed on Sunday. Post office and bank. Bus and train services (the railway station is just south of the centre of the village).

## STAGE 2
*Kingussie to Dalraddy*

| Distance | 12½ miles/20.1km |
|---|---|
| Map | OS Landranger 35 (Kingussie & Monadhliath Mountains) |

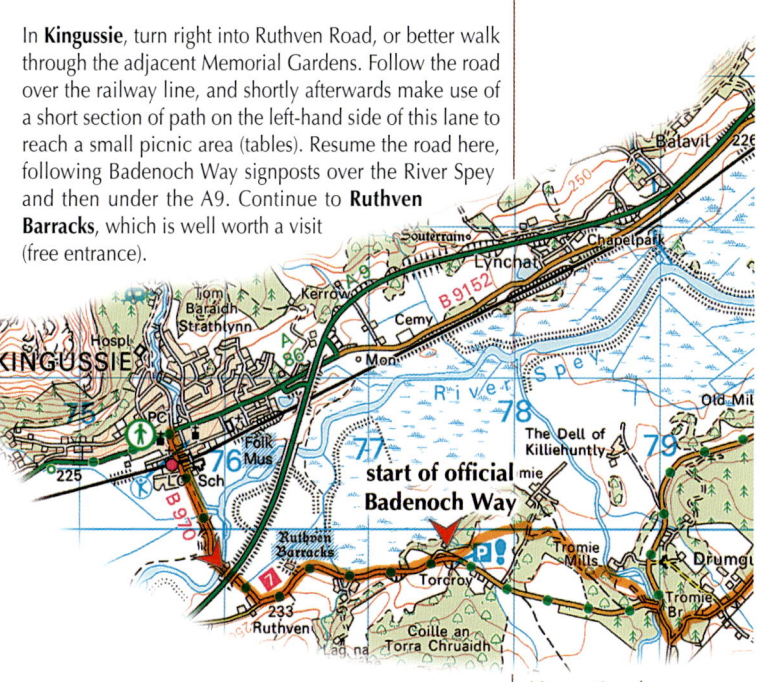

In **Kingussie**, turn right into Ruthven Road, or better walk through the adjacent Memorial Gardens. Follow the road over the railway line, and shortly afterwards make use of a short section of path on the left-hand side of this lane to reach a small picnic area (tables). Resume the road here, following Badenoch Way signposts over the River Spey and then under the A9. Continue to **Ruthven Barracks**, which is well worth a visit (free entrance).

*Map continued on page 91*

### RUTHVEN BARRACKS AND THE OLD SETTLEMENT OF RUTHVEN

Ruthven Barracks was one of four identical infantry garrisons built after the first Jacobite uprising in 1715. The locals adopted various delaying tactics during the

## THE SPEYSIDE WAY

building of the barracks, including kidnapping the masons! The barracks were completed by 1721, and by 1724 a stable block was added for cavalry using General Wade's new military roads that linked this barracks to the others. By August 1745 over 90 men had been withdrawn and only 14 remained to defend the barracks against Jacobite forces, so it is hardly surprising that on the second attempt in February 1746 the barracks fell. After defeat at Culloden Moor in April of that year, the retreating Jacobite troops set fire to the barracks, the result of which can be seen in the ruin of today.

The barracks were positioned on a natural mound, guarding one of the few reliable crossing places on the middle Spey. The medieval castle that had originally stood on the mound provided protection for the village that grew up around it. Weekly markets were recorded from 1685, and by the middle of the 18th century a grammar school had been established. The destruction of the barracks, bridging of the Spey in 1765 and development of the planned village of Kingussie all contributed to the disappearance of the community at Ruthven, which was complete by the end of the 18th century.

*Ruined guardhouse at Ruthven Barracks near Kingussie*

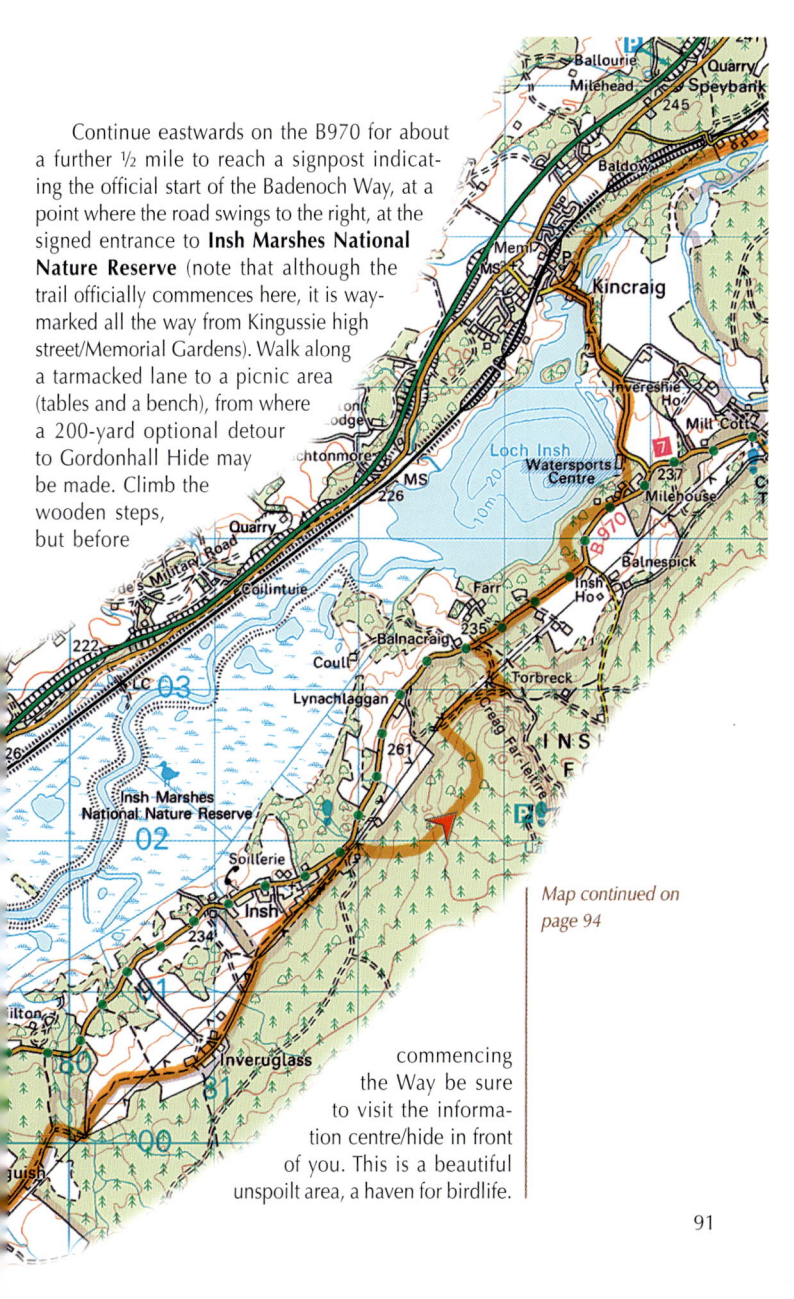

Continue eastwards on the B970 for about a further ½ mile to reach a signpost indicating the official start of the Badenoch Way, at a point where the road swings to the right, at the signed entrance to **Insh Marshes National Nature Reserve** (note that although the trail officially commences here, it is way-marked all the way from Kingussie high street/Memorial Gardens). Walk along a tarmacked lane to a picnic area (tables and a bench), from where a 200-yard optional detour to Gordonhall Hide may be made. Climb the wooden steps, but before commencing the Way be sure to visit the information centre/hide in front of you. This is a beautiful unspoilt area, a haven for birdlife.

*Map continued on page 94*

The RSPB reserve at **Insh Marshes** has hides for observing the birds. Seasonal flooding produces a large area of swamp and fen which together form the largest single unit of poor fen floodplain mire in the UK. In spring lapwings, redshanks and curlew nest, whilst in the winter the marshes are home to Icelandic whooper swans. The marshes, over 3 miles long and over ½ mile wide, have been designated a Special Area of Conservation and a National Nature Reserve, being one of the most important wetlands in Europe.

Follow the sign for the Invertromie Trail and also Badenoch Way waymarks (another short waymarked detour to Invertromie Hide is soon possible). Next comes another detour of only 100 yards or so to another picnic area and viewpoint, and very soon after there is yet another one (150 yards) to visit an old churchyard. All these trails are well waymarked. The trail undulates and is rather intricate to follow, but is all on good paths and the waymarking so good that getting lost would take quite an effort! Simply follow the white arrows of the Invertromie Trail and Badenoch Way waymarks.

*A section of boardwalk at Loch Insh*

Eventually reach the River Tromie. Follow this waterway to re-emerge on the **B970**. Just before joining this road ignore the white arrows of the Invertromie Trail, which bears to the right. Turn left over a bridge over the River Tromie and immediately leave the road by forking right at a signpost indicating the Badenoch Way and a couple of other SROW Society routes. After a few hundred yards, the right of way to Insh and the Badenoch Way to Dalraddy turn off the main track (which proceeds ahead to the Gaick and Minigaig Passes to the south) by turning sharply to the left, uphill on another track, now heading north-east and passing a marvellous stand of Scots Pines. The trail from here is straightforward on good paths, soon passing through a large section of woodland before emerging onto further moorland, from where there are open views to the Cairngorm mountains.

### CAIRNGORMS NATIONAL PARK

The Cairngorms National Park, established in September 2003, is, at nearly 1500 square miles, Britain's largest National Park. It covers a harsh and very mountainous area, with two-thirds of the park more than 2000ft above sea level and five of Scotland's six highest mountains (Ben Macdui – 4294ft (1309m), Braeriach – 4251ft (1296m), Cairn Toul – 4235ft (1291m), Sgor an Lochain Uaine – 4126ft (1258m) and Cairn Gorm – 4080ft (1244m)). This is the largest area of arctic mountain plateau ('montane zone') in Britain. The three major valley systems are the Spey, Dee and Don.

Nearly 40 per cent of the park is designated as important for nature heritage, and it is home to a quarter of Britain's threatened plant, bird and animal species. Golden eagle, capercaillie and osprey are all found in the park, as are pine martens and wildcats. The forests of the park, the most well known of which are the Rothiemurchus and the Abernethy, contain remnants of the original Caledonian pine forest. This huge area is sparsely populated, but about 16,000 people

*THE SPEYSIDE WAY*

live within the National Park boundaries, in towns and villages such as Newtonmore, Kingussie, Aviemore, Nethy Bridge, Grantown, Tomintoul and Braemar on the periphery of the mountains. The park receives about 1.5 million visitors a year, and constitutes 80% of the local economy.

After a while a number of dwellings are passed before the trail reaches another green SROW Society signpost. Follow the Way ahead signed to Insh and the B970, and later ignore another footpath sign at a picnic table, which indicates a footpath to the left (unless you wish to visit and walk through the village of Insh). The path eventually emerges on the B970 just northeast of Insh. Do not walk on this road, but immediately turn sharply to the right on a Badenoch Way signposted track. At a track junction in about 300 yards, turn left uphill. After a further few hundred yards be sure to follow carefully the Badenoch Way waymarks positioned on tall wooden posts, and leave the wide track for a good but narrow path on the left. A gentle climb follows up a wide, heather-covered clearing in a conifer plantation to reach another track. Turn left, downhill on this track. When high-tension electricity cables are encountered above, look out for a Badenoch Way waymarked path that leaves the track just before a huge pylon. Descend on this past the pylon to reach yet another track, where you turn left. Remain on this track, as the Badenoch Way descends to the B970 once more.

A few yards short of this road turn right on a path that parallels the B970 on the left for about 1/3 mile, before crossing the road at the **Old Farr Sawmill** and continuing parallel to the road, which is now on your right, once more entering the Insh Marshes Nature Reserve. Pass through some beautiful deciduous woodland to reach a path T-junction, where you turn left, but in 15 yards fork

*Wooded gentle hills west of Dalraddy Moor*

right again. The RSPB acquired this land from the Forestry Commission in 1987 and has since re-established the native birch and Scots pine woodland that you are currently enjoying and which supports a variety of bird species. Soon after Loch Insh comes into view between the trees, be sure to take a narrow path climbing to the right (look carefully for waymarks). This climbs back to the road. Turn left for about 100 yards to seek out the footpath sign at the house named **Inshbreck**. Follow this path, the Badenoch Way, between wooden fences.

The trail eventually descends to the shore of **Loch Insh**. To explore this area fully you should turn left, off the Badenoch Way (no dogs allowed). At the very least be sure to walk the boardwalk circuit before returning to the Badenoch Way.

**Loch Insh** is formed by a widening of the River Spey, south of the village of Kincraig. On the 700 acres of the loch a variety of water sports can be enjoyed, including sailing, canoeing, kayaking and rowing. The loch is also the starting point for local walks and cycle routes. There is restaurant and gift shop by the shore.

*THE SPEYSIDE WAY*

Continue ahead, passing to the immediate right of the **Boathouse Restaurant**, before following a surfaced path to the left of a narrow road. After a while cross over the road to resume the surfaced path, now with the road and a fence to your left. Later ignore the Public Footpath sign to Feshiebridge, but continue ahead on the path to the right of the road. When this path ends, cross the road to take a surfaced track on the left, which almost immediately swings to the right. Take the left fork at the small cemetery to descend on a grassy path to the narrow northern end of Loch Insh. Follow the shore of the loch to emerge on the road again, and then follow this into **Kincraig** village, crossing the long bridge over the Spey as the river leaves the loch.

### KINCRAIG

A small, pleasant village situated at the north-eastern end of Loch Insh. The mainline railway from Kingussie to Aviemore runs through the village, but alas there is no longer a station here.
   **Facilities**: independent hostel, hotels, B&Bs. Café in the village and on the banks of Loch Insh. Stores with post office, open 7 days a week. Buses.

About 50 yards after passing Kincraig Stores turn right on Speybank Walk. This road becomes quite a wide dirt track as it leaves the village. At a left bend in this track, leave it for the path ahead, also waymarked as Speybank Walk. This splendid path provides a panoramic view of the Spey and the distant Cairngorm mountains from the undulating bank of the River Spey. One of the ascents is quite steep, but leads to a seat at a wonderful viewpoint. The views of the river are seen to best effect in wintertime and in early spring, when the leaves, which obstruct the view, are absent from the trees. The path ends at a narrow minor road; continue ahead.

The lane descends to become a grassy dirt track, which is followed, keeping a field on your right and bank with silver birches on your left. Pass through a gate to enter woodland, but in 10 yards take the waymarked path on the right. There are many paths in these woods, so be sure to follow the Badenoch Way waymarking through them to exit the trees. Then bear left to pass through a wooden gate onto grassland, with the River Spey over to your right. About 35 yards after the gate be sure to bear left on the upper path. Care is required once again to follow the tall wooden posts bearing Badenoch Way waymarks, as the route makes several changes in direction before finally heading off to the north-east across the grassy sward of Dalraddy Moor. At the far corner of the moor, bear to the left in front of a conifer plantation and follow the path to the right of a caravan site to pass under the mainline railway line and emerge at a car park at **Dalraddy**. Here you will find a Badenoch Way information board. Bear right on the drive that exits from Dalraddy Holiday Park to reach the B9152 at NH 859 084.

## STAGE 3
### Dalraddy to Aviemore

| | |
|---|---|
| **Distance** | 3¾ miles/6km |
| **Map** | OS Landranger 35 (Kingussie & Monadhliath Mountains) |

This point at Dalraddy marks the very unsatisfactory official end of the Badenoch Way. The only direct way to Aviemore is right along the B9152, which can be quite busy, particularly in the tourist seasons, although most of the time it has light to moderate, rather than heavy traffic. Moreover, there are several tight bends in the road, which obscure the view of oncoming traffic, which increases the danger. It is advisable to arrange for transport from this point into Aviemore, but if you do decide to walk along this road then great care must be exercised at all times. There is a verge for much of the way, but you will have

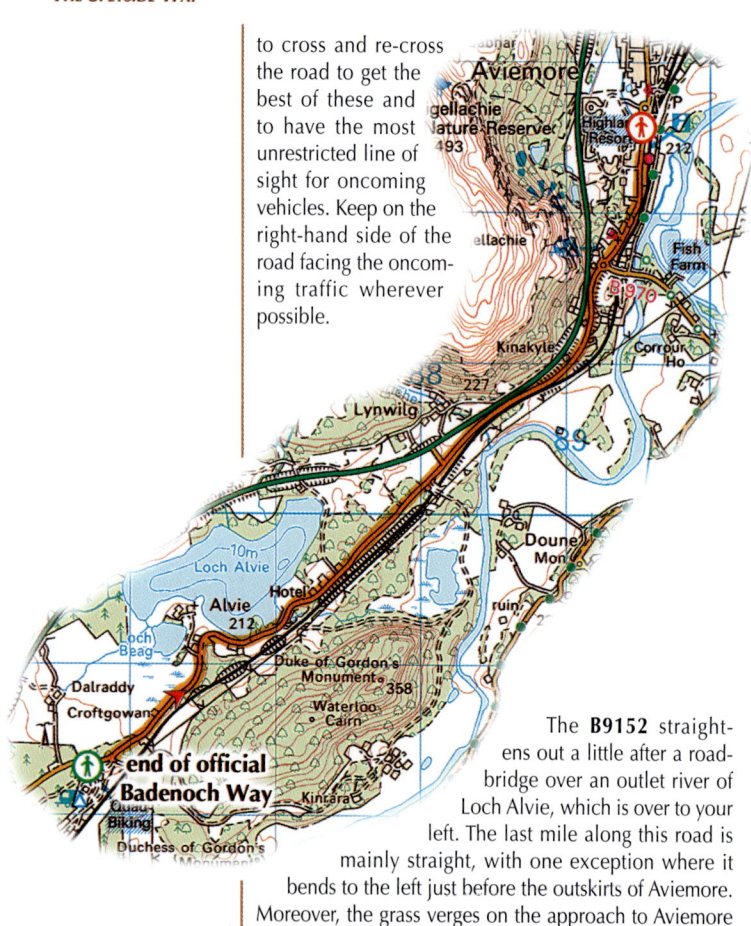

*THE SPEYSIDE WAY*

to cross and re-cross the road to get the best of these and to have the most unrestricted line of sight for oncoming vehicles. Keep on the right-hand side of the road facing the oncoming traffic wherever possible.

The **B9152** straightens out a little after a road-bridge over an outlet river of Loch Alvie, which is over to your left. The last mile along this road is mainly straight, with one exception where it bends to the left just before the outskirts of Aviemore. Moreover, the grass verges on the approach to Aviemore are mostly very wide ones, so allowing the pedestrian to keep further from the traffic. The road eventually reaches a mini-roundabout: continue ahead for the visitor centre, youth hostel and all the shops and facilities of the tourist centre of **Aviemore**.

For more information about Aviemore, see Speyside Way, Stage 1.

# SPEYSIDE WAY
## AVIEMORE TO BUCKIE

Despite its location in the mountainous Scottish Highlands and Moray, the Speyside Way is one of the easiest of Britain's official long distance trails to walk, being suitable for walkers of even modest abilities. High levels of fitness are not necessary and no special navigational competence is required, other than an aptitude for spotting signposts and waymarks and following the route described in this guidebook. The amount of ascent in its 66 miles is very modest, approximately 2600ft (790m) from Aviemore to Buckie, and about 600ft (180m) more if walking the opposite way, Buckie to Aviemore. Most of these climbs are concentrated in two areas, from Cromdale to Ballindalloch and from Craigellachie to Fochabers, when the Way leaves the valley bottom for stages across the low hills to the east of the river. A few ascents and descents are quite steep, but generally the gradients encountered along the main route of the Speyside Way are gentle, gradual ones.

The most difficult section of the main route of the Speyside Way is from the point where it leaves the A95 north of Cromdale until it rejoins the A95 a couple of

*A typical squeeze-stile on the Speyside Way as the route crosses farmland*

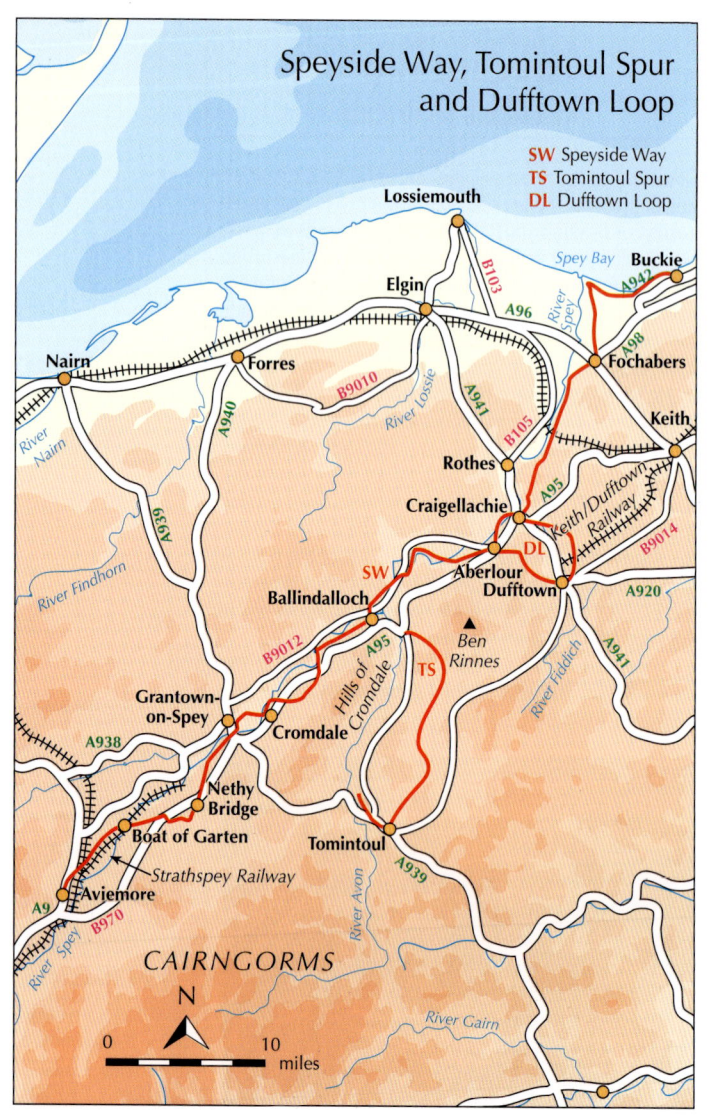

*THE SPEYSIDE WAY*

miles before Ballindalloch station. In this section there is a fair amount of ascent and descent, with one or two steep climbs; the trail constantly changes direction, and there are many metal squeeze-stiles to negotiate, making the walk both time consuming and rather tedious. Nevertheless the scenery, as elsewhere above the Spey valley, is ample recompense. Be sure to allow sufficient time for this section, as it will probably take longer than expected.

Most other sections of the Way offer easy walking on well-surfaced tracks and paths. The two major types of trail used on the Speyside Way are disused railway track beds and riverside paths, and these together account for over half of the route, with the last 5 miles consisting of coastal paths, tracks and minor roads. Woodland sections are plentiful, with an abundance of deciduous trees in the area, at their best with the fresh greens of spring and with the rich hues of the turning leaves during autumn time. Birches, silver birches, Scots pine, juniper and rowan are particularly attractive. Gorse and especially broom are frequently encountered along the Way (and on the Dava Way and MCT), the intoxicating smell of their bright yellow flowers being a delightful feature of a springtime walk along the trail.

### Attractions

Speyside is one the most beautiful regions of Scotland and possesses a rich, varied and abundant **wildlife** that can be enjoyed from the Way. The plaintive cry of the curlew and the call of oystercatchers are frequently heard when walking the Speyside Way, and there are many riverside birds, such as herons and dippers, to be enjoyed. Perhaps the most impressive and exotic species is the osprey, commonly seen in the area around Loch Garten during the spring and summer mouths, before they leave for their winter feeding grounds in West Africa.

These raptors are not the only ones who fish the rich waters of the Spey, as this is one of Scotland's finest angling rivers, fly-fishing for Atlantic salmon being a favourite **sport** in the region. Other popular sports and

## THE SPEYSIDE WAY

*Waiting for a steam train at Boat of Garten station*

pastimes in the surrounding mountain areas include hill walking, deer stalking, grouse shooting and skiing, with Aviemore being Scotland's premier skiing centre.

The Speyside Way is of particular interest to lovers of the Scottish 'water of life', single malt **whisky**. Speyside is at the very heart of whisky country and many distilleries are passed en route or can be reached by a short walking detour; many of them are open to the public and some of the most famous names in Scotch whisky offer free tours and tastings during the spring and summer months (see Appendix D).

The line of the **Strathspey Railway**, a great tourist attraction, is never far away on the first stretch of the Speyside Way from Aviemore to Boat of Garten, where the railway's principal station is located. If you are lucky you may catch sight of a steam train in full flight on this section of the walk.

### The route

The landscape slowly changes as the Way and the river head north-eastwards. By the time the Speyside Way leaves **Aviemore** much of the upland country with its hill farms and sheep rearing have been left behind, but both stock rearing and forestry are prevalent in the middle reaches of the valley. The lower stretches of the river, which have been receiving rich silt washed from the upper reaches of the river from time immemorial, have rich soils, so arable farming is common. Commercial fishing, from the small harbours on the Moray coast, has declined in the last few decades. The dunes of the coastal region form an ideal location for golf links, where that other Scottish sport is played with a passion.

A trek through Abernethy Forest National Nature Reserve leads to **Nethy Bridge**, but on the way an optional detour is possible to visit Loch Garten and its Osprey Centre. A disused railway line, forest tracks, rides and paths take the Speyside Way to the elegant town of **Grantown-on-Spey**, the 'capital' of Speyside. More forest tracks lead east and north-eastwards to a crossing of the Spey near **Cromdale**, after which the trail takes to the hill and farming country to the east of the Spey valley, before dropping back down to the river to **Ballindalloch** station. Easy, flat and pleasant walking follows along the track bed of the disused railway of the Speyside Line to enter the heart of whisky country and pass several of Scotland's most famous distilleries.

A stretch on riverside paths along the Spey, passing the Ranger headquarters of the Speyside Way at Aberlour, leads to **Craigellachie**, once an important junction of three lines in the heyday of the railway. A quiet lane leads out of Craigellachie and offers good views across the Spey valley before forest tracks take the walker around the western slopes of Ben Aigan to drop to **Boat o' Brig**, a ferry-crossing point in days gone by. A scenic high road follows to the town of **Fochabers**, before paths close to the River Spey head for the Moray coast at **Spey Bay**, famous as the landing site in Scotland of Charles II in 1650 and an estuary rich in wildlife. A final walk along the coast on a route similar to the Moray Coast Trail reaches the terminus of the Speyside Way at the small, now unworked, harbour of Buckpool in the town of **Buckie**, from where public transport can be taken home.

## THE SPEYSIDE WAY

*Speyside Way*

The Speyside Way has a distinctive **logo** which consists of an upright bootprint. On the front of this foot are two symbols that are a feature of the route, a distillery pagoda and a steam engine, the latter emphasising the fact that an appreciable length of the Way follows disused railway lines, and the former that this is the whisky centre of the world. On the heel of the foot are wavy lines, symbolising ripples on the river with a leaping salmon.

### STAGE 1
*Aviemore to Boat of Garten*

| | |
|---|---|
| **Distance** | 6 miles/9.7km |
| **Maps** | OS Landranger 36 (Grantown, Aviemore & Cairngorm area) |

### AVIEMORE

The arrival of the railway at Aviemore in the late 1800s acted as a spur to growth, as was the case in many of the old settlements along the Spey. By 1892 it was an important junction for travel to Perth and Inverness. Aviemore's development as a Victorian mountain resort was underpinned by the construction of hotels such as the Cairngorm, which still serves tourists today. The Aviemore Centre was built in 1964 at a time when the Cairn Gorm ski area was being developed. More recent building in Aviemore has helped to soften the architectural scars of this 1960s development.

**Facilities**: SYHA hostel, bunkhouse, several hotels, B&Bs. Cafés. Tesco supermarket, many shops, especially those offering outdoor clothing and equipment. Pharmacy, post office, two banks. Mainline train station and Strathspey Railway. Long-distance and local bus services. Theatre. Swimming pool. Cairngorm Brewery is open for tours weekdays throughout the year; shop.

## SPEYSIDE WAY STAGE 1 – AVIEMORE TO BOAT OF GARTEN

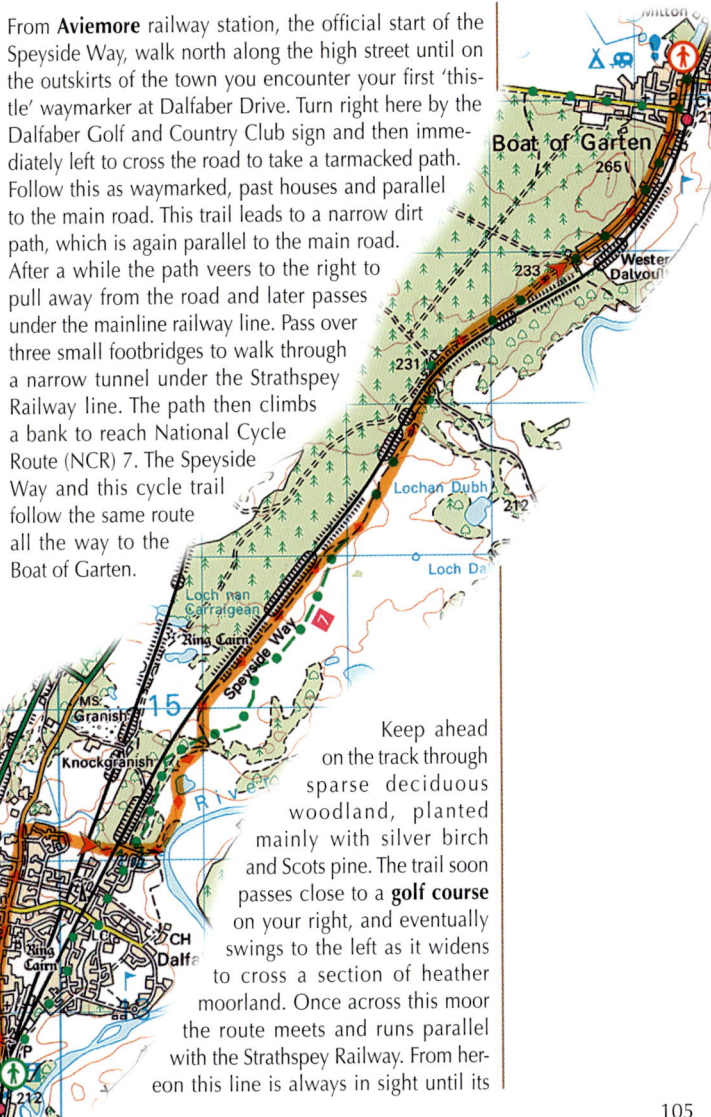

From **Aviemore** railway station, the official start of the Speyside Way, walk north along the high street until on the outskirts of the town you encounter your first 'thistle' waymarker at Dalfaber Drive. Turn right here by the Dalfaber Golf and Country Club sign and then immediately left to cross the road to take a tarmacked path. Follow this as waymarked, past houses and parallel to the main road. This trail leads to a narrow dirt path, which is again parallel to the main road. After a while the path veers to the right to pull away from the road and later passes under the mainline railway line. Pass over three small footbridges to walk through a narrow tunnel under the Strathspey Railway line. The path then climbs a bank to reach National Cycle Route (NCR) 7. The Speyside Way and this cycle trail follow the same route all the way to the Boat of Garten.

Keep ahead on the track through sparse deciduous woodland, planted mainly with silver birch and Scots pine. The trail soon passes close to a **golf course** on your right, and eventually swings to the left as it widens to cross a section of heather moorland. Once across this moor the route meets and runs parallel with the Strathspey Railway. From hereon this line is always in sight until its

# THE SPEYSIDE WAY

*Passing a traditional highland cottage on the approach to Boat of Garten*

station is reached at the Boat of Garten, and if you are lucky you will see some of its fine steam trains go past. Eventually meet and pass through a gate to bear left on a track which passes under a stone arch beneath the railway line. Continue ahead, now with the railway line on your right, following a sign for the Kinchurdy Road. The track eventually becomes metalled as it passes through the outskirts of Boat of Garten, passing a number of old and modern houses. Continue to a T-junction at **Boat of Garten**. The post office and village store is directly ahead and The Boat hotel, bar and restaurant is to the right.

## BOAT OF GARTEN

This scenic village was known as Gart until 1863, when it was renamed Boat of Garten, the same name as the ferry and newly built railway station. The word 'boat' therefore refers to the ferry that used to operate here across the River Spey in the days when there was no road bridge across the river (Boat of Cromdale, east of Grantown, and Boat o' Brig, south of Fochabers in the latter stages of the walk, are comparable examples). The village is now famous for its steam railway and the RSPB reserve at nearby Loch Garten, where osprey breed.

**Facilities:** independent hostel, hotel, B&Bs, campsite. General stores and post office. Local buses and Strathspey Steam Railway station. Community garden next to railway station.

*Interesting carved bench in Boat of Garten community garden (Beryl Castle)*

## STAGE 2
*Boat of Garten to Nethy Bridge*

| | |
|---|---|
| **Distance** | 4½ miles/7.2km |
| **Maps** | OS Landranger 36 (Grantown, Aviemore & Cairngorm area) |

The **Strathspey Steam Railway** is a local tourist attraction, popular with both young and old visitors, but especially with steam enthusiasts. A daily 20-mile return service is operated between Aviemore, Boat of Garten and Broomhill stations in July and August, and a weekend and selective weekday service from April to October. Steam trains take 1½ hours to travel from one end of the line to the other. The line was originally opened by steam enthusiasts between Aviemore and Boat of Garten in 1978, and was extended to Broomhill in 2002. The next major project is to extend the line by four miles to Grantown-on-Spey, but this requires significant engineering work and is not expected to be completed until 2012 at the earliest.

*The Speyside Way*

In **Boat of Garten**, turn right at the T-junction to pass the Strathspey railway station and the Boat of Garten community garden and picnic spot. Be sure to have a peek at the latter, as this little garden is a delight and the benches quite unique! There follows a section of road walking, heading first north and then east to cross over the River Spey. The old wooden bridge here was not replaced until 1974. Be mindful of traffic until a path is reached which is fenced off from road, but runs parallel to it. When this emerges onto a road, you part company with NCR 7, which heads towards Coylumbridge. Turn left to locate a footpath which parallels the road that heads towards Loch Garten. You are now in the **Abernethy Forest National Nature Reserve**, which at is the largest area of Caledonian pine forest remaining in the UK.

The **Abernethy Forest National Nature Reserve** covers an area of 14,500 acres and is a unique mix of woodland and northern bog. The diversity of wildlife is immense, including small mammals such as red squirrel and pine martens, birds such as capercaillie, crossbill, crested tit, osprey and goldeneye, and there are said to be 300 species of moths, 280 types of fly, 128 varieties of spider and 900 different types of beetle in the reserve. Beetles include the Timberman with its impressive long antennae and camouflage colouring. The best time to see birds, plants and insects is April to July. The Abernethy Information Centre is in Nethy Bridge village and is open from April to October.

From here, the Speyside Way follows the route of the waymarked 'Blue Trail' to the Osprey Centre on Loch Garten. Before the end of this section, do take the short boardwalk

## SPEYSIDE WAY STAGE 2 – BOAT OF GARTEN TO NETHY BRIDGE

detour on the right of the trail to enjoy the reed-rich lochan, abundant with wildlife. Shortly after this lochan, the Speyside Way crosses the road to reach a trail junction: the 'Blue Trail' continues ahead here to the Osprey Centre in a little over ½ mile (well worth the detour if you have a few hours to spare), but the Speyside Way takes a path to the left, where there is an Abernethy Forest information board. This path leads through conifer trees to a wide fire break. Here the route swings to the right to follow the line of high-tension electricity cables on huge pylons.

*Bog pool surrounded by ancient pines at Abernethy Forest*

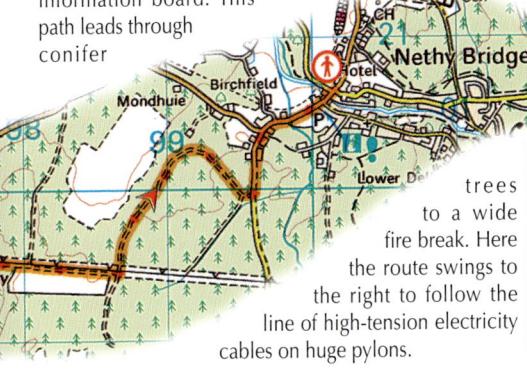

109

The **Osprey Centre** at the RSPB reserve here is the place to visit if you wish to see ospreys. When these magnificent birds returned to breed in Scotland, they came here to the ancient Caledonian pinewood forest near Boat of Garten. Non-invasive CCTV has been installed so that it is possible to make close-up observations of the ospreys, when the Osprey Centre is open between April and the end of August. In early morning in April and May, it is also possible to see capercaillies. Binoculars, telescopes and guided walks are available to assist with identification of the large range of other birds that feed in the woods and on the lake, including crested tits, goldeneye and crossbills. The Osprey Centre is closed in the autumn and winter, but visitors can still walk on the trails and observe many species, including wild geese and Whooper swans.

If don't have the time to visit the Osprey Centre you may nevertheless be lucky enough to spot one of these majestic birds flying amongst the trees in this area. Eventually the trail turns left as waymarked, to pass under the power lines and become a forest track that heads towards Nethy Bridge. The track leads to a road in about ¾ of a mile. Cross this lane to bear left on a path that parallels the road and later joins it on the outskirts of Nethy Bridge. Continue ahead to a road junction, where you turn right. This leads to the bridge and River Nethy in the centre of the village of **Nethy Bridge**, where you should find a grocery shop, picnic tables and public toilets.

## NETHY BRIDGE

It is thought that even in Pictish times there was ferry that crossed the Spey here. The focal point of this pleasant village is now the bridge designed by Telford in 1820. Although tranquil today, industrialisation came early here, with sawmills established by 1728, and in 1730 there was an iron furnace nearby which used local charcoal to smelt iron ore from the Cairngorms.

There is an 'Explore Abernethy' exhibition in the community centre, open Saturday to Wednesday from Easter until October.

**Facilities**: Bunkhouse, two hotels, B&Bs. Nearby campsite. General store and post office. Buses.

## STAGE 3
*Nethy Bridge to Grantown-on-Spey*

| | |
|---|---|
| **Distance** | 6 miles/9.7km |
| **Maps** | OS Landranger 36 (Grantown, Aviemore & Cairngorm area) |

At **Nethy Bridge** cross the bridge over the River Nethy, a tributary of the River Spey, and immediately turn left on the road signposted to Dulnain Bridge (no Speyside Way waymark here in May 2009). After about 200 yards turn right onto a track (Abernethy Bunkhouse is located here in the old Nethy station building). The trail now follows the line of the disused railway, which offers easy and pleasant walking, with views of low hills to the left. The disused railway line reaches **Balliefurth Farm** (information board), and from here the trail follows a footpath enclosed between fences before returning to the grassy track of the disused railway. Pass under a superb stone bridge that spans the old line and note, but ignore, the footpath fingerpost for the Bacharn Trail to Nethy Bridge on the right.

The waymarked 8½-mile **Bacharn Trail** offers an alternative route to the Speyside Way between Nethy Bridge and Grantown-on-Spey, passing through woodland, open hills and Revack Gardens. It is possible to return on a 13-mile route utilising the Speyside Way and a linking path at Boat of Balliefurth. Revack Gardens has pleasant walks, a plant centre, gift shop and tearoom for visitors.

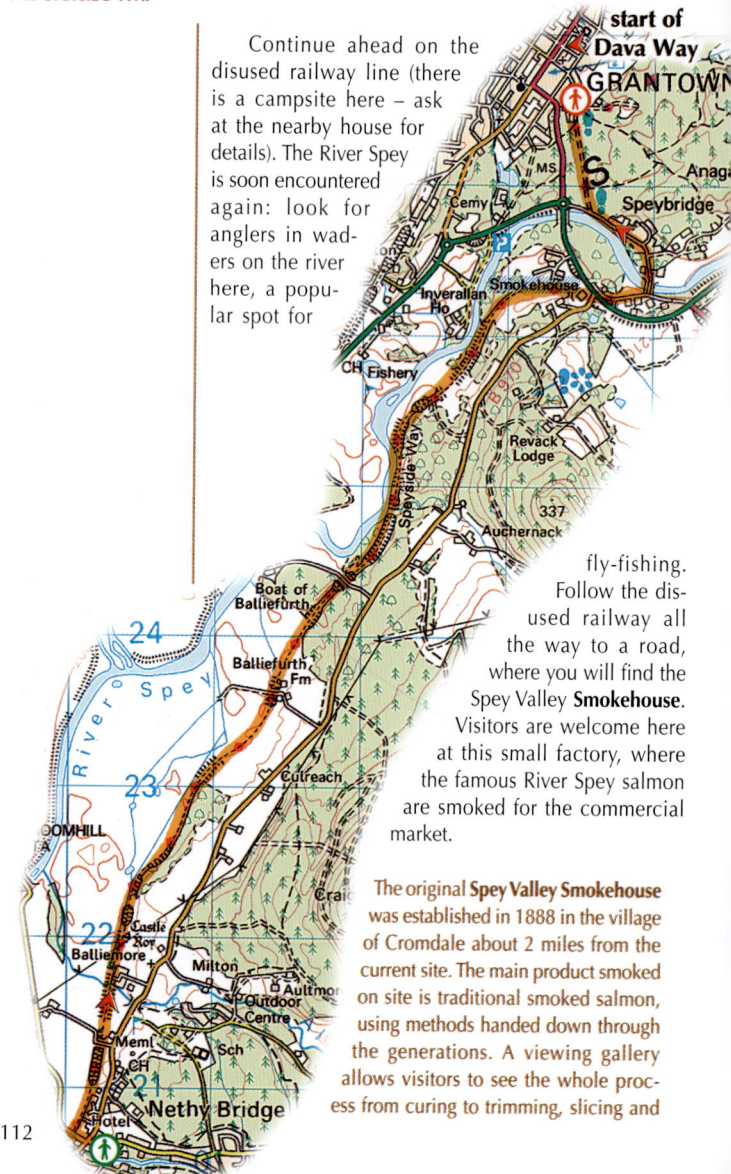

*THE SPEYSIDE WAY*

Continue ahead on the disused railway line (there is a campsite here – ask at the nearby house for details). The River Spey is soon encountered again: look for anglers in waders on the river here, a popular spot for fly-fishing. Follow the disused railway all the way to a road, where you will find the Spey Valley **Smokehouse**. Visitors are welcome here at this small factory, where the famous River Spey salmon are smoked for the commercial market.

The original **Spey Valley Smokehouse** was established in 1888 in the village of Cromdale about 2 miles from the current site. The main product smoked on site is traditional smoked salmon, using methods handed down through the generations. A viewing gallery allows visitors to see the whole process from curing to trimming, slicing and

## SPEYSIDE WAY STAGE 3 – NETHY BRIDGE TO GRANTOWN-ON-SPEY

packing, while the audio-visual presentation tells the basics about the rearing of farmed salmon. The site is open to visitors, Monday to Friday throughout the year. As well as salmon-related products, other locally produced foods are also for sale.

Turn left on the road to cross the **A95** with care. Bear right on the tarmacked drive that soon bends to the left and leads to the Old Spey Bridge. Cross the River Spey on this fine old bridge and follow the road ahead. After just over ½ mile turn right off this road onto a forest track which bears to the left in 20 yards at a T-junction. Follow this track northward through woodland. Keep ahead at cross-tracks to reach the entrance to Anagach Woods.

**Anagach Woods** are owned by the local community of Grantown-on-Spey. The almost 1000-acre woods contain three generations of Scots pine trees and date back to the inception of Grantown. The woods contain an extensive network of waymarked paths and tracks, and are home to a variety of wildlife, including the capercaillie.

*Looking towards the River Spey after passing Balliefurth Farm*

## THE SPEYSIDE WAY

*High street, Grantown-on-Spey*

The Speyside Way goes off to the right at this point, but to visit **Grantown-on-Spey** (¼ mile) continue ahead up Forest Road: keep ahead at the next cross-roads (Woodside Avenue/South Street junction) to reach the high street.

### GRANTOWN-ON-SPEY

The plans for Grantown-on-Spey were laid out by Sir James Grant in 1765. He intended this to be an industrial town with mills, factories, a hospital and an orphanage, but today the 'Capital of Strathspey', the largest town on the Speyside Way after leaving Aviemore, is a tourist town of elegant stone buildings, mainly dating from the Georgian and Victorian periods. Grantown Museum explains the history of Grantown and the Clan Grant. Open weekdays from March to December. Admission charge.

*The southern end of the Dava Way can be joined at Grantown-on-Spey.*

**Facilities**: independent hostel, hotels, B&Bs, campsite. Cafés, restaurants, fish and chip shop. Co-op food shop, open 7 days a week, plus many other shops. Pharmacy, post office, banks. Local bus services. ◄

## STAGE 4
*Grantown-on-Spey to Cromdale*

| | |
|---|---|
| **Distance** | 3½ miles/5.6km |
| **Maps** | OS Landranger 36 (Grantown, Aviemore & Cairngorm area) |

After your visit to **Grantown-on-Spey**, retrace your steps back to the point where you left the Speyside Way (at NJ 034 276). Follow the wide track signposted as 'Speyside Way to Cromdale'. Soon you reach a junction of four tracks: take the left-hand track passing to the side of a metal gate. On reaching an open area, bear to the left. Pass a golf clubhouse and later, on reaching another track junction, bear left underneath Scots pines. Continue through the trees of the **Anagach Woods** and at the next junction bear left again. Bear right at the next track T-junction by a wooden seat. The trail eventually emerges from the forest at a gate, at which point the village of

*Woodland and river in Anagach Wood*

Cromdale, nestling below the sweep of the Cromdale Hills, is seen over to the right. Continue, now with pasture on your right, to cross a small tributary of the Spey, after which bear right to follow this burn alongside Crow Wood, so reaching the River Spey at a large iron girder bridge.

Cross the Spey over this bridge, the **Boat of Cromdale** crossing. Note the fine stone church and graveyard on its far bank. To continue along the Speyside Way, follow the roadside path ahead, but about 500 yards after crossing the bridge over the river, take a path which takes you left, bypassing **Cromdale** to the north. If you want to visit the village ignore this turning, and keep ahead on the lane for a further 500 yards to reach a road T-junction with the A95. The bulk of the village lies to the left here. The Haugh Hotel is in the centre of Cromdale, at the junction of Lethendry Road and the high street, not 1 mile to the north-east as shown on at least one map!

This variant is marked on Landranger 36 and Explorer 419.

### Alternative return to the Speyside Way

Note that if **Cromdale** village is visited, then it is not necessary to return to the line of the disused railway to continue the Speyside Way; it can be rejoined further along (on Stage 5). For the alternative route, walk up Lethendry Road, leaving Cromdale on this quiet and narrow minor lane. Follow it via **Claggersnich**, **Wester** and **Easter Rynaballoch** to rejoin the standard route of the Speyside Way between **Balnallan** and **Millton** (see below). This route would have to be used if the standard trail through the trees on the western slopes of Tom an Uird was temporarily closed due to forestry operations.

*The old church and graveyard at Cromdale*

## CROMDALE

The old Cromdale school is now an outdoor centre.
**Facilities**: Haugh Hotel has accommodation, a restaurant and serves food, including bar meals, to non-residents. It is closed on Mondays. There is other limited B&B accommodation in the area. Post office, but no shop. Local bus services.

*THE SPEYSIDE WAY*

## STAGE 5
*Cromdale to Ballindalloch station*

| | |
|---|---|
| **Distance** | 11 miles/17.7km |
| **Maps** | OS Landranger 36 (Grantown, Aviemore & Cairngorm area) and 28 (Elgin and Dufftown) |

The **Battle of Cromdale** took place at the Haugh of Cromdale on 30th April and 1st May 1690, in the early days of the Jacobite struggles. The Jacobite army of 800, led by General Buchan, was met at Cromdale by Sir Thomas Livingston, who had a larger force as well as cavalry. Fortunately for the Jacobites, after they started to retreat a thick fog came down, compelling Livingston to discontinue the pursuit. The defeat at Cromdale effectively ended the rebellion in Scotland. However, propaganda for the Jacobites declared the action a victory, and a song was composed in its honour, the last verse of which reads:

The loyal Stewarts, with Montrose,
So boldly set upon their foes,
And brought them down with Highland blows
Upon the Haughs of Cromdale.
Of twenty-thousand Cromwell's men,
Five-hundred fled to Aberdeen,
The rest of them lie on the plain,
Upon the Haughs of Cromdale.

The path just outside **Cromdale** soon bears left to pass under a bridge to join the line of the disused railway. Within a few yards you pass alongside the beautifully restored and now private Cromdale railway station. Please keep off the platform unless invited onto it by the owner, who is often on the premises and usually delighted to show interested people around the outside of his unique home. A booklet, 'The Speyside Line, the

## SPEYSIDE WAY STAGE 5 – CROMDALE TO BALLINDALLOCH STATION

Railway from Craigellachie to Boat of Garten', on sale here, will tell you all you need to know about the history and engineering of the railway.

After admiring the former station continue along the line of the old railway, which runs parallel to, but some distance from, the main A95 road, over to your right. After about 1¼ miles this trail meets the road. Turn right on the grass verge alongside the road for about 250 yards, before crossing the road with great care to take the track opposite, so commencing the hardest section of the Speyside Way, beneath the towering Cromdale Hills to the east, a route that is often quite tortuous to follow. **Special care with navigation is essential** from this point until the River Spey is again encountered a little before Ballindalloch station, and do be prepared for some fairly steep and long ascents.

The track climbs into the woodland that covers the slopes of Tom an Uird (1375ft, 419m). After an initial steep climb the trail levels, although it does continue to undulate somewhat through the conifer trees along the lower slopes of the hill. After a final substantial climb to a height of 845ft (258m) the track descends to exit the forest at a large gate/metal squeeze-stile, the first of many along this section of the walk. Another metal squeeze-stile leads to a path between fences, which descends quite steeply in places to a narrow **lane** that runs up from the

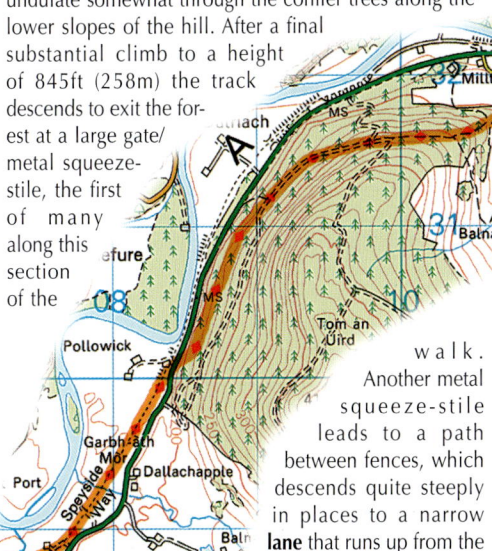

*Map continued on page 120*

## THE SPEYSIDE WAY

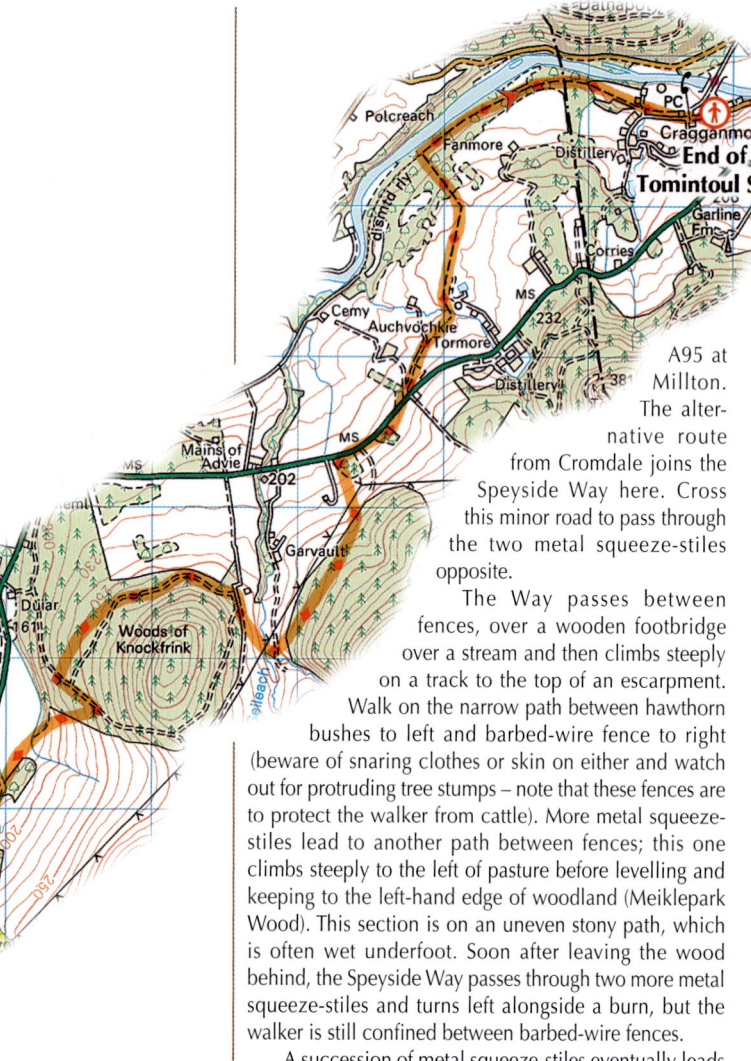

A95 at Millton. The alternative route from Cromdale joins the Speyside Way here. Cross this minor road to pass through the two metal squeeze-stiles opposite.

The Way passes between fences, over a wooden footbridge over a stream and then climbs steeply on a track to the top of an escarpment. Walk on the narrow path between hawthorn bushes to left and barbed-wire fence to right (beware of snaring clothes or skin on either and watch out for protruding tree stumps – note that these fences are to protect the walker from cattle). More metal squeeze-stiles lead to another path between fences; this one climbs steeply to the left of pasture before levelling and keeping to the left-hand edge of woodland (Meiklepark Wood). This section is on an uneven stony path, which is often wet underfoot. Soon after leaving the wood behind, the Speyside Way passes through two more metal squeeze-stiles and turns left alongside a burn, but the walker is still confined between barbed-wire fences.

A succession of metal squeeze-stiles eventually leads to a track; bear right here to cross the stream over a culvert

## SPEYSIDE WAY STAGE 5 – CROMDALE TO BALLINDALLOCH STATION

*A tributary of the Spey on the lower slopes of the Hills of Cromdale*

and once more enter a path enclosed between fences. Follow this as it changes direction several times, eventually leaving the confines of the fences behind to cross a gully and climb a grassy track, before another metal squeeze-stile leads to yet more trail between fences. The way eventually leads to a grassy path alongside conifer woods. Bear right uphill, with the trees on your left.

There follows possibly the hardest climb on the Speyside Way between Aviemore and Buckie; be sure to look back from time to time to enjoy the expansive views of the Spey valley unfolding below. Climb to a Speyside Way fingerpost and here bear left on a track alongside a conifer plantation. This track soon descends between tall pine trees. Turn right at a track junction to climb again as the trail circuits **Knockfrink Hill** (1246ft, 380m). After a right bend in the track look out for a gate through a deer fence on your left; once through this follow yet another confined path between fences. Pass through two metal squeeze-stiles, cross a track and then descend to cross two streams by means of a wooden footbridge over the **Burn of Coire Seileach**. Follow the dirt track ahead for a

*A short climb on the path near Garvault*

few hundred yards before turning sharply to the right on a grassy track. Soon leave this on the left to enter a large conifer wood by a fieldgate. Now begin a long and steep climb through the trees, which some may consider to be the hardest climb on the Speyside Way.

Climb to a Speyside Way fingerpost at a wide forest track. Bear left along this, gradually descending through Garvault Plantation. After almost ½ mile watch carefully for a Speyside Way fingerpost that will direct you left off the track. A narrow path descends through trees, under high-tension electricity cables, through two metal squeeze-stiles (do not take a stile on the left here, down to the track in front of Airdbeg Cottage), and downhill on a thin path to the **A95**. Bear right on a path that runs alongside and to the right of this main road. After about ½ mile, near the top of the hill and ¼ mile before **Tormore Distillery**, cross the A95 with care and follow a deer-fence-enclosed path around the edge of pasture to meet an earthen track. Turn right along this track, but soon leave it on the right for another fence-enclosed path. Remain on this trail as it descends all the way to the River Spey.

Designed by Sir Alfred Richardson, the **Tormore Distillery** buildings are built around a square which includes a belfry with chiming clock. Although it opened as late as 1959, it was the first new distillery on Speyside in the 20th century. Its water source is the Achvochkie Burn, which is crossed on the descent from the A95 to the River Spey on the Speyside Way. It is not open to the public.

Bear right to follow the river, mainly hidden in the trees to the left, downstream. You have joined the old railway line that leads in about 1¼ miles to **Ballindalloch station**, near Cragganmore, where there are toilet facilities and water, as well as free camping for Speyside Way walkers. ▶

Ballindalloch station is also at the end of the Tomintoul Spur, which could be joined at this point.

## STAGE 6
*Ballindalloch station to Aberlour*

---

**Distance**      10 miles/16.1km
**Maps**          OS Landranger 28 (Elgin and Dufftown)

The spur route of the Speyside Way from Tomintoul joins the main route at **Ballindalloch station**, near Cragganmore, so walkers following the route to Buckie should be careful not to follow the Speyside Way signs of the Tomintoul trail. ▶ Instead, remain on the disused railway line, which soon crosses the River Spey by way of a huge metal girder bridge. The walking now could not be easier, or more pleasant, along a good surfaced track. In just over 1½ miles you pass **Blacksboat**, where there is a water tap and

Cragganmore Distillery is a few yards down the road from the station (for more information see The Tomintoul Spur).

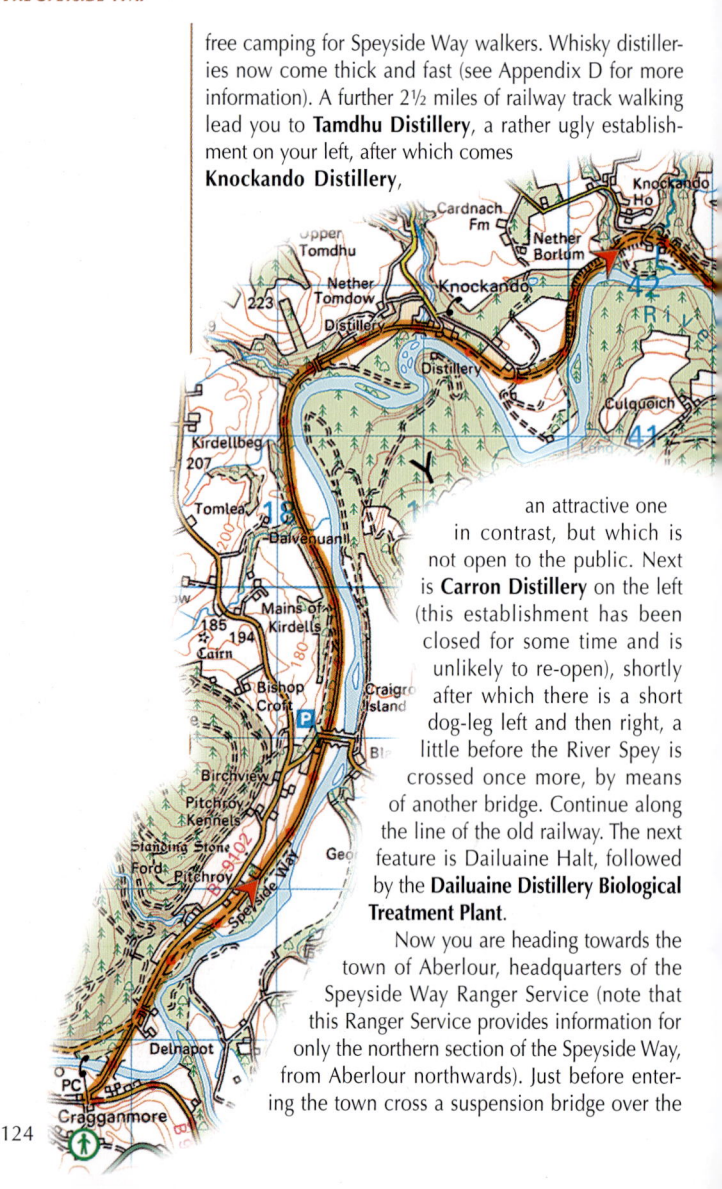

free camping for Speyside Way walkers. Whisky distilleries now come thick and fast (see Appendix D for more information). A further 2½ miles of railway track walking lead you to **Tamdhu Distillery**, a rather ugly establishment on your left, after which comes **Knockando Distillery**, an attractive one in contrast, but which is not open to the public. Next is **Carron Distillery** on the left (this establishment has been closed for some time and is unlikely to re-open), shortly after which there is a short dog-leg left and then right, a little before the River Spey is crossed once more, by means of another bridge. Continue along the line of the old railway. The next feature is Dailuaine Halt, followed by the **Dailuaine Distillery Biological Treatment Plant**.

Now you are heading towards the town of Aberlour, headquarters of the Speyside Way Ranger Service (note that this Ranger Service provides information for only the northern section of the Speyside Way, from Aberlour northwards). Just before entering the town cross a suspension bridge over the

## SPEYSIDE WAY STAGE 6 – BALLINDALLOCH STATION TO ABERLOUR

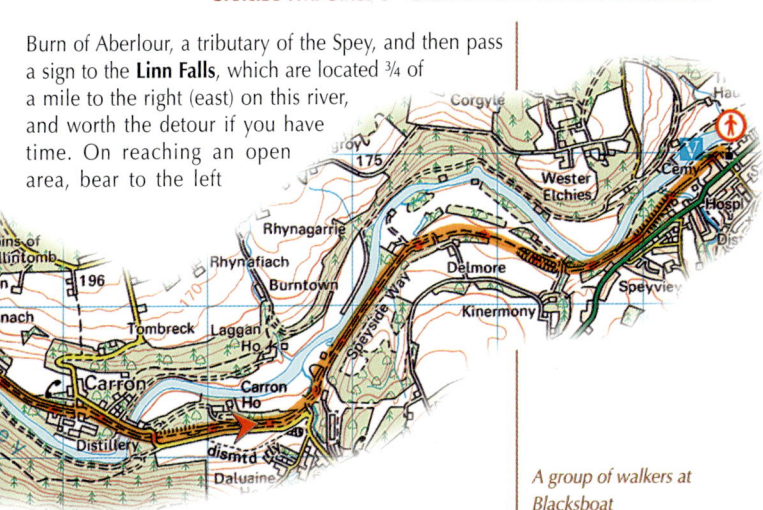

Burn of Aberlour, a tributary of the Spey, and then pass a sign to the **Linn Falls**, which are located ¾ of a mile to the right (east) on this river, and worth the detour if you have time. On reaching an open area, bear to the left

*A group of walkers at Blacksboat*

125

towards the suspension bridge over the Spey. Do not cross this bridge, but continue along the right bank of the river. The old railway station building, situated over the grass on your right, houses the **Speyside Way Visitor Centre**, definitely worth a visit if open. Head over to the right, up Elchies Road or through the Square, to reach the high street of **Aberlour** at the town's centre, where all kinds of facilities will be found, including cafés, pubs, hotels and B&Bs.

### ABERLOUR

The village was founded by Charles Grant in 1812 and was named officially Charlestown of Aberlour, after his son Charles. Aberlour, as it is more generally known, is now famous for its shortbread (see below) and for its whisky (Aberlour and Glenallachie distilleries, see Appendix D), but in former times it was known for its orphanage. This establishment was founded by a Miss MacPherson and Canon Charles Jupp in 1875, when it opened its doors to four 'mitherlessbairns', but by the mid-1950s it was home to over 1000 children at any one time. Changes in the 1960s resulted in the charity dispersing the children to smaller family-style units around Scotland, until the orphanage closed in 1967. Only the orphanage clock tower remains in Aberlour, although the Aberlour Childcare Trust continues work with disadvantaged children in Scotland.

The Alice Little Park surrounds the old railway station that has been converted to become the Speyside Way Visitor Centre (open April to October, generally from 10am to 5pm). This centre, which is the base of the Speyside Way Ranger Service for the northern half of the route, has informative displays and a DVD about the Way.

**Facilities**: hotels, B&Bs, caravan/campsite. Cafés and restaurants. Co-op food store and other shops. Pharmacy, bank and post office. Local buses. Swimming pool. ◄

At Aberlour you can leave the main Speyside Way and detour along the Dufftown Loop (nearly 12 miles), which heads up to Dufftown and then rejoins the Speyside Way at Craigellachie. See Dufftown Loop for full details.

## SPEYSIDE WAY STAGE 7 – ABERLOUR TO CRAIGELLACHIE

*The 'mash tun' in Aberlour*

**STAGE 7**
*Aberlour to Craigellachie*

| | |
|---|---|
| **Distance** | 2 miles/3.2km |
| **Maps** | OS Landranger 28 (Elgin and Dufftown) |

After a visit to **Aberlour**, return to the River Spey to resume the Speyside Way. The trail follows the river for a further 2 miles to the village of Craigellachie. On the way pass the famous Walkers Shortbread factory on the outskirts of Aberlour. The river is always in sight over to your left.

There can be few more iconic tourist symbols of Scotland than a tartan-embellished tin of shortbread, and the most famous company producing this product is undoubtedly **Walkers of Aberlour**. In 1898 Joseph Walker had perfected his recipe for shortbread and started to sell his product in the locality. Such was local demand that he soon had to purchase both a horse

*The Speyside Way*

and cart and a larger shop in Aberlour, a visit to which became a 'must see' destination for guests at the local shooting parties. Today his descendants still manufacture shortbread, cakes and biscuits, including some for the Prince of Wales' Duchy Original brand. Over 60% of Scottish shortbread, exported to more than 40 countries, is manufactured by Walkers. A shop specialising in Walkers' products will be found on the main street in Aberlour.

Before reaching **Craigellachie** the old railway goes through a cutting and then a brick-arch tunnel, the latter about 40 yards long. Later the trail passes through a shorter corrugated-iron-surfaced tunnel, before reaching the Craigellachie Hotel, which offers teas, coffee, meals and accommodation. Pass under a road (A941) and continue to pass under a second one to enter Fiddich Park. Here will be found public toilets (open April to October), a water tap and free camping for Speyside Way walkers. Nearby is a very good pub, the Fiddichside Inn, handsomely situated along the water's edge.

## CRAIGELLACHIE

Its name means 'rocky hill' in Gaelic, which no doubt refers to the cliff on which most of the village is situated. One of the Spey's most famous tributaries, the Fiddich, joins the Spey alongside the Speyside Way, just outside the village. There was already a ferry across the Spey and a small settlement here by 1750, but in 1814 the Spey was bridged at Craigellachie by Thomas Telford.

The Speyside Cooperage (see below) is just outside the village, which boasts two distilleries, Craigellachie and Macallan (see Appendix D).

**Facilities**: hotel, B&B, post office. Free camping for Speyside Way walkers in Fiddich Park.

## STAGE 8
*Craigellachie to Fochabers*

| | |
|---|---|
| **Distance** | 13 miles/20.9km |
| **Maps** | OS Landranger 28 (Elgin and Dufftown) |

**Speyside Cooperage** (½ mile south of Craigellachie on the A941) is the only cooperage in Britain with a visitor centre, which is open weekdays throughout the year. The cooperage was set up as a family business in 1947, and the current establishment was built in 1992. In the first decade of the 21st century it was sold to a French Bordeaux company that owns other cooperages in Scotland. Over 100,000 casks are made or repaired here annually. The 'Acorn to Cask' exhibition explains the lifecycle of a cask, and it is possible to watch the coopers and apprentices at work. There is a charge for admission. Gift shop and café.

Leave Fiddich Park in **Craigellachie** close to its camping area and cross the bridge over the River Fiddich. Take the road on the left, signposted to Arndilly, opposite the Fiddichside Inn. The Speyside Way follows this quiet lane for a few miles. Ignore another minor road on the right after about ½ mile, and after a further similar distance ignore a track, also on the right, the latter signposted to Tominachty. The lane you are following is lined with some superb specimens of beech and birch trees. Pass the private **Arndilly House**, where there is a

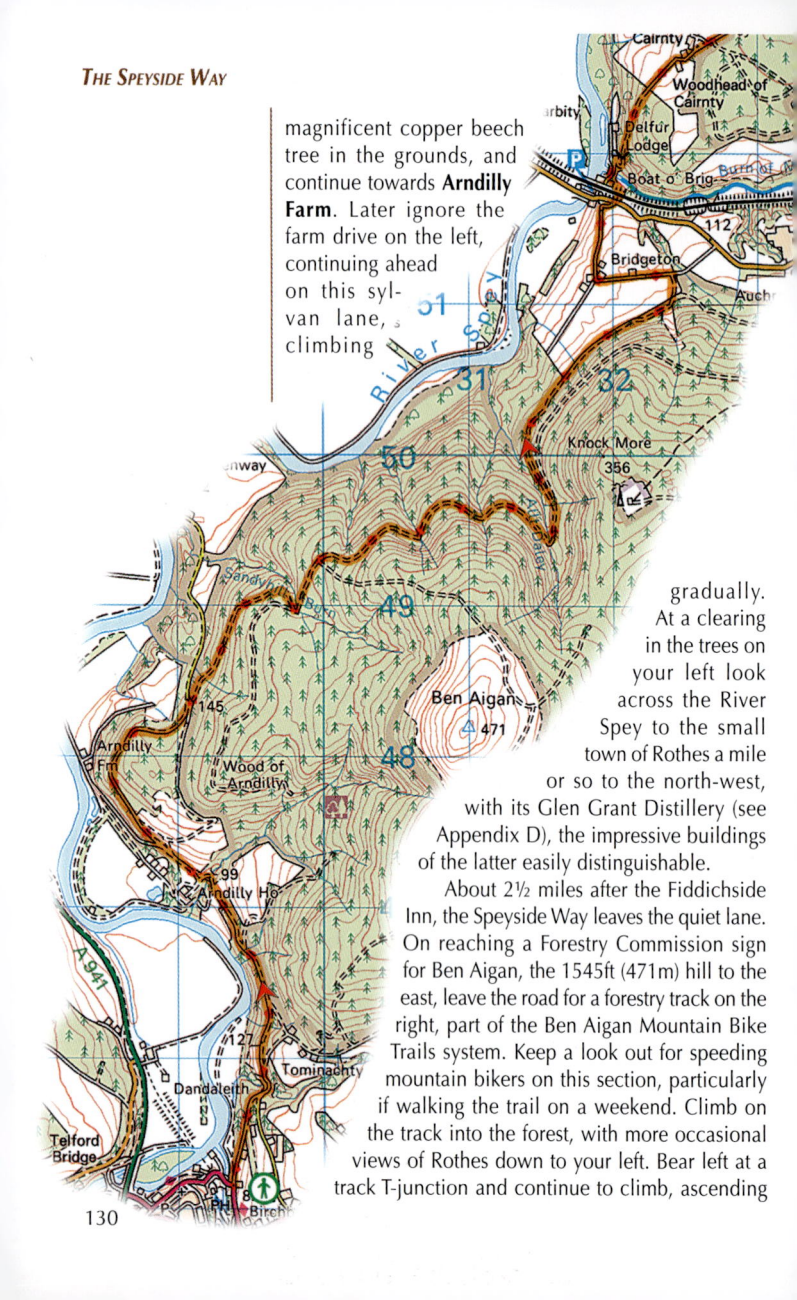

*The Speyside Way*

magnificent copper beech tree in the grounds, and continue towards **Arndilly Farm**. Later ignore the farm drive on the left, continuing ahead on this sylvan lane, climbing gradually. At a clearing in the trees on your left look across the River Spey to the small town of Rothes a mile or so to the north-west, with its Glen Grant Distillery (see Appendix D), the impressive buildings of the latter easily distinguishable.

About 2½ miles after the Fiddichside Inn, the Speyside Way leaves the quiet lane. On reaching a Forestry Commission sign for Ben Aigan, the 1545ft (471m) hill to the east, leave the road for a forestry track on the right, part of the Ben Aigan Mountain Bike Trails system. Keep a look out for speeding mountain bikers on this section, particularly if walking the trail on a weekend. Climb on the track into the forest, with more occasional views of Rothes down to your left. Bear left at a track T-junction and continue to climb, ascending gently to a short detour path on the left – this leads to seats and a picnic table at a viewpoint overlooking the steep ravine of Red Sheugh and down to the River Spey. Shortly after this, the high point of the climb is reached at around 900ft (275m). The track undulates from now on and offers good views of the Spey valley and your first glimpses of the sea in the Moray Firth.

The trail eventually begins a long, gradual descent into the Spey valley. After a sharp bend in the track, as it crosses the **Allt Daley** burn, look out for the Speyside Way signpost indicating a narrow track heading down to the left. This leads down into the valley, the path eventually skirting land belonging to the Speyside Gun Club. A red flag will be flying if firing is taking place, but even then, provided you keep strictly to the waymarked trail, you should not be in any danger. Turn left at a track T-junction, soon leaving the Ben Aigan Forest. Turn left at a second track T-junction onto a sandy track in open country, following a line of overhead electrical cables and soon passing **Bridgeton** Farm. Turn right at the entrance to Bridgeton Mains. The Way soon bends to the right on a descent towards the River Spey. Turn left at the next T-junction in front of and above the B9103 road, and after about 100 yards turn right onto a narrow footpath which descends to the road.

Turn right onto the **B9103** (take care – no pavement), but leave it in 30 yards to take another road on the left, at the **Boat o'Brig Speyside Way car park**. Pass under the bridge and remain on the quiet lane, soon climbing again quite steeply. The gradient eases near the summit of Tor Hill. Ascend, passing **Woodhead of Cairnty**,

*The Earth Pillars rock formations alongside the Spey, can be visited by following the footpath from the car park and are well worth seeing.*

and continue on to pass the **Mains of Cairnty** and, much later, the house of **Culfoldie**. From here the lane, which carries very little vehicular traffic, descends very steeply, and this is followed by an equally steep re-ascent to the **Earth Pillars car park**. ◄ The Speyside Way continues to follow this narrow minor road ahead.

After Speyside Cottage the road descends again; leave it at **'The Pines'** by turning left off the road onto a track, but 25 yards later turn right onto a grassy path. Follow this to a T-junction of paths in a wood; turn right here (no Speyside Way waymark in May 2009), climb some steps and continue along a path between fence and trees. At a cross-path at a green fingerpost, turn right on a path to the right of houses to reach a road on the outskirts of the town of Fochabers. Walk ahead on this road (Spey Road), which becomes West Street. Leave it where the road swings to the left, by turning right over a small bridge. Immediately after this bridge turn left on a path to continue the Speyside Way, but to visit **Fochabers** town centre continue ahead, shortly reaching the high street.

*A rest stop by a picnic table in Ben Aigan Wood (Beryl Castle)*

## SPEYSIDE WAY STAGE 8 – CRAIGELLACHIE TO FOCHABERS

*Looking across to Bridgeton Farm and Boat o' Brig from the lower slopes of Knock More (Beryl Castle)*

**Note**: this section from 'The Pines' to Fochabers was severely damaged in the floods of late 2009. In future, the route into Fochabers may simply continue along the minor road turning left just as the village is reached.

### FOCHABERS

The name Fochabers is thought to derive from the Gaelic 'foth', meaning 'land', and 'abar', meaning 'marsh'. The original buildings of the old town stood too close to Gordon Castle for the 4th Duke of Gordon's liking, so in 1776 he had plans for a new town drawn up by John Baxter and the inhabitants were moved. There is a fine Georgian church (1798) with a clock tower and the Gordon Chapel. Another church in Fochabers has been converted to the Fochabers Folk Museum. Baxters Highland Village is just outside Fochabers on the other side of the River Spey (see below).

**Facilities**: hotel, B&Bs, caravan/camping site. Cafés ('The Quaich' can be recommended for good and cheap meals). Fish and chip shop. Co-op food store and other shops. Pharmacy, bank, post office. Local buses.

*The Speyside Way*

## STAGE 9
*Fochabers to Spey Bay*

| | |
|---|---|
| **Distance** | 5 miles/8km |
| **Maps** | OS Landranger 28 (Elgin and Dufftown) |

*A walker on the path through woodland after leaving Fochabers (Beryl Castle)*

The tourist destination **Baxters Highland Village** (on the A96 west of the River Spey, ½ mile from the centre of Fochabers) offers a variety of shops stocked with a range of Baxters food products, speciality foods, whiskies, clothing, cookware and gifts. The George Baxter's Cellar Shop stocks all of the Baxters food range produced in Fochabers, and it is possible to discover the history of the Baxter family and their food production in the old grocery shop originally opened by George Baxter in 1868. There are also restaurants on the site, which is open to visitors every day.

After a visit to **Fochabers** town return to the point where you left the Speyside Way. The path follows a stream along the edge of the town. Cross a road and continue following this burn downstream. Bear right on meeting the Spey at the 'Famous Fochaberians Memorial Garden'. Continue along the Spey to pass under two roads, a minor one followed immediately by the A96 (T). At the far side of the latter bear right into **Bellie Wood**. After this attractive woodland section the path is squeezed for a while between the River Spey on the left and the B9104 road on the right, before the trail leaves the river with a right–left dog-leg and heads once more into woodland, **Warren Wood**.

Keep left at the next junction. The pleasant track passes through swathes of yellow broom, a heady perfume and blaze of colour when in flower. Keep to the main track through the forest, eventually returning to the bank of the River Spey, now at its widest, only a couple of miles from the sea. After a little over ½ mile look out for a Speyside Way 'thistle' marker post that indicates a path to the right, off the main track. Bear right at the next T-junction and keep left at the following Y-junction. Banks of yellow gorse and broom line this fenced track between rich arable fields.

The trail runs alongside **Culriach Wood**, rich in water-loving alder and willow, crosses the Aberdeen to Inverness National Cycle Track and reaches Spey Bay Wildlife Reserve. Keep ahead at the next junction, now heading for the buildings of Spey Bay seen ahead. Eventually **Spey Bay** is reached at a road T-junction by Tugnet House. The Speyside Way is joined by the Moray Coast Trail (fulmar waymarks) just before Spey Bay, and the two paths now follow the same route for most of the way between Spey Bay and Buckie. Turn left at the junction to reach, in about 100 yards, the Whale and Dolphin Conservation and Wildlife Centre, the Tugnet Ice House, toilets and café.

*Looking across the Spey to Kingston from Tugnet*

The **Wildlife Centre** at Tugnet, Spey Bay, is managed by the Whale and Dolphin Conservation Society (WDCS), an organisation that has been active in the Moray Firth area for over 20 years, sponsoring research into conservation and working to achieve greater protection for whales and dolphins in Scottish waters. The Wildlife Centre is housed in old buildings that originally were part of the fishing station at Tugnet. This closed in 1991, and the Wildlife Centre opened 6 years later. Highlights of the site include an Underwater World experience based in the old ice house, listening to live underwater sound obtained from a 'sonobuoy', using the centre's binoculars and telescopes to spot bottlenose dolphins, seals and other wildlife, and relaxing in the Café Wild. There is also a sculpture park here and several interesting interpretative boards. The site, café and shop are open every day, 10.30am to 5pm, from April to October, and at weekends from November to March.

**Tugnet Ice House** is reputedly the largest industrial ice house in Scotland. Built in 1830, it has six chambers, with only a third of the building visible above ground. Ice gathered in the winter from specially cut channels in the Spey was stored in the ice house to keep the salmon catch fresh until it was shipped to market. It has now been acquired by WDCS and is open to the public.

### SPEY BAY

**Facilities**: These are few. There is a B&B, but no campsite. The hotel at Spey Bay was closed in about 2006, but was bought in 2009 and so may open again in the future (not open at time of writing).

## STAGE 10
*Spey Bay to Buckie*

| | |
|---|---|
| **Distance** | 5 miles/8km |
| **Maps** | OS Landranger 28 (Elgin and Dufftown) |

After a visit to the wildlife centre and café, head eastwards along the road into **Spey Bay** village. Bear right at the hotel, away from the coast for a few hundred yards to a Speyside Way waymark indicating a path on the left. This path winds through conifer woods to the landward side of the golf links, although the latter are completely hidden from sight by the trees. When the golf course is finally spotted on the left, the path pulls away from it, continuing through the trees and eventually emerging into open country. Turn right here on the lower footpath (not on the upper track). This soon swings to the left to join a disused railway line. Follow this towards the coastal village of Portgordon. Eventually the trail emerges onto a road, which is followed to the esplanade in **Portgordon**.

*The Speyside Way*

## PORTGORDON

Portgordon was founded on an uninhabited site in 1797 by the 4th Duke of Gordon. He arranged for the construction of the harbour, which for over 50 years was the most important on this section of the Moray coast. Mainly a fishing port, it was also used to import coal for industries in Moray. However, by 1857 its importance was declining after a harbour was built at nearby Nether Buckie (now known as Buckpool, the end of the Speyside Way), and by 1877 the huge Cluny harbour at Buckie was becoming established. Portgordon's harbour remained active, although declining, until it was badly damaged by a storm in 1953. It has since been repaired and is now the base for a few leisure craft and some small-scale fishing.

**Facilities**: B&Bs, a shop, local buses.

Walk along the front to the little harbour of Portgordon, where a Speyside Way sign informs you that it is only 53 miles back to Aviemore on this trail! Take the tarmacked lane between the houses and the sea. On leaving the town this becomes an earthen track and then soon a footpath along the coast (keep an eagle eye for seals along this section, resting on the coastal rocks). The

## SPEYSIDE WAY STAGE 10 – SPEY BAY TO BUCKIE

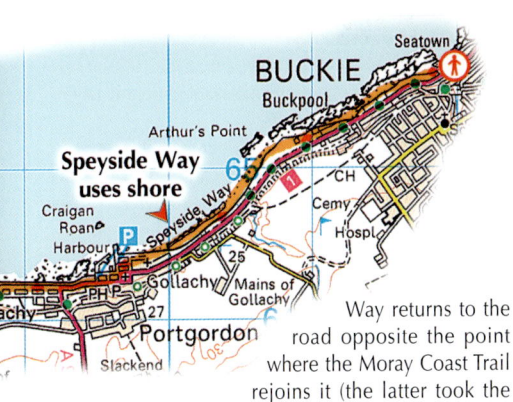

*Lobster pots, harbour and houses at Portgordon*

Way returns to the road opposite the point where the Moray Coast Trail rejoins it (the latter took the National Cycle Route out of Portgordon), and the two walking trails now share the same route between here and Buckie.

After a short distance the Speyside Way takes a path along the coast again, rejoining the road at the 'Welcome to Buckie' road signpost. Walk along the pavement into the Buckpool area of the town. Later leave the pavement on the left for a final footpath section, passing a

*THE SPEYSIDE WAY*

> The terminus of the Speyside Way is to be moved into Buckie town centre at some point but if so this will be waymarked.

fingerpost directing the way to the Speyside Way terminus at **Buckpool** harbour. This official end of the Speyside Way is now soon reached. Here there is an erroneous sign indicating only 55 miles back to Aviemore on the Speyside Way. The town centre of **Buckie** is soon reached by taking any road off to the right, away from the coast. ◄

## BUCKIE

Buckie lies either side of the mouth of the Burn of Buckie. It was formed from an amalgamation of several separate fishing villages, including Nether Buckie (now known as Buckpool). The new town of Buckie began to form on the ridge above the fishing villages in the late 18th and early 19th centuries, developed by the Gordons of Cluny, who also built the huge harbour in 1877, at the great expense of £60,000. They had previously tried to develop the harbour at Buckpool in 1857, but this had problems with silt, and in the 1970s it was filled in and turned into the pleasant park area where the Speyside Way now ends.

Cluny harbour was initially one of the finest harbours in Scotland and is still a very active one. It retains a fishing fleet and also has a shipyard, which builds and repairs fishing boats and repairs lifeboats (all this will be seen if you continue eastwards along the MCT). Buckie and District Fishing Heritage Centre (in summer, open weekdays 10am to 4pm and Saturday 10am to 1pm) is located in the town and has free admission (donation requested).

**Facilities**: hotel and B&Bs. Cafés and restaurants. Co-op food store and many other shops. Bank and post office. Local and long-distance bus services (fairly frequent bus services from Buckie to Inverness or Aberdeen, from where there are good bus and train connections to all parts of the UK).

# TOMINTOUL SPUR
## TOMINTOUL TO BALLINDALLOCH STATION

The Tomintoul Spur is a scenic delight, a walk for connoisseurs of the lower rolling hills of the Eastern Highlands. Although the Tomintoul Spur encounters the main Speyside Way only at its northern terminus at Ballindalloch station, the route is considered by many to offer the finest section of walking on the whole trail. It particularly appeals to hillwalkers, as it traverses the moorland and hill country to the east of the Spey and provides views of the Cairngorm Mountains to the south-west and the Hills of Cromdale, nearer at hand, to the west. Although it involves considerably more ascent and descent in its 15 miles than the main route of the Speyside Way (see the 'Summary of ascent' table in 'The routes in this guidebook'), it always remains below the 2000ft contour and its climbs are gradual ones on good paths. Another of its advantages is that the Spur avoids the

*Speyside Way marker post on the summit of Carn Daimh*

hardest section of the main Speyside Way trail between Cromdale and Ballindalloch station.

The Spur starts its journey at Tomintoul, which lies at a height of 1168ft (356m) above sea level, reputedly the highest village in the Highlands. After crossing Conglass Water, a tributary of the River Avon, it begins a slow, gradual climb to its highest point on the summit of Carn Daimh (1870ft, 570m), a panoramic viewpoint. The Way then descends to Glen Livet, where it offers the opportunity for a tour of the eponymous distillery, at approximately the half-way stage of the walk. After crossing the River Livet, another tributary of the Avon, the Spur climbs again, this time over the Deskie and Cairnacay hills, before making a final descent to Strath Avon. It follows the Avon, which is itself a tributary of the Spey, passing the old Bridge of Avon, to Ballindalloch station, near the Cragganmore Distillery in the Spey valley.

Many will consider starting their Speyside Way journey at Tomintoul and continuing to the Moray Firth and Buckie, a distance of 50 miles that involves approximately 2950ft (900m) of ascent (about 1050ft (320m) more if walking in the reverse direction, from Buckie

*A happy worker in Tomintoul tourist office (Beryl Castle)*

## TOMINTOUL SPUR (S TO N) – TOMINTOUL TO BALLINDALLOCH STATION

to Tomintoul). Another possibility is to start the walk at Newtonmore or Aviemore, and at Ballindalloch turn south for a hike over the hills to finish at Tomintoul. For those who want this north–south option a description of the Tomintoul Spur from Ballindalloch to Tomintoul follows the main route description below.

### TOMINTOUL

The name Tomintoul is derived from the Gaelic and means 'mound of the barn'. The village, which lies above Strath Avon to the south-east of Grantown and is separated from the Spey valley by the Cromdale Hills, was planned in 1776 by the 4th Duke of Gordon. He attempted to establish a flax and linen industry here, but this was unsuccessful. Today the village is surrounded by the Crown Estate of Glenlivet, which helps attract many visitors for outdoor activities. There is an excellent museum and visitor centre (open April to October) in the village.

**Facilities**: SYHA hostel, hotels, B&B, unserviced campsite (adjacent to Glenlivet Estate Office) – free to Speyside Way walkers. Cafés. Post office and store and other shops. An infrequent bus service

## SOUTH TO NORTH: STAGE 1
*Tomintoul to Glenlivet Distillery*

| | |
|---|---|
| **Distance** | 7½ miles/12km |
| **Maps** | OS Landranger 36 (Grantown, Aviemore & Cairngorm area) |

From the central square in **Tomintoul** walk north-north-east along Main Street. At the end of the village follow a path on the right-hand side of the road for about 250 yards to where the A939 bends to the left, and where

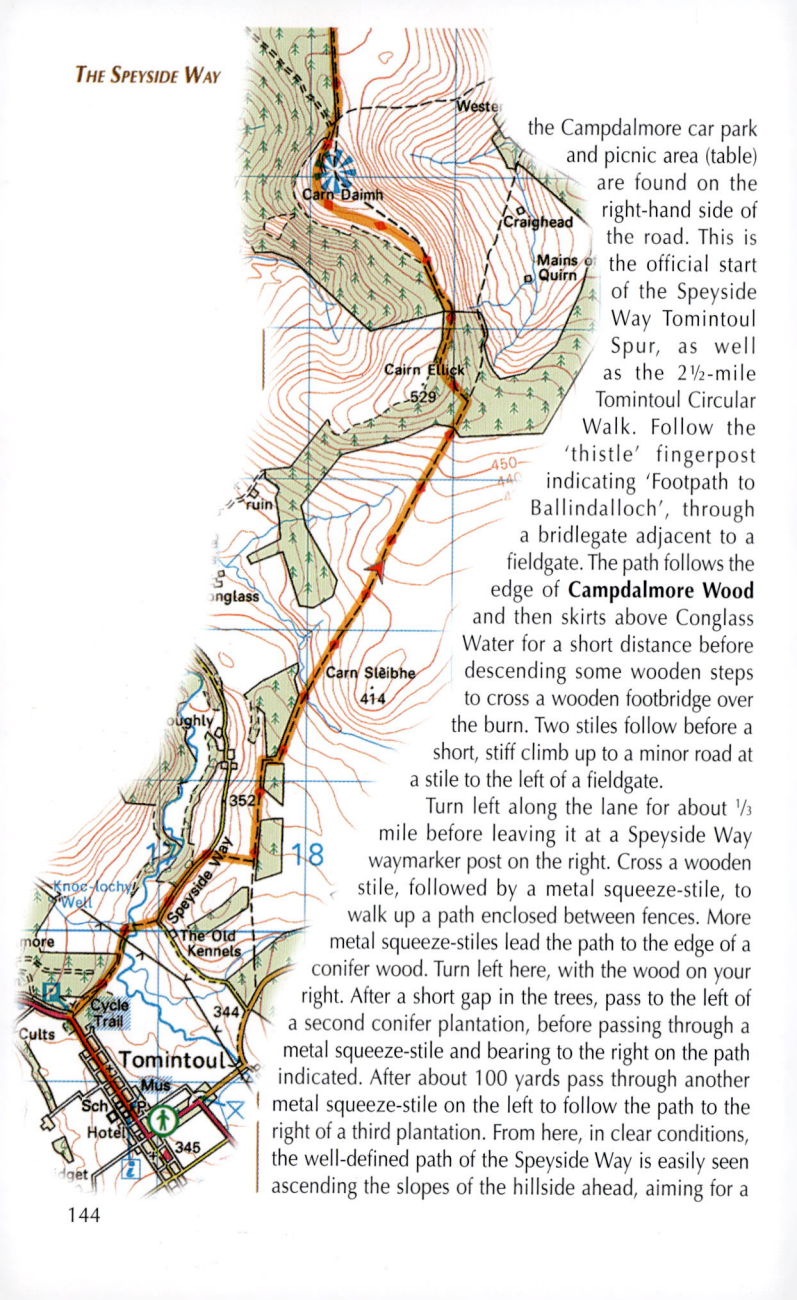

## THE SPEYSIDE WAY

the Campdalmore car park and picnic area (table) are found on the right-hand side of the road. This is the official start of the Speyside Way Tomintoul Spur, as well as the 2½-mile Tomintoul Circular Walk. Follow the 'thistle' fingerpost indicating 'Footpath to Ballindalloch', through a bridlegate adjacent to a fieldgate. The path follows the edge of **Campdalmore Wood** and then skirts above Conglass Water for a short distance before descending some wooden steps to cross a wooden footbridge over the burn. Two stiles follow before a short, stiff climb up to a minor road at a stile to the left of a fieldgate.

Turn left along the lane for about ⅓ mile before leaving it at a Speyside Way waymarker post on the right. Cross a wooden stile, followed by a metal squeeze-stile, to walk up a path enclosed between fences. More metal squeeze-stiles lead the path to the edge of a conifer wood. Turn left here, with the wood on your right. After a short gap in the trees, pass to the left of a second conifer plantation, before passing through a metal squeeze-stile and bearing to the right on the path indicated. After about 100 yards pass through another metal squeeze-stile on the left to follow the path to the right of a third plantation. From here, in clear conditions, the well-defined path of the Speyside Way is easily seen ascending the slopes of the hillside ahead, aiming for a clearly visible V-shaped 'nick' in the forestry plantation on the skyline. The reason for this clearly visible path soon becomes evident, as after the wood the trail consists of long sections of boardwalks over a boggy area for about ⅓ mile. After the boardwalk, the path over heather moorland is both clearly visible on the ground and well waymarked with 'thistle' signposts.

The Speyside Way enters the conifer plantation by crossing a stile at the aforementioned 'nick' in the trees and then follows a wide but often wet and boggy track. After a few hundred yards be sure to turn left at a Speyside Way fingerpost indicating the route to Ballindalloch (the path ahead leads to Tomnavoulin and its Distillery – currently not in production – in a couple of miles). Climb on the track through the trees, ignoring another track to the left at the top of the climb (this track to the left leads in a few hundred yards to the small, low cairn in a clearing on the summit of Carn Ellick, 1735ft, 529m). The Speyside Way follows the muddy track ahead, slightly downhill through the plantation. The summit of Carn Daimh (1870ft, 570m) should be glimpsed to the left through the trees. This is the next objective, the highest point on the whole of the Speyside Way.

Leave the forest by a stile to the left of a fieldgate and climb on the good path to the summit of **Carn Daimh**, which is classed as a 'Marilyn' as it has a drop on all sides in excess of 150m or 500ft. The summit of the hill offers extensive views, from the high Cairngorm plateau to the southwest to the prominent Corbett of Ben Rinnes (2755ft, 840m) in the north-east. A large cairn crowns the summit of Carn Daimh, adjacent to which is a toposcope. Sadly, the plinth of the top of this, which would have identified the view, was missing

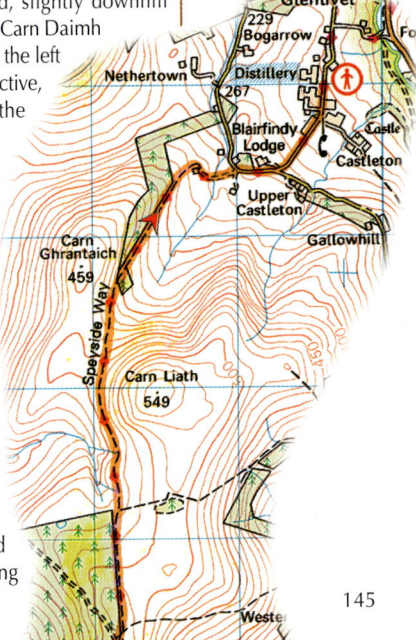

*Orientation table and large summit cairn on Carn Daimh*

in May 2009, presumed stolen. Hopefully there will be a new one in place by the time of your visit.

### GLENLIVET CROWN ESTATE

The Glenlivet Estate covers 58,000 acres of hill, moor, woodland and strath of the rivers Avon and Livet, from the Hills of Cromdale in the west to the Ladder Hills in the east, and includes the settlements of Tomintoul, Tomnavoulin and Bridgend of Glenlivet. All of the estate is above 600 feet and much of it considerably higher, so that snow often remains here until late spring. Acquired by the Crown Estate in 1937, it encourages sustainable economic development, and a Ranger Service is provided to encourage visitors to walk, cycle, horse ride or ski, with leaflets available describing several cycle routes and waymarked walking trails. The Ranger base

## Tomintoul Spur (S to N) – Tomintoul to Ballindalloch Station

and information centre for the estate is on the outskirts of Tomintoul.

The estate has worked in partnership with the Glenlivet Distillery to waymark three new routes retracing the footsteps of three renowned whisky characters, the George Smith Smugglers' Trail (4 miles), Robbie MacPherson Smugglers' Trail (7 miles) and Malcolm Gillespie Smugglers' Trail (6 miles). Several of Tomintoul's community paths also pass through the estate, including Blairfindy Moorland Walk (5 miles) and Tomintoul Circular Walk (2½ miles).

Do not cross the stile in the fence ahead, but follow the Speyside Way path northwards, downhill with the wire on your left. After an initial descent the path is sheltered for a while by another conifer plantation on your left. You will arrive at a path junction where a path to the right is signposted as the Robbie McPherson Smugglers' Trail, which leads to Clash Wood and, in a couple of miles, to Tomnavoulin. However, the Speyside Way continues ahead along the side of the trees. At the end of the plantation pass through the gate to take the path ahead, contouring the western slopes of **Carn Liath** (1801ft, 549m). On this section the Speyside Way follows the same route as the local Blairfindy Moorland Walk.

On reaching the edge of woodland pass through a metal squeeze-stile and follow the path gently downhill, with trees to your left and a wire fence to your right, aiming for the buildings of Glenlivet Distillery seen clearly in the glen below. The path is narrow, a little rough, and goes along a sloping bank, which makes it a bit difficult, but it leads to a metal squeeze-stile, which in turn leads out onto a dirt track. This heads down to a stile to the left of a gate and so out onto a minor road by a small car park (space for two cars only). Turn right along this narrow metalled lane, passing Glenlivet House on your left. At the entrance gate to the latter, turn left downhill on another tarmacked lane. This leads down to the **Glenlivet Distillery**, where a free recommended tour and whisky sample can be enjoyed.

George Smith, the founder of the **Glenlivet Distillery**, was the first person to take out a licence under the 1823 act of Parliament that set a basis for alcohol taxation, thus allowing legal distillation. His neighbours, who had illegal stills, tried to burn his distillery down, but using a pair of pistols (on display in the Glenlivet Reception Centre) Smith managed to dissuade them. The distillery moved to its current location in 1858 and was allowed the appellation 'The Glenlivet' in 1880. Its water source is Josie's Well. It remained in the Smith family until 1975, and today is owned by Pernod Richard. There is a free one-hour guided tour and tasting available from Easter until October (Monday to Saturday 9.30am to 4.00pm, and Sunday 12pm to 4pm), which includes access to a hands-on exhibition that tells the story of Glenlivet and its environment. A coffee shop and gift shop is also open for visitors.

## SOUTH TO NORTH: STAGE 2
*Glenlivet Distillery to Ballindalloch station (Cragganmore)*

| | |
|---|---|
| **Distance** | 7½ miles/12km |
| **Maps** | OS Landranger 36 (Grantown, Aviemore & Cairngorm area) and 28 (Elgin & Dufftown) |

Walk down through the buildings of the **Glenlivet Distillery**. A couple of hundred yards after the last buildings, turn right onto a narrow lane that descends to become a dirt track that further descends to cross a footbridge over the River Livet. On the far side of the river, bear left onto a grassy path that follows the Livet downstream. Steps and a stile lead to the B9008 at **Tombreckachie**, where the Burn of Tervie meets the River Livet. Turn left for an optional detour of about ⅓ mile along this road to visit the famous Packhorse Bridge at Bridgend of Livet.

**joins Speyside Way here**

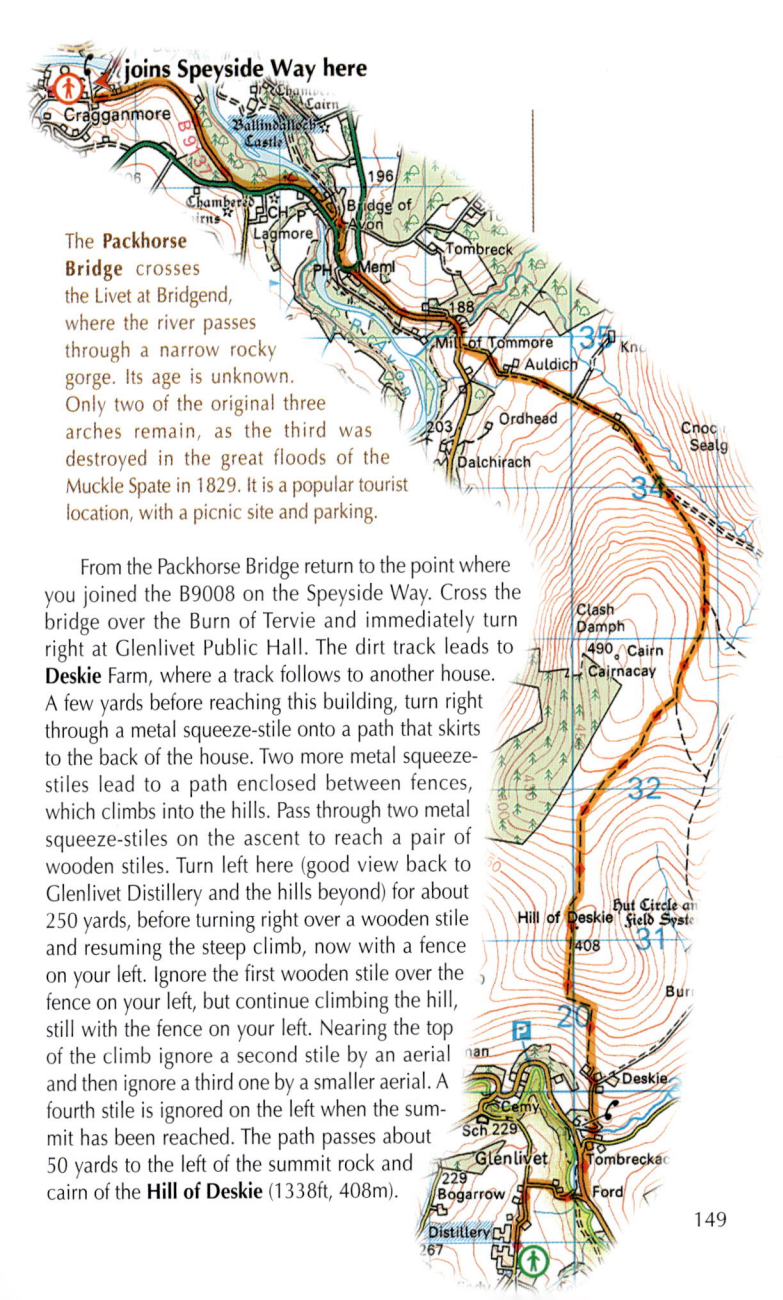

The **Packhorse Bridge** crosses the Livet at Bridgend, where the river passes through a narrow rocky gorge. Its age is unknown. Only two of the original three arches remain, as the third was destroyed in the great floods of the Muckle Spate in 1829. It is a popular tourist location, with a picnic site and parking.

From the Packhorse Bridge return to the point where you joined the B9008 on the Speyside Way. Cross the bridge over the Burn of Tervie and immediately turn right at Glenlivet Public Hall. The dirt track leads to **Deskie** Farm, where a track follows to another house. A few yards before reaching this building, turn right through a metal squeeze-stile onto a path that skirts to the back of the house. Two more metal squeeze-stiles lead to a path enclosed between fences, which climbs into the hills. Pass through two metal squeeze-stiles on the ascent to reach a pair of wooden stiles. Turn left here (good view back to Glenlivet Distillery and the hills beyond) for about 250 yards, before turning right over a wooden stile and resuming the steep climb, now with a fence on your left. Ignore the first wooden stile over the fence on your left, but continue climbing the hill, still with the fence on your left. Nearing the top of the climb ignore a second stile by an aerial and then ignore a third one by a smaller aerial. A fourth stile is ignored on the left when the summit has been reached. The path passes about 50 yards to the left of the summit rock and cairn of the **Hill of Deskie** (1338ft, 408m).

Make a gentle descent from the summit of the hill for about 100 yards to a fence corner, where you climb a pair of wooden stiles on the left and turn right, with a fence on your right. From this point ignore any stiles over, and gates through, the fence on the right, always keeping to the left of the fence as you ascend the eastern slopes of **Cairnacay** (1607ft, 490m). The trail passes about 450 yards to the east of the summit. Arrive at a 'thistle' mark-erpost and a sign that directs you to 'follow and keep to the side of the fence away from cattle' – this at a point at which the fence you have been following for so long comes to an abrupt end!

The sparse, dead remnants of an ancient forest of trees lies between here and the flat, wide summit area of **Cairnacay**. Those with time and a care to explore will find a number of cairns spread over the forlorn summit area of this hill, some large, some small, some expertly built, others less so. One may speculate as to who built them, when and for what purpose. Take care if you do explore, as there is no path across the heather

*The old packhorse bridge at Glenlivet (Beryl Castle)*

## TOMINTOUL SPUR (S TO N) – TOMINTOUL TO BALLINDALLOCH STATIONSTATION

and the terrain is rough underfoot, so accurate navigation is of the utmost importance. The prominent high summit which lies some 3½–4 miles to the east-north-east is mighty Ben Rinnes, at 2755ft, 840m, the highest mountain in these parts, and the second highest in old Banffshire. After your summit adventure return to the above mentioned 'cattle' notice, before continuing.

Follow the 'thistle' Speyside Way waymarker posts on a good path that descends towards the north. Keep to this path, eventually joining a track that continues the descent. This track becomes a metalled lane at a small car park on the left. Continue ahead down this minor road. Pass the House of **Auldich** before emerging on the B9008. Turn right along this road until you reach the A95, where you turn left, signposted to Grantown-on-Spey. Take care along both the B9008 and the A95, keeping to the grass verges of these roads.

Pass over the River Avon on the modern road bridge, but then take the steps down on your right to explore the old stone-arched **Bridge of Avon**, with the turreted circular gatehouse on the far bank of the river. There is a garage, food shop and post office opposite the bridge. Continue along the A95 for about another ½ mile, passing the Lady Macpherson-Grant Hall and keeping to the wide grass verge on the left-hand side of the road. Shortly after passing the Ballindalloch Castle Golf Course, turn right onto the B9137, signposted to Cragganmore and the Speyside Way. ▶ After about ¾ mile you reach **Ballindalloch station** (Cragganmore) and the main route of the Speyside Way. Cragganmore Distillery is a few more yards down this road.

Turn back to Speyside Way Stage 6 to continue on the route to Buckie.

**Cragganmore Distillery** was opened in 1869 by John Smith. It was the first distillery that was built to take advantage of the new railway in Speyside. The water is drawn from the Craggan Burn. It passed out of family control in 1923 and is currently owned by Diageo. The visitor centre opened in 2002 and is open on weekdays from May to October. There is an admission charge.

*THE SPEYSIDE WAY*

## NORTH TO SOUTH: STAGE 1
*Ballindalloch station (Cragganmore) to Glenlivet Distillery*

| | |
|---|---|
| **Distance** | 7½ miles/12km |
| **Maps** | OS Landranger 28 (Elgin & Dufftown) and 36 (Grantown, Aviemore & Cairngorm area) |

*See page 149 for route map.*

Leave **Ballindalloch station** on the B9137 and follow it for ¾ mile to its junction with the A95. Turn left on this, keeping to the wide grass verge and passing Lady Macpherson-Grant Hall and a garage, food shop and post office. Just before crossing the modern road bridge over the River Avon, go down the steps to inspect the old stone-arched bridge over the river, with the small turreted gatehouse, on the far bank. Continue along the main road for over ½ mile to leave the A95 by turning right onto the B9008. Take care along both the A95 and the B9008, keeping to the grass verges.

After about ½ mile turn left onto the minor road to the house of **Auldich**, and continue past this house until the tarmac turns to a dirt surface, after a small parking

*The old Bridge of Avon, south-east of Ballindalloch station*

## TOMINTOUL SPUR (N TO S) – BALLINDALLOCH STATION TO TOMINTOUL

*Speyside Way signpost on the trail between Tomintoul and Glenlivet*

area. Climb on this track, eventually leaving it for a Speyside Way waymarked path on the right. This path climbs the eastern flanks of **Cairnacay** (1607ft, 490m) until a fence is reached. Follow this by keeping it always on your left, ignoring any unmarked stiles and gates in this fence. Follow the fence for a considerable distance until finally reaching a waymarked stile, crossing over the fence here, so that now it is on your right-hand side. Pass to within 50 yards of the summit rock and cairn of the **Hill of Deskie** (1338ft, 408m), which is over to your left, and then descend quite steeply to reach a house before the farm of **Deskie**.

Take the path behind the house to pick up a dirt track, which descends to the B9008 road at **Tombreckachie** by Glenlivet Public Hall (an optional detour to the Parkhorse Bridge at Bridgend of Livet can be made from here – see above ('South to north', Stage 2) for details. Turn left on this road over the bridge over the Burn of Tervie and then soon leave it by climbing over a stile on the right of the road, going down some steps and then along a path heading upstream alongside the River Livet. After about 400 yards cross the suspension footbridge over the River Livet and climb quite steeply up to a road near the **Glenlivet Distillery** ('South to north', Stage 1). Turn left here to walk up through the buildings of the distillery and perhaps take a free one-hour tour with free tastings of their products.

*The Speyside Way*

## NORTH TO SOUTH: STAGE 2
### *Glenlivet Distillery to Tomintoul*

**Distance**      7½ miles/12km
**Maps**          OS Landranger 36 (Grantown, Aviemore & Cairngorm area)

*See pages 144 and 145 for route map.*

The trail now heads south over the hills to Tomintoul. Leave the **distillery** heading south on the road to reach a T-junction, with the entrance to Glenlivet House on your right. Turn right on the road here to reach, after about 400 yards, a small car park on the left, where there is also a stile to the right of a gate. Follow the dirt track to a metal squeeze-stile. The path from here is rather narrow, a little rough and is along a sloping bank. There are trees to your right and a wire fence on your left. Pass through a metal squeeze-stile, climb and then contour the western slopes of **Carn Liath** (1801ft, 549m). The Speyside Way eventually reaches a conifer plantation. Keep the trees to your right until you reach a signpost that indicates a trail to the left down to Tomnavoulin. Now head out onto the open hillside to climb to the summit of **Carn Daimh** (1870ft, 570m), the highest point on the Speyside Way.

Descend the south-east ridge of the hill on a good path to reach a stile to the right of a fieldgate. Now maintain direction through the plantation heading up hill. At the top of the climb ignore another track on the right (this leads in a short distance to the summit of Carn Ellick (1735ft, 529m). The often wet and muddy track leads through the forest to exit the plantation at a stile. Here a good path leads out onto open hillside. Descend south-westwards on this path, which after a while becomes a long boardwalk over a boggy area. The trail eventually descends to run alongside a conifer plantation.

Keep the trees on your right to the end of this first plantation, after which a waymarked dogleg leads to a path that follows the right-hand of two further plantations.

## Tomintoul Spur (N to S) – Ballindalloch Station to Tomintoul

*The gatehouse on the east side of the Bridge of Avon*

Before the end of the third plantation take a path on the right that descends between fences to reach a minor lane at a wooden stile. Turn left along the road for about ⅓ mile to reach a stile by a fieldgate on the right-hand side of the road. Follow the sign here that indicates that the route descends the steep bank to cross the Conglass Water by an excellent wooden footbridge. The trail then follows the meandering stream southwards, soon after which it skirts the edge of **Campdalmore Wood** to reach a bridlegate adjacent to a fieldgate. This leads out to a car parking area and the A939 at the official end/start of the Tomintoul Spur. Turn left on the road soon reaching the first buildings of **Tomintoul**. Follow Main Street to reach the central square of the village, where all facilities will be found.

## THE SPEYSIDE WAY

*The clock tower in the centre of Dufftown*

# DUFFTOWN LOOP

## ABERLOUR–DUFFTOWN–CRAIGELLACHIE

The Speyside Way, Stage 6, ends at Aberlour, from where walkers can make a pleasing detour around the Dufftown Loop. The Loop runs 9 miles (plus an extra ½ mile if you visit Dufftown centre) from Aberlour, via Dufftown, to Craigellachie, where it rejoins the Speyside Way. The complete circuit – from Aberlour to Craigellachie and back to Aberlour via the Spey valley – is nearly 12 miles in length and forms an excellent day walk.

Originally, in the early days of the Speyside Way, a Dufftown Spur provided an alternative starting point for the offical trail. The route from Dufftown followed Glen Fiddich to Craigellachie, where it met the main route of the Speyside Way to Buckie. Unfortunately, due to continuing erosion by the River Fiddich, this route has now lost its Speyside Way designation, so no longer carries the Speyside Way 'thistle' waymarks. Nevertheless, it

*Dufftown*

*The Speyside Way*

remains open and is passable with care except in severe weather conditions.

An alternative and very pleasant route, waymarked by the SROW Society, now exists over the low hills between Aberlour and Dufftown, and this, coupled with the old Speyside Way Spur route along Glen Fiddich, creates an excellent loop. It forms a much more interesting walk from Aberlour to Craigellachie than the official two-mile stroll along the Spey, and as a bonus provides an opportunity to visit one of Scotland's most famous distilleries, Glenfiddich, one of the few family-owned distillery companies remaining in the Highlands.

Remember that the Dufftown Loop from Aberlour to Craigellachie does not carry the Speyside Way 'thistle' waymark.

## STAGE 1
*Aberlour to Dufftown*

| | |
|---|---|
| **Distance** | 4½ miles/7.2km |
| **Maps** | OS Landranger 28 (Elgin & Dufftown) |

From the Speyside Way Visitor Centre in **Aberlour** walk up to the high street where, on the corner of Victoria Terrace and the high street, there is a sign that indicates 'Public Path to Dufftown, 4 miles'. Cross the high street to walk up Queens Road opposite. At the Fleming Hospital bear to the right on Chapel Terrace and then in 150 yards left into Allachie Drive. Climb on this road above the Spey valley to the south-east of Aberlour. Keep to the metalled lane, ignoring side tracks as this narrow lane skirts to the north of the **Wood of Allachie**. After about ½ mile this lane becomes a track that turns sharply to the left just before the large house of **Gownie** seen ahead. Do not walk up to this house, but instead take the track which heads to the right (signposted as 'Public Path to

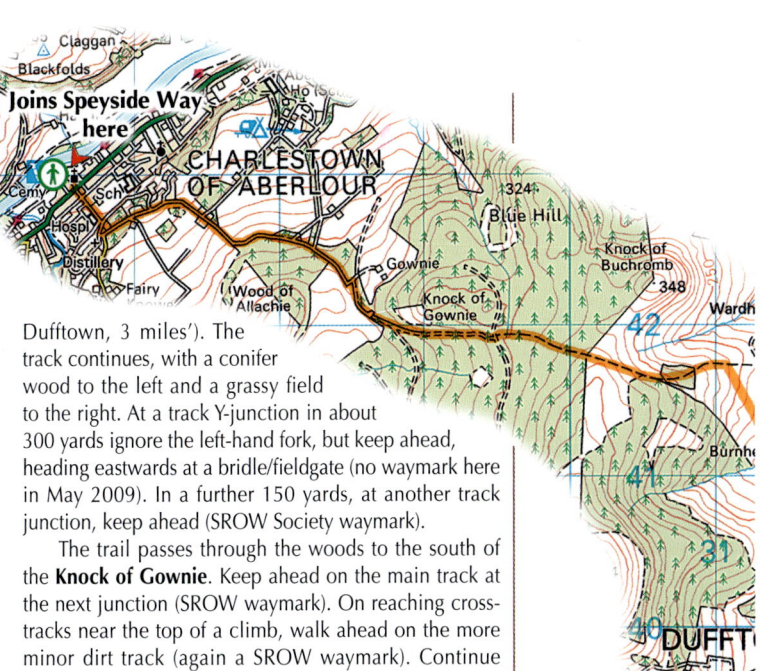

Dufftown, 3 miles'). The
track continues, with a conifer
wood to the left and a grassy field
to the right. At a track Y-junction in about
300 yards ignore the left-hand fork, but keep ahead,
heading eastwards at a bridle/fieldgate (no waymark here
in May 2009). In a further 150 yards, at another track
junction, keep ahead (SROW Society waymark).

The trail passes through the woods to the south of
the **Knock of Gownie**. Keep ahead on the main track at
the next junction (SROW waymark). On reaching cross-
tracks near the top of a climb, walk ahead on the more
minor dirt track (again a SROW waymark). Continue
ahead at the next junction where there is a very old
and small 'Aberlour–Dufftown' wooden signpost. The
path climbs through the forest, eventually exiting via a
fieldgate/bridlegate/stile complex onto open gorse and
heather-covered moorland. Now begin the descent into
Glen Fiddich. Further downhill follow a SROW waymark
through another small section of woodland, after which
the town of Dufftown in Glen Fiddich lies spread out
below you.

Follow the path south-eastwards towards it. The
Glenfiddich Distillery is easily distinguished just to
the north of the town. Descend a broad grassy sward
between young trees to reach an earthen cross-track. Do
not take this, but follow the grassy path ahead (SROW
waymark) heading south. Soon cross the next track (large
stone cairn) and keep ahead on a grassy path between
fences. The town comes ever closer into view on your
left. Remain on the track as it curves to the left, joins
another path and heads for the town. Cross a small bridge

*Map continued on page 160*

*THE SPEYSIDE WAY*

over a stream, pass Dufftown Football Club grounds and walk ahead to the high street.

Turn left here to continue the walk to the Glenfiddich Distillery and on to Craigellachie, but turn right onto the high street to visit **Dufftown** town centre, with its prominent clock tower in which is located the Tourist Information Centre.

### DUFFTOWN

An old poem states that 'Rome was built on seven hills; Dufftown was built on seven stills'! Today there are nine distilleries in or close to Dufftown, and not surprisingly it is known as the Malt Whisky Capital of the World. Dufftown, or Balvenie as it was originally called, was founded in 1817 by James Duff, 4th Earl of Fife, to provide employment for locals after the Napoleonic Wars.

**Facilities**: hotels and B&Bs. Cafés and restaurants. Co-op food store and other shops. Bank and post office.

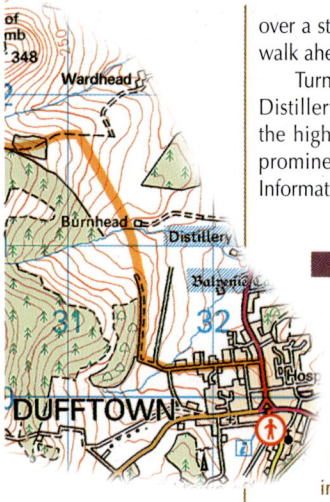

*Glenfiddich Distillery on the outskirts of Dufftown (Beryl Castle)*

## DUFFTOWN LOOP STAGE 2 – DUFFTOWN TO CRAIGELLACHIE

*The still room at Glenfiddich Distillery*

**STAGE 2**
*Dufftown to Craigellachie*

| | |
|---|---|
| **Distance** | 4½ miles/7.2km |
| **Maps** | OS Landranger 28 (Elgin & Dufftown) |

After a visit to **Dufftown** retrace your steps to the point where you joined the high street, but this time keep ahead along it, following the pavement out of town to reach the **Glenfiddich Distillery** (see Appendix D) after about ½ mile. Balvenie Castle is nearby.

**Balvenie Castle**, one of the oldest stone castles in Scotland, was built in the latter half of the 13th century by the Comyn Earls of Buchan. After the middle of the 15th century, James II granted the castle to the Earl of Atholl, who transformed it from a medieval stronghold to a Renaissance residence. But a new house was built nearby, and by 1720 the castle had been abandoned

161

and soon started to fall into decline. Today the castle is managed by Historic Scotland, and with its vast curtain wall is still an impressive sight.

After a recommended free tour of Glenfiddich Distillery and possibly a visit to Balvenie Castle, continue along the pavement, north along the A941, for about a ¼ mile to Dufftown railway station on the Keith and Dufftown Railway.

The **Keith and Dufftown Railway** is Britain's most northerly heritage railway. The 11-mile line was reopened by volunteers during 2000/2001. Between Keith and Dufftown it passes forests, farmland, lochs and glens, castles and distilleries. Trains run on the line at weekends from April until September.

Walk along the platform to follow the signs for the Isla Way, 3¾ miles to Craigellachie. There is a warning notice that states: 'The path ahead was damaged by landslides in November 2002. Minimal clearance works

*The River Fiddich between Glenfiddich Distillery and Craigellachie*

## DUFFTOWN LOOP STAGE 2 – DUFFTOWN TO CRAIGELLACHIE

have been carried out and following a Health and Safety Inspection the footpath has been re-opened for walkers only. The footpath could be subject to further landslides and therefore you should take particular care if you decide to walk the route.' Proceed carefully, particularly in very wet or windy weather. If there are signs closing the path at the time of your visit, then you must not continue. If you have any queries contact the Speyside Way Route Manager, tel. 01340 881266.

The **Isla Way** is a 13-mile walking or cycling route which links the two famous whisky distillery towns of Dufftown and Keith, using woodland tracks, meandering country paths and minor roads to explore old Banffshire. The route travels between Keith's Reidhaven Square and Dufftown's old clock tower. Three stations of the Keith and Dufftown Railway service the short trail. Its name comes from the valley that the trail and the railway pass through, Glen Isla, in which runs the River Isla.

After about ½ mile you reach a green Isla Way fingerpost. This trail takes the path to the right to Loch Park (3½ miles) and Drummuir (4½ miles) from this point. Your route, however, keeps ahead on the path signposted to Craigellachie, 3¼ miles. There follows a very pleasant walk on a good path down Glen Fiddich, through attractive deciduous woodland. You should, after about ¾ mile, come to a short section (about 30 yards long) bearing a sign warning that this is a landslip area. The River Fiddich runs in the glen below, an idyllic

## THE SPEYSIDE WAY

setting, particularly in springtime, with new leaves on the trees and the singing of a variety of bird species (the autumn tree colours, too, are stunning). The trail follows the line of a disused railway along the glen.

About 2½ miles from Glenfiddich Distillery the trail is bridged over the River Fiddich, so from here to Craigellachie the river is now on your left. The trail eventually recrosses the River Fiddich and enters Fiddich Park, where the Speyside Way is rejoined at the Speyside Way camping area and car park, near the Fiddichside Inn, on the north-eastern outskirts of **Craigellachie**. From here you can either continue along the Speyside Way (see The Speyside Way, Section 8, above) towards Buckie or return to Aberlour following the Way back along the valley to complete the Loop.

*A tour group inside Glenfiddich Distillery*

# THE DAVA WAY

*New pond in 'breathing spaces' nature area at Dunphail Sidings (Beryl Castle)*

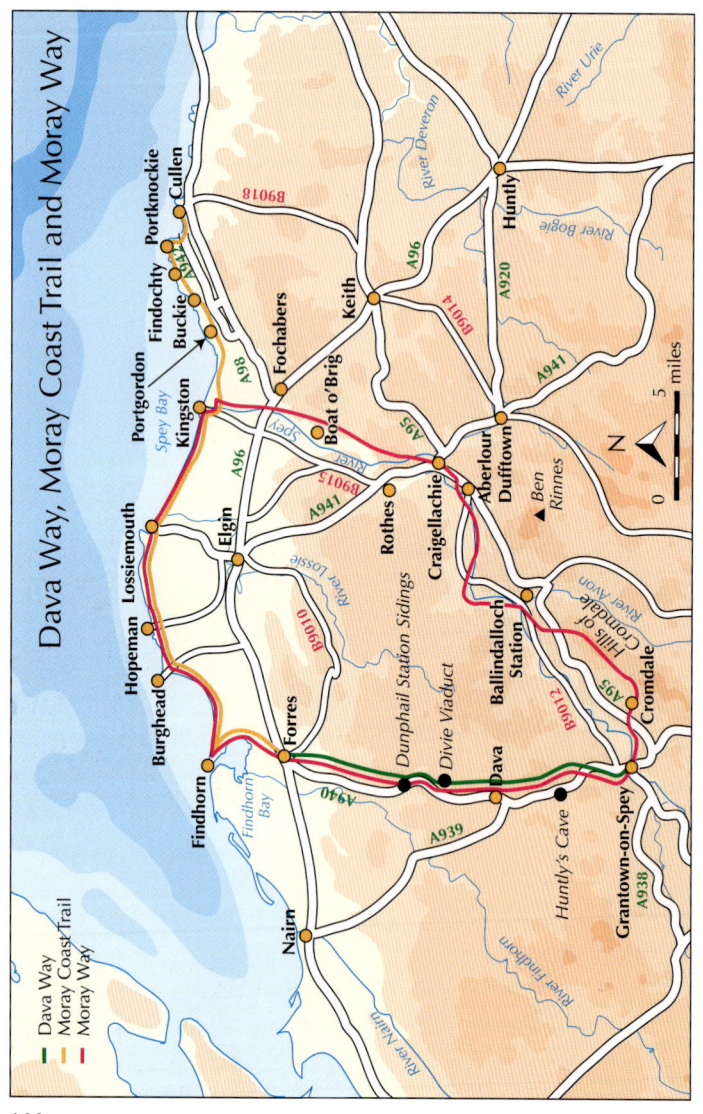

# THE SPEYSIDE WAY

## Dava Way, Moray Coast Trail and Moray Way

# INTRODUCTION

The Dava Way (25 miles/40km) follows the line of a disused railway from Grantown-on-Spey to the town of Forres, a few miles south of the Moray coast. Although an easy trail to walk, in its southern half it traverses some remote and wild moorland landscape. Views of the surrounding hills, moorland and distant mountains are panoramic and extend from the Cairngorm mountains and Cromdale Hills in the south to the distant mountains of the northern Highlands in Sutherland and Caithness. You can expect to see red deer roaming the hills and moorland to either side of the line, as well as various raptors in the skies above your head. The northern half of the route crosses more fertile country and large areas of deciduous woodland. It forms a vital link in the Moray path network, linking the Speyside Way at Grantown with the Moray Coast Trail at Forres.

The Dava Way was officially opened on 18th September 2005 as a rural multi-user route. The former railway line it follows was a section of the Highland

*The track heads north towards Dava Moor*

*Dava Way sign (Dava Way Association)*

Railway, which ran for just over 100 miles from Dunkeld in Perthshire, south of Pitlochry, to Forres, and was built in the very short space of less than 2 years in the 1860s. Many of the bridges and other structures associated with the railway are still standing today.

Named after the hamlet of Dava through which it passes, the Dava Way offers generally easy walking and mountain biking, mostly on a surface of compacted railway track bed, although there are occasional rough, soft and wet sections to negotiate, which are worse after heavy rain and during the winter months. As one might expect from a railway line, the amount of ascent/descent is negligible. The route is also promoted for horse riders; although relatively few of these will probably be encountered, cyclists are quite often seen.

The trail is diverted away from the line of the old railway from time to time, notably at Lady Catherine's Halt, Dava hamlet and Squirrel Neck Bridge, to avoid private property or very wet or even flooded sections of the line. Do look out for these diversions, following the description in this guidebook and the Dava Way waymarks carefully. The Squirrel Neck Bridge deviation in particular offers a very pleasant sylvan walk. Navigation along the route is fairly straightforward, and the Way is waymarked with a triangular logo, depicting a railway viaduct and a bootprint.

This guidebook describes the route of the Dava Way for walkers; there are a few short, but obligatory, clearly waymarked routes for cyclists and horse riders to ensure they avoid sensitive areas, and further information on these alternative sections can be obtained from the Dava website or from the free Dava Way leaflets available from TICs locally. Long distance runners who are looking for a good off-road route of almost marathon length would also find the trail to their liking (a marathon race from Grantown to Forres was held on 17th September 2006 to mark the anniversary of the opening of the Dava Way the previous year).

**Facilities:** none for the route's entire length between Grantown and Forres, both of which have abundant accommodation, cafés, restaurants and shops.

## STAGE 1
*Grantown-on-Spey to Dava*

| Distance | 8¾ miles/14.2km |
|---|---|
| Maps | OS Landranger 36 (Grantown, Aviemore & Cairngorm area) and 27 (Nairn & Forres) |

Start your walk from the main square in the centre of **Grantown-on-Spey**, at the traffic lights near to the post office. Head north-west along Seafield Avenue. After passing Grantown-on-Spey Caravan Park (tent camping as well as caravans) the road swings to the left and climbs to pass under Dulicht Bridge. At the far side of the bridge is the first green fingerpost of the Dava Way that indicates the official start of the route. Here too is an information board on the Dava Way and another on the local 'Viewpoint Walk'. Pass through a kissing gate to climb up to the old railway line. Within a few hundred yards, a path leaves the track on the left to climb to a series of three viewpoints, from where there are good views down to Grantown and of the distant Cairngorm mountains. The Hills of Cromdale lying to the east are also prominent; this range rises to over 2300ft (700m) and separates the Spey valley from Strath

For more about Grantown-on-Spey, see Speyside Way Stage 3.

*Lady Catherine's Halt, north of Grantown-on-Spey*

## THE SPEYSIDE WAY

Avon. It is only a short detour up to the first viewpoint, so at least take time out for this, as the fine view offers adequate recompense for the extra effort required. The full 'Viewpoint Walk' is 2 miles in length (allow 1–1½ hours).

Return to the railway line to continue along the Dava Way, where attractive deciduous woodland lines the bank. The trail soon passes through an impressive rock cutting and then through a kissing gate to cross a track and resume the old railway line, now parallel to a road, the A939, for a little over ½ mile. A bridge takes the railway line over this road at **Lady Catherine's Halt**. This unusual and attractive Grade A listed building was built to allow the gentry of nearby Castle Grant to board and alight from the trains.

The top turrets of **Castle Grant**, ½ mile east of Lady Catherine's Halt, can be seen from the Dava Way. The original tower was built in the 15th century by the Comyns of Badenoch. Previously named Castle Freuchie, it became the principal residence of the Grant chiefs of Strathspey in 1693. Although the Grants were government supporters, the castle was occupied by Jacobites during both the 1715 and 1745 Jacobite uprisings. In 1765 Sir Ludovic Grant was responsible for extending the tower into the castle which remains today. It was refurbished in the 1990s and is now a private residence.

About 150 yards after the bridge, leave the railway line by a narrow path on the left which leads to a track at a path/track T-junction; turn left onto the track to reach

## Dava Way Stage 1 – Grantown-on-Spey to Dava

a stone gateway immediately in front of the main road. Turn right here (no waymark in May 2009) on a path that runs alongside the road, but is separated from it by a drystone wall. Follow this to reach a dirt track, and turn right through a metal fieldgate to follow this track away from the road for 30 yards and then left through a small gate to follow a narrow path through trees. This reaches a metalled lane at a **telephone box** by a Dava Way fingerpost (Forres 21 miles/Grantown 3 miles).

Turn right along this lane, away from the main road. After about 600 yards, just before a farmhouse, turn left (Forres now signposted as only 20 miles, though Grantown is still only 3 miles back!). Pass through a wooden gate to follow a path through woodland, which soon bears to the right and later to the left to rejoin the railway line. (The long term-intention of the local authorities is to make the Dava Way follow the old railway line exactly in this area, in which case this detour will become unnecessary.) **Note** that the route of the Dava Way is marked erroneously on current OS maps, showing it following the railway line, rather than the detour.

After about ½ mile pass through a metal fieldgate to re-enter woodland, and in a further 200 yards reach a Dava Way information board (Forres 19 miles from here). A footpath crosses the railway line here. Turn right on the path for a 200-yard detour to **Huntly's Cave** rock outcrop. This most impressive crag above a deep, narrow gorge is well worth the short detour. It is a popular spot for a picnic and to watch local climbers test their skills. Take care near the edge of the rock escarpment. A steep path descends to the left, and from this a good view is obtained of this popular crag shattered with numerous cracks, which offer several good climbing lines.

**Huntly's Cave** is the traditional hiding place of the 2nd Marquis of Huntly, Lord Lewis Gordon, when pursued by the Earl of Argyll in the 17th century. The cave, or what remains of it, is surrounded by rugged crags on the steep side of the glen. The Marquis married Mary Grant in 1644, sister of James 7th Laird of Grant. She is said to have given him aid in the cave whilst he was in hiding in fear of his life.

After a possible 'elevenses' or picnic lunch at Huntly's cave, return to the railway line and continue northwards. The railway line soon passes through another cutting, after which a metal gate leads out onto the section approaching wild Dava Moor. After a while pass a 'Summit 1052ft' sign, and 100 yards after this the A939, which has been alongside the track for some distance, curves away to the left. The climb out of Grantown-on-Spey is now complete – it required two engines to pull the trains up the incline. The Dava Way continues ahead across the moor, as straight as a die.

**The Inverness and Perth Junction Railway**, opened in 1863, required 8 viaducts, 126 bridges over rivers and 119 road bridges. The railway reduced the time it took to move livestock from the Moray Firth to the markets of the south from the 4 weeks required for droving to one day by railway. A few years after opening, 21,000 sheep were carried in one week. The line merged with several others in 1865 to form the **Highland Railway**, and in 1923 became part of the LMS (London, Midland and Scottish) Railway. The section between Forres and Aviemore was closed in 1965.

**Dava Moor** is a blaze of colour in the spring and early summer, with the bright yellow of the broom dominating. Buzzards and lapwings can frequently be seen in the skies overhead. This section across the wide, expansive moorland is a delight in good conditions, but in adverse weather one would be fully exposed to the elements. The hill to the west, Craig Tiribeg at 1594ft (486m), is the highest point on the western moor and towers above the 2-mile long Lochindorb, which has the ruins of a castle on its tiny island. The line eventually curves slightly to the left, enters an area of conifer trees and meets a metal gate in a wooden fence. Pass through this gate and immediately turn left off the railway line onto an earthen track (the railway line goes on to meet the Dava station buildings which are now private property). In 100 yards, at a track T-junction, turn left onto a gravel track near **Dava**.

## STAGE 2
### Dava to Dunphail

| | |
|---|---|
| **Distance** | 6½ miles/10.5km |
| **Maps** | OS Landranger 27 (Nairn & Forres) |

About 50 yards before meeting the main road at the tiny settlement of **Dava**, turn right at a Dava Way signpost, off the track and onto a path through the woods (walkers only – cyclists and horse riders must use the alternative waymarked route). The path leaves the wood and climbs to rejoin the line of the railway north of the old station building. Turn left along the line and pass to the left of another private house. From here, on a clear day, there are good long distance views of the mountains of the north-west Highlands, with both the Munros of Ben Wyvis (3431ft, 1046m) and Ben More Assynt (3273ft, 998m) visible, the latter over 60 miles away in Sutherland. Continue ahead on the old line, soon soft underfoot and flanked with conifer trees. The trail is now heading towards the **Knock of Braemoray**, a prominent hill that dominates the view as it stands proudly at 1492ft (455m) above the moderately flat surrounding moorland. Those

*The Speyside Way*

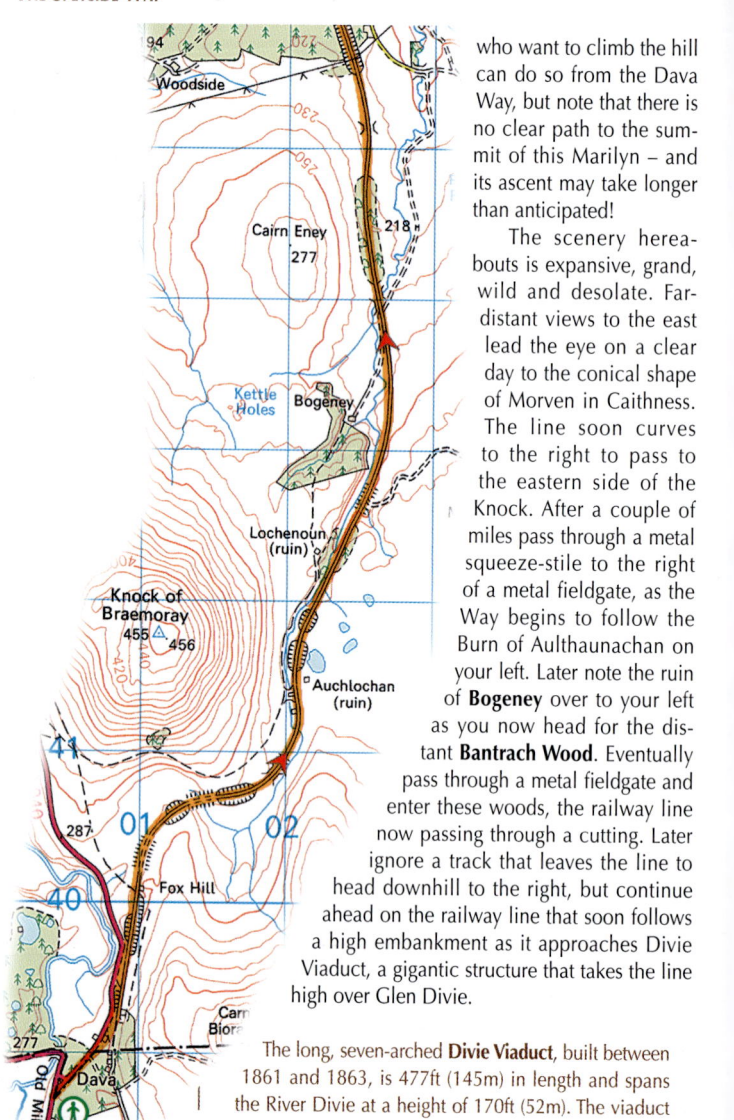

who want to climb the hill can do so from the Dava Way, but note that there is no clear path to the summit of this Marilyn – and its ascent may take longer than anticipated!

The scenery hereabouts is expansive, grand, wild and desolate. Far-distant views to the east lead the eye on a clear day to the conical shape of Morven in Caithness. The line soon curves to the right to pass to the eastern side of the Knock. After a couple of miles pass through a metal squeeze-stile to the right of a metal fieldgate, as the Way begins to follow the Burn of Aulthaunachan on your left. Later note the ruin of **Bogeney** over to your left as you now head for the distant **Bantrach Wood**. Eventually pass through a metal fieldgate and enter these woods, the railway line now passing through a cutting. Later ignore a track that leaves the line to head downhill to the right, but continue ahead on the railway line that soon follows a high embankment as it approaches Divie Viaduct, a gigantic structure that takes the line high over Glen Divie.

The long, seven-arched **Divie Viaduct**, built between 1861 and 1863, is 477ft (145m) in length and spans the River Divie at a height of 170ft (52m). The viaduct

## DAVA WAY STAGE 2 – DAVA TO DUNPHAIL

*Looking down on houses from the Divie Viaduct*

carried the Inverness and Perth Junction Railway (see above), the first turf of which was cut by the Countess of Seafield on 17th October 1861 (interestingly, she obstructed the Great North of Scotland Railway at Cullen – see notes on Cullen at the end of the MCT). The line was completed and formally opened less than 2 years later, on 9th September 1863. The building of the viaduct itself, a tremendous piece of Victorian engineering, took almost as long, the foundation stone being laid by Lady Elma Bruce on 20th October 1861, and the work being completed on 3rd August 1863.

After the viaduct, the line soon passes through another cutting, this one rather wet and muddy underfoot, even in relatively dry conditions. But this sometimes unpleasant section is soon passed as the Way approaches Dunphail. The wonderful mixed woodlands, a feature of this region of Scotland, are a particular delight in this area. Just before Dunphail Sidings are reached the trail makes a short

*The Speyside Way*

diversion to avoid a wet cutting, so follow the Dava Way waymarks which direct you slightly to the right, away from the line onto a pleasant woodland path. This later bends to the left to rejoin the bed of the old railway track at **Dunphail** Sidings and Picnic Area (tables), where there are Dava Way information boards and a large car park.

## STAGE 3
*Dunphail to Forres*

| | |
|---|---|
| **Distance** | 9½ miles/15.3km |
| **Maps** | OS Landranger 27 (Nairn & Forres) |

Follow the old railway line north from **Dunphail**, passing under a stone road bridge. The line passes through an area abundant with gorse and broom, which add a blaze of yellow in season. The Way negotiates several metal fieldgates, and another long, wet and muddy section is encountered on the approach to **Peathillock Bridge**, under which the trail passes.

The nearby Logie Steading and its associated walks can easily be visited by a detour from the Dava Way or, alternatively, they make a very good half-day out. To reach the Steading from the Dava Way (about ¾ mile) take the minor lane over Peathillock bridge and walk through Peathillock farmyard to reach the A940, Forres to Grantown road. Cross over this with care to pass through East Lodge gate and take the track down to the visitor centre.

The **Logie Steading heritage centre** explains the history and ecology of the area, and there are also craft and bookshops, plus an excellent café. The two main riverside walks are to Randolph's Leap and to Sluie. Randolph's Leap is a narrow, steep-sided spectacular gorge, with many rock pools and small cascades (the walk to the Leap is accessed from the visitor centre).

## DAVA WAY STAGE 3 – DUNPHAIL TO FORRES

The Sluie walk starts further north from the A940 near the Mains of Sluie and is a forest walk leading to the River Findhorn, said by some to be Scotland's finest river.

On a clear day you should catch sight of the sea in the Moray Firth and the mountains to the north of the Firth. This lush section of the walk is in complete contrast to the bleak moorland that now lies to the south. Here is rich pasture and arable land, particularly around the area of Logie. Ahead and to the left is the dramatic wooded gorge of the River Findhorn, which can be visited by detours from the Way. The railway often lies on a shallow embankment as it passes through this pastureland, with several gated crossing points (pay particular attention to fasten all gates, as plenty of cattle roam this area). The line enters **Cowgreens Wood** and crosses a small burn. It may look harmless when you cross it, but in 1997 the water in spate caused severe damage to the railway embankment.

Follow Dava Way signposts, which will direct you across the Half Davoch road (from here it is 6 miles to the centre of Forres). After about ⅓ mile, ignore a forest track on the right, but continue ahead along the line of the railway. After a while you will cross the Altyre Burn by means of a metal bridge.

*Yellow gorse lines the disused railway, north of Dunphail Sidings*

*THE SPEYSIDE WAY*

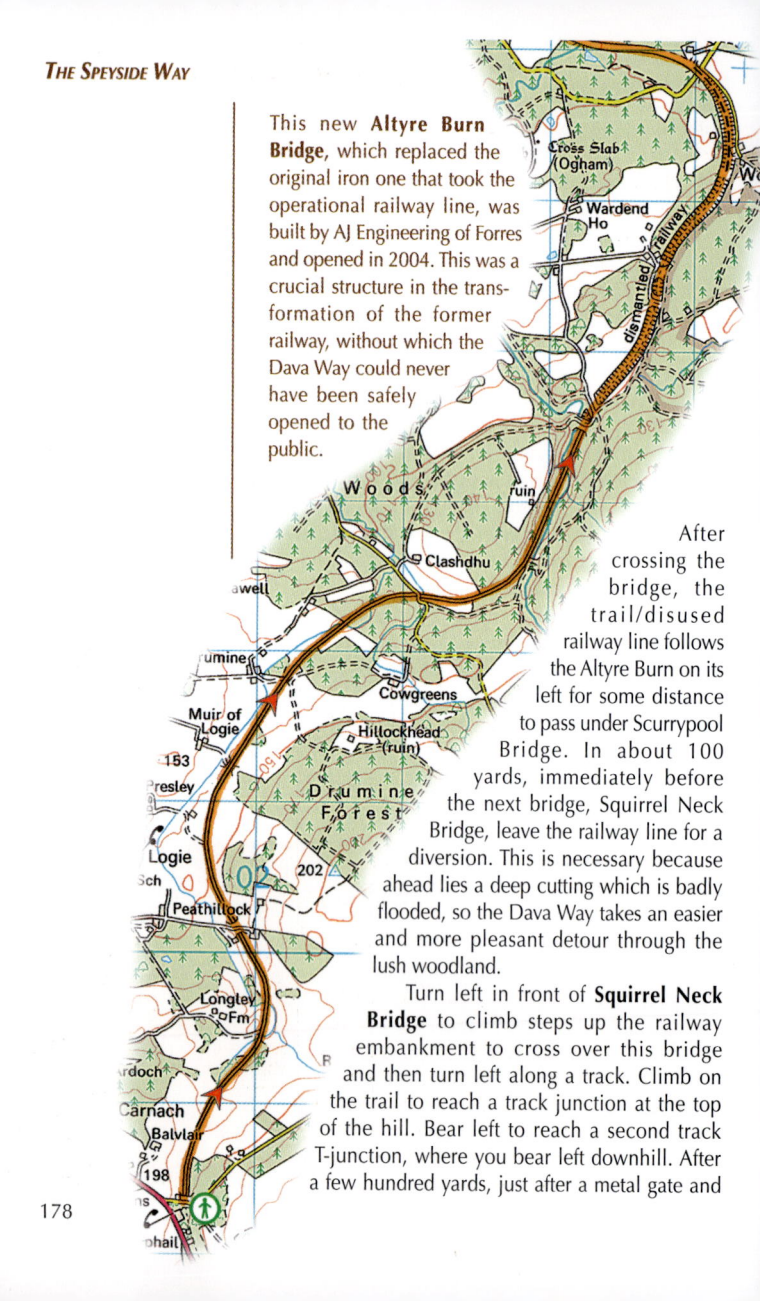

This new **Altyre Burn Bridge**, which replaced the original iron one that took the operational railway line, was built by AJ Engineering of Forres and opened in 2004. This was a crucial structure in the transformation of the former railway, without which the Dava Way could never have been safely opened to the public.

After crossing the bridge, the trail/disused railway line follows the Altyre Burn on its left for some distance to pass under Scurrypool Bridge. In about 100 yards, immediately before the next bridge, Squirrel Neck Bridge, leave the railway line for a diversion. This is necessary because ahead lies a deep cutting which is badly flooded, so the Dava Way takes an easier and more pleasant detour through the lush woodland.

Turn left in front of **Squirrel Neck Bridge** to climb steps up the railway embankment to cross over this bridge and then turn left along a track. Climb on the trail to reach a track junction at the top of the hill. Bear left to reach a second track T-junction, where you bear left downhill. After a few hundred yards, just after a metal gate and immediately before a cottage, be sure to leave this track by taking a descending path on the left through woodland. This path undulates through the woods for about ½ mile, with the railway cutting to your left, after which a track comes in from the right. Here are no less than four Dava Way marker posts in quick succession directing the walker onto a path sharply to the left. Two more marker posts direct you back onto the line of the old railway.

The next stage of the walk follows the longest and highest embankment section of the whole route from Grantown-on-Spey to Forres, and as a result offers good views, particularly over to the right to Rafford, with its church clearly visible and with Blervie Castle perched on the hill above the village. The railway soon takes a bridge over the **Rafford Road**, shortly after which a green fingerpost is encountered, indicating a path to the right to Rafford in ¾ mile. Ignore this, but keep ahead on the Dava Way. About ½ mile later the line crosses the Mosset Burn and then leaves woodland to cross open fields. Soon you will reach a no doubt welcome Dava Way bench, where a rest can be taken before the last section of the walk into town.

The trail crosses a wide sandy drive and then passes to the right of the **Dallas Dhu Distillery**. Later the railway passes under a stone bridge, and a 100 yards later you fork left to reach the end of the railway line at a Dava Way information board and a flight of steps which lead to a suburban road.

**The Dallas Dhu Distillery** (Dallas Dhu means 'black water valley' in Gaelic) was built in 1898 by Wright and Greig, whisky blenders in Glasgow, to provide whisky for their popular Roderick Dhu blend. The water source was the Altyre Burn. In 1983 United Distillers closed the distillery, but Historic Scotland purchased it and reopened it as a 'living museum' in 1988, a perfectly maintained

*Dallas Dhu Distillery on the approach to Forres (Beryl Castle)*

'time capsule' which could be used to produce whisky again. It sells a rare and first-class malt. It is open daily from April to October, and at weekends and a few weekdays from November to March. There is an admission charge.

Turn right along this road, following the signpost to Forres Town Centre. Follow the road, Mannachie Avenue, through a housing estate. Where the road swings sharply to the left, look for a waymarked path between houses, ignoring the path on the right into Sanquhar Woodlands. This leads to Loch View. Walk ahead along this road to bear left, opposite Beechway, downhill. Follow this lane as it bends to the left past Sanquhar Weir and Reservoir, and then to the right past Forres Academy. Now follow the road, Sanquhar Road, northwards on a path alongside Roysvale Park. Continue past another school on your left, before reaching a staggered five-way road junction at a small roundabout. Bear left following the signs for **Forres** town centre and Falconer Museum. Climb on this road, Tolbooth Street, to reach the high street, so completing the Dava Way.

*For details of Forres, see under Moray Coast Trail, Stage 1.*

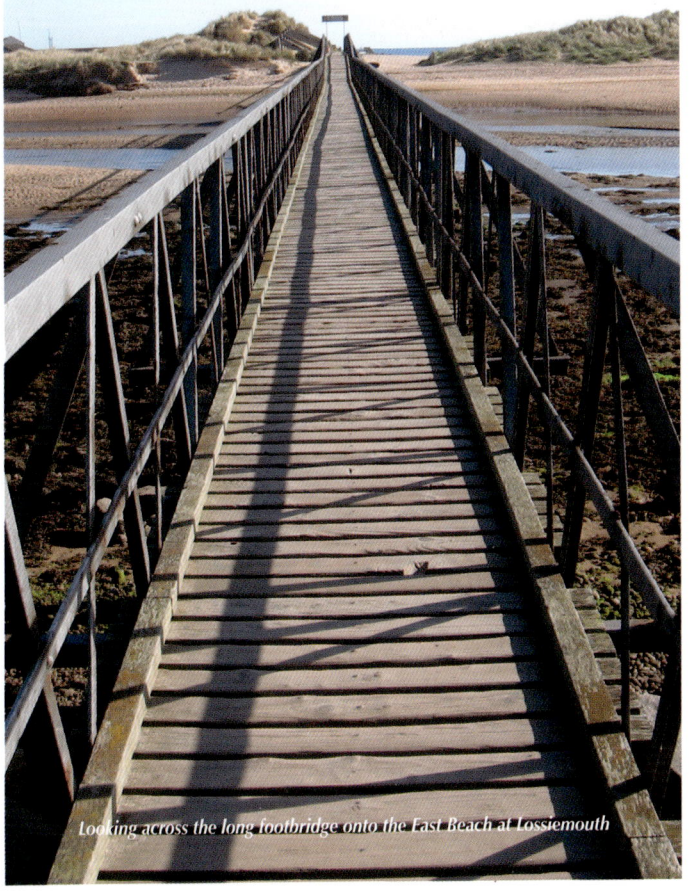

# THE MORAY COAST TRAIL

*Looking across the long footbridge onto the East Beach at Lossiemouth*

# INTRODUCTION

The Moray Coast Trail (MCT) is a walking (and partly multi-user) route that stretches for nearly 50 miles from Forres and Findhorn Bay in the west of Moray, past Burghead, Lossiemouth, Garmouth and Spey Bay, Buckie, Findochty and Portknockie to finish at the coastal village of Cullen on the eastern edge of the Moray district. The route, opened in 2004, consists of a continuous trail of paths, tracks and minor lanes, all of which can be walked and some cycled (a mountain bike or at least an on road/off-road hybrid bicycle is the most suitable). These link the numerous coastal villages, towns, beaches, cliffs and headlands of Moray. The trail is signposted and waymarked from Findhorn to Cullen with a distinctive logo showing a white fulmar on a blue background, a bird frequently seen in the skies and on the rocky headlands, sea stacks and skerries of this coast.

*Moray Coast Trail sign (Moray Coast Trail Association)*

The coastal landscape of Moray is a very varied one, from huge bays and mudflats to coastal cliffs and sea stacks, from deciduous and pine woodlands to long white sandy beaches. Some of the picturesque fishing villages, such as Findochty in the east, would not be out of place on the Cornish coast. The Moray coast is the north of Scotland's best kept coastal secret, far less well known than some other coastal areas of Britain, but equally as fine – locals would say that there is no better, more beautiful and varied stretch of coastline in the UK.

Between Forres and Garmouth, the MCT forms part of the new Moray Way (see Introduction, 'The official trails of Speyside and Moray') walking and cycling trail, opened in 2010, a circular route that uses sections of the Speyside Way and MCT and the whole of the Dava Way. The MCT is also part of the much longer Moray Firth Trail, that stretches around the north-eastern coast of Scotland, for 470 miles from to Duncansby Head near John o'Groats to Cullen. The Moray Firth Trail is not a continuous route, but rather a network of paths around the

Firth in the regions of Caithness, Sutherland, Easter Ross, Cromarty Firth and the Black Isle, Inverness to Nairn and to Forres, and then the Moray Coast to Cullen. It is itself part of the very much longer North Sea Trail, a coastal route of some 3100 miles (5000km) through the six European countries that border the North Sea: Norway, Sweden, Denmark, Germany, the Netherlands and UK.

Wildlife is in abundance along the rich coastal waters of the Moray Firth and is one of the major attractions of walking the coast. Dolphins, grey seals, fulmars, puffins, herons, salmon, oystercatchers and many more species may be seen from the trail. The lucky and patient may even spot otters playing and feeding in these waters. The Moray coast is very rich in archaeological remains, particularly those of the enigmatic Picts, the farmer and hunter descendants of the native Iron Age tribes of northern Scotland who lived in the region from the first to the ninth century AD. Their language does not survive, and no written records have ever been found. But they did leave behind several Pictish forts (such as that at Burghead) and many elaborately carved standing stones. But the abandoned remains of much more recent times are also very evident, particularly of World War II coastal defences.

One note of caution is necessary, as the coast of northern Britain demands to be treated with respect, if

*Rocky coastline east of Hopeman*

*The Speyside Way*

a safe journey is to be enjoyed. Beware of fast-moving rising tides – it is best to check on the tide times published in local newspapers (see also www.tidetimes.org.uk). Secondly, take great care if exploring mudflats, tidal estuaries and estuarine sand bars; these can often be unstable and dangerous. Also, take care on coastal cliffs, particularly in high winds, heavy rain, wet and slippery underfoot conditions and when a thick fog blankets the coast. By keeping strictly to the paths and tracks of the MCT you will not be, under normal conditions, exposed to any untoward dangers. Gales are not uncommon on these coasts, so come prepared and retreat if necessary.

## STAGE 1
*Forres to Findhorn*

**Distance**      6 miles/9.7km
**Maps**          OS Landranger 27 (Nairn & Forres)

### FORRES

There was a royal castle at Forres from AD900, although no ruins remain today. Forres was made a Royal Burgh in 1496 by James IV of Scotland, and this established it as an important centre for trade. Today it has a population of 9000 and a thriving tourist trade. Local attractions include Grant Park with its sunken gardens, Nelson Tower (built to commemorate the Battle of Trafalgar), Brodie Castle (Tower House owned by the National Trust for Scotland) and Falconer Museum. A rather gruesome reminder of less tolerant times is the Witches' Stone on the high street, the site of a barbaric burning of 'witches' in the 16th century.

**Facilities**: hotels and B&Bs. Cafés. Supermarket, Co-op food store, numerous other shops. Pharmacies, banks, post office. Mainline trains and both local and long distance bus services.

## Moray Coast Trail Stage 1 – Forres to Findhorn

*The Witches' Stone, memorial to the victims of less tolerant times, Forres (Beryl Castle)*

Note that there are **no MCT signposts or waymarks** on this first section of the trail from Forres to Findhorn. The route is entirely on minor metalled roads, pavement footpaths and shared cycleways. The views of the massive Findhorn Bay, teeming with wildlife, nevertheless make this a very worthwhile section to walk.

There are two possible routes out of **Forres**. The recommended route visits the Sueno's Stone, one of the region's most important ancient monuments. Those wishing to visit the Benromach Distillery (visitor centre and guided tours) should take the other option (see below). Both routes meet up about 1½ miles north of Forres.

For the **route via the distillery**, start from the Falconer Museum in the centre of town. Cross the high street and take North Street opposite. At its end turn right for 30 yards and then left down a No Through Road. Bear left at Lea Road for 40 yards, before crossing the footbridge over the river on your right. On the far bank turn right onto Invererne Road to emerge onto Forres bypass, the A96. Cross this busy road with great care, followed by the railway line at a level crossing. Follow the sign to **Benromach Distillery**.

*THE SPEYSIDE WAY*

*Church on Forres high street seen from Grant Park (Beryl Castle)*

The **Benromach Distillery** was built in 1898 by Duncan McCallum of the Glen Nevis Distillery and F Brinkman, a spirit dealer from Edinburgh. It soon closed and did not reopen until 1907, closures and reopening being a feature of this distillery's history. Gordon and MacPhail purchased the site in 1992 after another closure, and the distillery was not fully operational until 1998. The Benromach Distillery and Malt Whisky Centre opened in 1999; it can be visited on weekdays throughout the year, plus Saturdays and some Sundays in the summer season. There is a charge for admission.

After visiting the distillery continue on the quiet lane, which is also part of National Cycle Route 1. After about a mile the recommended route described below joins from the right, just after Mill of Grange. Continue towards Kinloss as described below.

The **recommended route** leaves the Falconer Museum in the centre of Forres and follows the high street heading east. After passing Grant Park, on your right, and the Witches' Stone, the road splits. Take the left fork, Findhorn Road, and follow it for about 200 yards to the **Sueno's Stone**.

## MORAY COAST TRAIL STAGE 1 – FORRES TO FINDHORN

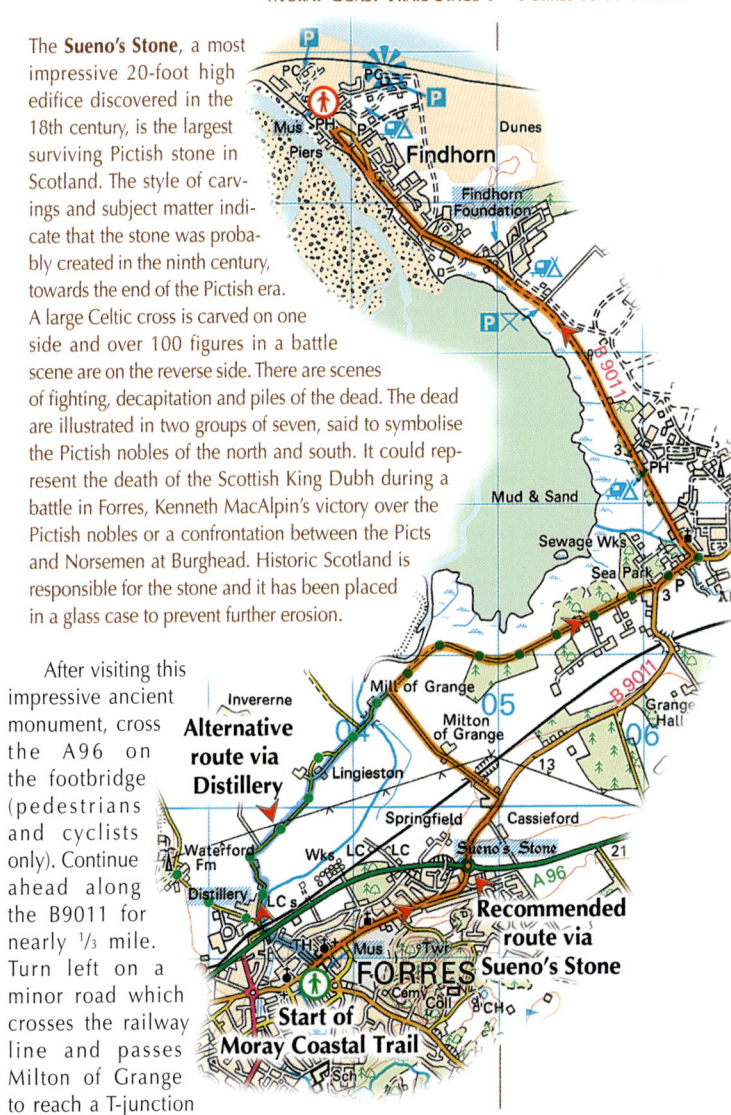

The **Sueno's Stone**, a most impressive 20-foot high edifice discovered in the 18th century, is the largest surviving Pictish stone in Scotland. The style of carvings and subject matter indicate that the stone was probably created in the ninth century, towards the end of the Pictish era. A large Celtic cross is carved on one side and over 100 figures in a battle scene are on the reverse side. There are scenes of fighting, decapitation and piles of the dead. The dead are illustrated in two groups of seven, said to symbolise the Pictish nobles of the north and south. It could represent the death of the Scottish King Dubh during a battle in Forres, Kenneth MacAlpin's victory over the Pictish nobles or a confrontation between the Picts and Norsemen at Burghead. Historic Scotland is responsible for the stone and it has been placed in a glass case to prevent further erosion.

After visiting this impressive ancient monument, cross the A96 on the footbridge (pedestrians and cyclists only). Continue ahead along the B9011 for nearly 1/3 mile. Turn left on a minor road which crosses the railway line and passes Milton of Grange to reach a T-junction

## THE SPEYSIDE WAY

*The route via the distillery joins this route here.*

after just over ½ mile. ◀ Turn right onto another minor road, part of National Cycle Route 1, and follow it for 1¼ miles to **Kinloss**. These backwater lanes carry little traffic. Hereabouts is a flat landscape, reminiscent of Holland, with a myriad of narrow water channels draining into the massive area of mudflats that is Findhorn Bay, rich in wildlife.

The trail reaches a T-junction with the **B9011**. Turn left along this road, on the joint footpath/cycleway, following NCR 1 signposted to Findhorn. Pass a petrol station (drinks and snacks for sale in the small shop), and at the junction with the B9089 turn left, still on NCR 1 to Findhorn, still a joint footpath/cycleway. After passing Seaview Caravan Park (tents welcome) the trail soon runs close to the mudflats of **Findhorn Bay**, with its abundant wading birds. The peace and tranquillity of the scene may alas be broken by the occasional roar of a jet engine from adjacent RAF Kinloss, where the RAF's Nimrod MR2 aircraft are based. Follow the sign for 'Aircraft Viewing and Bird Hide'. Enthusiasts of both hobbies, bird watching and aircraft spotting, are commonly seen in this area, one of the very few places in Britain where such disparate pastimes are in such close proximity.

*Findhorn Bay*

**Findhorn Bay** was designated a local **nature reserve** by Moray Council in 1998. It is a spectacular, almost landlocked tidal basin, and provides a good habitat for wading birds throughout the year, with large numbers of migratory birds passing through in spring and autumn. Common birds of the bay include greylag geese, pinkfooted geese, oystercatchers, widgeon, shelduck, cormorant, curlew, dunlin, redshank and bartailed godwit. In winter great quantities of geese take up residency in the bay. Together with the neighbouring Culbin Sands RSPB reserve it has been recognised as a Site of Scientific Interest (SSSI) and a European Community Special Protection Area (SPA).

The trail reaches Findhorn Local Nature Reserve Bird Hide. If you have time spend a while here observing the birds; this hide is also a good place to shelter from the rain and wind in bad conditions! After the hide another campsite is passed, Findhorn Bay Holiday Park. Here also is the **Findhorn Foundation and Community**, which among other things has open to the public a café, shop, and art and crafts studios (see below). Cross over the road with care here to continue on the cyclepath/footpath to **Findhorn**, ¾ mile distant. Cyclists must soon rejoin the main carriageway, but walkers keep to the pavement footpath through the village. At a Y-junction in the village take the left fork signposted to Harbour Bay Heritage Centre and toilets. Cross to a MCT fingerpost, which will probably be the first one encountered. This indicates the way to Roseisle and Burghead in 7 miles.

## FINDHORN

In the 1600s, the original fishing village was buried by sand dunes, and its replacement was engulfed by floods in 1701, so the picturesque village seen today is its third incarnation. In its past Findhorn has been an important centre for fishing and shipbuilding, but these activities have today been replaced by sailing and watersports. Internationally, the area is famous because of the Findhorn Foundation (see below). The Heritage Centre and Icehouse (open 2–5pm every day in June, July and August; weekends only in May and September; closed in the winter months) is of interest.

**Facilities**: hotel, pubs, B&Bs, 2 caravan/camping sites. Fish and chip shop. Community shop at The Park, Findhorn Foundation.

The **Findhorn Foundation** is a spiritual community, ecovillage and international centre for holistic education. The Park is a 30-acre site situated on the original caravan park where Peter and Eileen Caddy and Dorothy Maclean moved in 1962 and attracted a small community that today has grown to several hundred people. The Park has over 90 ecological structures encompassing houses, workshop spaces, the 'Living Machine' sewage treatment centre and electricity-generating wind turbines. Local, national and international visitors are welcome for the day or longer, and many come to attend a wide range of courses that cover topics such as sustainable living and exploring spirituality (www.findhorn.org). The cafés and shops are open to visitors.

## STAGE 2
*Findhorn to Burghead*

| | |
|---|---|
| **Distance** | 7¼ miles/11.7km |
| **Maps** | OS Landranger 27 (Nairn & Forres) and 28 (Elgin & Dufftown) |

The **Moray Firth** ('firth' is an Old Norse word meaning 'arm of the sea') is a transition zone where salty water mixes with fresh water to create varied habitats, ranging from mudflats and salt marsh in the estuary of the firth to sand dunes, rocky shores and cliffs at its outer edge. Each supports a wide range of sea life, birds, animals and insects. Many visitors come to this area to watch Cetaceans (whales, dolphins and porpoises) either from the coastline or on boat trips. Dolphin species include bottle-nosed, Risso's, whitesided and common. Minkie, orca and pilot whale species are also occasionally seen, as are basking sharks. This coastline is famed for its seal colonies, both eastern Atlantic common and Atlantic grey seals; look out for them on the coastal rocks as you walk the MCT. A plethora of birds also makes this area a haven for birdwatchers. Cormorants, eider ducks, fulmars, various gull species, gannets, guillemots, kittiwakes, razorbills, red-throated divers, scoters, snow bunting and wigeon can be seen at different times of the year, either around the cliffs or out in the firth.

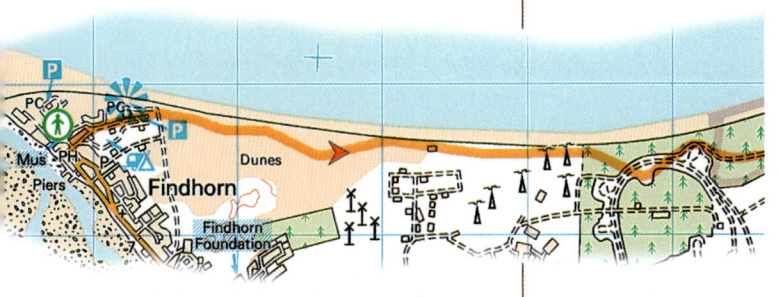

Follow the path alongside the harbour at **Findhorn**, turning right at a second MCT fingerpost. Turn left at a crossroads, and in 20 yards bear right to Findhorn Heritage Centre. A few yards later look out for the waymarker post carrying the bird logo and another for the North Sea Trail Coastal Path. Follow this path, now heading east through gorse and sand dunes, soon bearing to the right as indicated by a MCT fingerpost.

*Map continued on page 192*

The area of **dunes** at Findhorn has been owned by the Findhorn Dunes Trust since 2002. A Site of Outstanding Landscape Value, it is little changed since the last Ice Age 10,000 years ago, although the dunes are constantly evolving. The land is managed to protect its diversity, encompassing sheltered hollows and pine woodland.

*The Speyside Way*

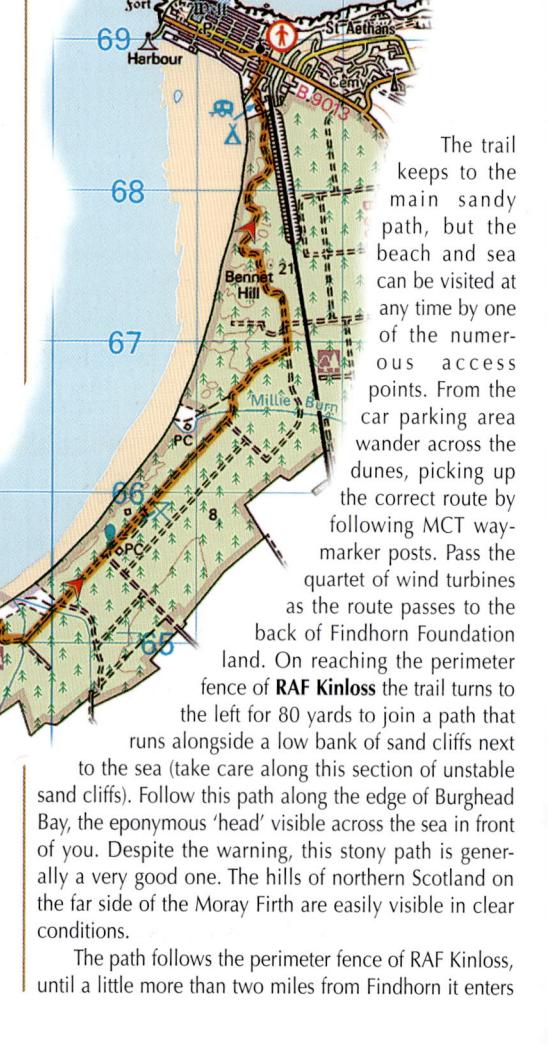

The trail keeps to the main sandy path, but the beach and sea can be visited at any time by one of the numerous access points. From the car parking area wander across the dunes, picking up the correct route by following MCT waymarker posts. Pass the quartet of wind turbines as the route passes to the back of Findhorn Foundation land. On reaching the perimeter fence of **RAF Kinloss** the trail turns to the left for 80 yards to join a path that runs alongside a low bank of sand cliffs next to the sea (take care along this section of unstable sand cliffs). Follow this path along the edge of Burghead Bay, the eponymous 'head' visible across the sea in front of you. Despite the warning, this stony path is generally a very good one. The hills of northern Scotland on the far side of the Moray Firth are easily visible in clear conditions.

The path follows the perimeter fence of RAF Kinloss, until a little more than two miles from Findhorn it enters a strip of coastal conifer **woodland**, with a beautiful sandy beach over to the left. After a while the sandy path improves to become a sandy track which heads inland slightly into somewhat denser conifer forest. Later, on reaching a clearing, take a waymarked right fork and keep to the main track as it heads to right and left. The trail eventually becomes a very good dirt track that runs north-eastwards through the forest. Ignore any side turns (there are several other waymarked trails in these popular woods), and continue ahead to reach **Roseisle Forest Car Park** and MCT fingerpost (2½ miles to Burghead). Continue ahead on a short section of narrow metalled road through the car park, where there are picnic tables and toilets (closed in winter). There is also access to the beach from here.

Continue straight ahead through this large car parking area, taking the pine-needle-strewn path heading north-north-east and signposted to Burghead. Walk through the very attractive Roseisle Forest, where you will

*Looking across scrub into Burghead Bay*

find both Scots and Corsican pine. Ignore any side trails and paths, but follow the signposts for Burghead. About a mile after the car park you will reach a fingerpost indicating 'MCT: Burma Road to Burghead, 1¼ miles'.

> The **Burma Road**, a trail through the coastal woodland of Roseisle, south of Burghead, acquired its name during the D-Day invasion rehearsals, which involved thousands of troops in Burghead Bay in 1944. There was no path as we know it today, and because the route was so impenetrable and insect infested, the troops gave it the nickname of the Burma Road, the horrors of which were then making the wartime headlines. Roseisle Forest is today no more insect infested than other parts of Scotland!

Turn left at the fingerpost to follow this trail. Once more ignore any side turnings in this scented pine forest, always keeping to the main track. The Burma Road undulates and twists and turns for a mile, eventually emerging from the forest at a caravan site. Walk through this site to reach a MCT fingerpost indicating ½ mile to Pictish fort and 2¼ miles to Hopeman. Walk down into the village of **Burghead** to a second fingerpost. To visit the harbour and Pictish fort follow the harbour wall to the left, but to continue the MCT turn right as indicated by the fingerpost for the trail to Hopeman. Although a detour from the main trail, the Pictish fort, on the headland, has a visitor centre and viewing tower, and is worth a visit if time is available – the main route can be rejoined by continuing eastwards along the front.

## BURGHEAD

The quiet fishing village of Burghead was once the site of the biggest Iron Age fort in Britain. Sitting on a peninsula it was a 7½ acre easily defended site for the early Picts, from the fourth to the seventh century AD. Much of the fort was destroyed in the ninth or tenth century,

*The harbour and houses of Burghead*

but a map of 1747 still showed collapsed stonework. The old village and land were purchased by William Young of Inverugie for the building of the new planned village of Burghead, between 1805 and 1809. During this work the fort's ramparts of earth and stone were levelled into the fort's ditches to provide a level site for building, and stone was reused to build the harbour designed by Thomas Telford. Hence, little is visible of the fort today.

During the 19th-century destruction of the fortress, 30 Pictish stones were discovered inscribed with pictures of bulls, but today only six remain. The fortress well was cleared during restoration, revealing a flight of 20 steps down into a stone tank; today, Burghead Well is a tourist attraction and it is worth obtaining the key to explore it. A visitor centre is located in a restored Martello tower, by the site of the old Pictish fort.

Warehouses, a coastguard station and a fish-curing unit supported the development of Burghead as a major herring port in the 19th and 20th centuries. Although fishing has declined in importance, boats still work

*THE SPEYSIDE WAY*

from this port. Around the harbour are the maltings and the granaries. The granary, built by Telford, has been converted to flats, whilst the maltings was built over the old rope factory. Over 100,000 tonnes of barley is malted each year, enough for the production of over 100 million bottles of whisky!

Another tourist attraction at Burghead is the Burning of the Clavie. It is not known if this event is Pictish, Celtic, Viking or Roman in origin, but it takes place on the night of 11th January (the original Hogmanay before the calendar changed in 1660). The 'clavie' is a half-barrel filled with wood shavings and tar, nailed onto a carrying post. Once lit, a group of men take it in turns to carry the barrel clockwise around the town and then onto nearby Doorie Hill.

**Facilities:** B&B, caravan/camping site. Cafés. Co-op food store and other shops. Post office. Buses.

## STAGE 3
### Burghead to Lossiemouth

| | |
|---|---|
| **Distance** | 9¼ miles/15km |
| **Maps** | OS Landranger 28 (Elgin & Dufftown) |

In **Burghead**, walk up Park Street, crossing Grant Street, Dunbar Street and King Street, thereby cutting across the Burghead peninsula to the north shore, where you will find a green fingerpost indicating ¼ mile (left) to the Pictish fort (those that have visited the latter will rejoin the route here). But to continue the MCT, head east along the coast following the sign to Hopeman in 2¼ miles. This is a bracing walk along a very fine section of rocky, shelving coastline, in marked contrast to the previous section through the coastal woodland of Roseisle Forest. Some of the coastal cliffs around here are popular with local climbers. Pass under two stone arches and continue ahead, still with the sea to your left, through a tunnel of gorse, heady with the scent of its bright yellow flowers in springtime. On reaching a stone bridge over the path, take the ramp to its right to arrive at the houses on the outskirts of the village of **Hopeman**.

## HOPEMAN

The village was originally called Newtown of Hopeman when it was established in 1805 by William Young of Inverugie to house the quarry workers from his newly opened sandstone quarries nearby (one of these is passed on the MCT east of Hopeman). In 1836 the Inverugie estate was acquired by Admiral Duff of Drummuir, and he quickly constructed the harbour at Hopeman. By 1880 over 100 fishing boats operated from the port, and several fish-curing businesses had been established. The harbour gradually silted up during the 20th century, the few remaining commercial boats leaving the harbour in the 1980s, but leisure craft still use it. The beach has some very attractively painted beach huts.

**Facilities**: B&B, campsite, post office, shops and tearoom.

*Looking across Hopeman Bay (Beryl Castle)*

*The Speyside Way*

Follow the cycle trail on a road parallel with the coast. Walk to the end of this road, Duff Street, to turn left to walk towards the harbour. Opposite the entrance to Hopeman's pretty harbour, turn right immediately in front of 'Harbour House'. Now walk along Findlay's Bay, above Hopeman East Beach. Look out for the petrified pre-dinosaur reptile footprints in the rock alongside the path. Follow the sign for Daisy Rock and Braemou Well (the latter is off the path to the right). There follows a most scenic stretch of sandstone coastal cliffs, squeezed between golf course and sea. This leads to a track where a green signpost indicates the way to the left to Lossiemouth in 4¾ miles. The track passes above Cove Bay and its caves and approaches **Clashach Quarry**. At the entrance to this quarry, the MCT takes the track to its right. This soon narrows to a footpath which climbs and follows the perimeter fence of the quarry, down to your left. This good path soon becomes hemmed in between large clumps of yellow gorse (whin) above head height.

On reaching a path T-junction turn left past a squat lookout tower and viewpoint, descend a flight of steps and continue along a lower coastal path, passing above Gows' Castle sea stack, with a tall white lighthouse now in view ahead. Follow this undulating coastal path. Caves and rock arches are a feature of this spectacular section of coast at **Covesea**. There are several caves in the cliffs below, one of which was found to contain headless prehistoric human skeletons and some primitive early rock paintings. It is possible to explore the area

## MORAY COAST TRAIL STAGE 3 – BURGHEAD TO LOSSIEMOUTH

more thoroughly and search out some of the caves, but take great care if you do so, as some of the faint paths come to abrupt drops and the rocks are often slippery. Between early spring and autumn many fulmars will be seen gliding in the skies above and nesting on the coastal cliffs and rock sea stacks.

For the MCT keep to the main coastal path, later forking left at a waymarker post to head towards the lighthouse. Drop almost to sea level to follow a grassy path just behind a shingle beach. Follow this narrow path through the grassy dunes, above a large pristine sandy beach, heading towards the white column of the **Covesea Lighthouse** seen ahead. When you get close to it you

*Map continued on page 200*

*Covesea Lighthouse*

*THE SPEYSIDE WAY*

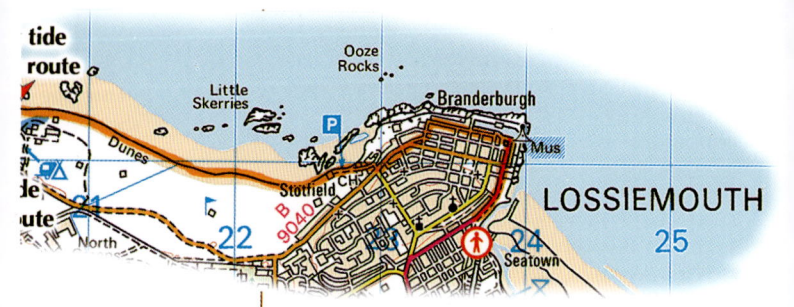

come to a green fingerpost which indicates that it is 2 miles ahead to Lossiemouth. Alternatively, if the sea is rough and the tide fully in, there is a waymarked high-tide route to the right.

Assuming the tide is low and the sea well out, continue on the coastal path, soon dropping down to Lossiemouth West Beach. Enjoy the walk along this huge beach with its superb stretch of sands, much frequented by locals when the weather is fine. Nearing the end of the beach, on the approach to Lossiemouth, take to the grass to the right of the beach where a sandy path will be found. This path leads to a car park at the Ponderosa Beach Café (open all year) and toilets, at the western side of the town of **Lossiemouth**. At the far end of the car park is a memorial to the Stotfield fishing disaster of 1806.

Walk up the ramp by the side of the golf course and at the top, just before the main road, turn left onto a minor road parallel with the sea. This soon becomes a dirt track to the left of houses. Follow it to a large grassy area by a beach bar. Walk diagonally left across the grass to pick up the coastal path at the far side of this pub. This soon returns to a road; walk eastwards along this, passing to the rear of the harbour. At its far end bear to the left, near the harbour entrance, and follow the road round to the right to pass the Fisherman's Museum. Continue along Pitgaveny Street which leads into Clifton Road, and next turn left into Seaton Road, passing public toilets. Turn left to head towards the very long wooden footbridge over the river and sands.

## LOSSIEMOUTH

Established in the mid-18th century, Lossiemouth has grown from a small port serving Elgin to a thriving port in its own right. A modern marina has been developed in its twin-basined harbour. On the West Beach on the outskirts of Lossiemouth is the memorial to the Stotfield fishing disaster of Christmas Day 1806, when 21 men and lads, the entire able-bodied male population of Stotfield, died when their boats were engulfed by a violent storm. Stotfield village is now part of Lossiemouth. Ramsay Macdonald, the labour party's first Prime Minister, was born and brought up in Lossiemouth.

**Facilities**: hotels, B&Bs, caravan/camping site. Cafés. Fish and chip shop. Shops, bank, post office. Bus services.

## STAGE 4
*Lossiemouth to Buckie*

| | |
|---|---|
| **Distance** | 15¼ miles/24.6km |
| **Maps** | OS Landranger 28 (Elgin & Dufftown) |

**RAF Lossiemouth** is the largest and busiest fast-jet base in the Royal Air Force. Several squadrons of Tornado GR4s are based here, together with a Sea King Search and Rescue Flight. The station is a major administrative centre of the RAF, with over 2800 military personnel and civilians involved in the operation of the base.

Cross one of Britain's longest pedestrian footbridges to step out across **Lossiemouth East Beach**, a wide and long stretch of sand as equally impressive as Lossiemouth West Beach, particularly at low tide when the sea recedes considerably. When the beach begins to narrow take one of several sandy paths to climb over the first ridge of the dunes, behind which will be found a sandy path running

*THE SPEYSIDE WAY*

parallel with the sea. Follow this south-eastwards, with a conifer plantation over to your right. After a while the best path is to be found on the landward side of the shingle embankment that edges the coast.

Pass an old World War II pillbox and then follow a line of large concrete block defences that links a series of other pillboxes, an unpleasant reminder of the last major global conflict. This area of the coast was heavily fortified and defended in the 1940s, and the MOD still owns a great deal of the land in this region. The route now approaches a MOD Firing Range, Danger Area. The MCT follows the line of concrete defences/pillboxes for several miles.

On approaching the MOD Firing Range keep an eye open for any red flags flying on tall white flagpoles. If they are seen to be flying, then you must keep away from the area: in this case look out for alternative waymarks, diversions and instructions directing you safely past the range. Never touch any item that looks suspicious – it may be old ordnance. If approached by MOD personnel please follow their instructions exactly.

These **World War II coastal defences** are a reminder that in 1940 there was a real fear that Hitler would invade the UK from Norway via the Moray Firth beaches, an anxiety perhaps heightened by the fact that there were suspicions of influential German sympathisers in this area. The Moray pillboxes and anti-tank obstacles were constructed at high speed from a mixture of brick, stone and concrete breeze. On the MCT today long lines of them remain on the section between Lossiemouth and Kingston, but there were originally very many of these defences along other stretches of the Moray coast, the highest concentration being in Burghead Bay. Amazingly, 18,000 pillboxes were built in the UK during 1940, so these were only a small fraction of the total. The other tangible remains of this time are the stumps of the anti-glider posts which can still be seen in Burghead Bay.

Provided no red flags are flying, continue along the MCT, looking out for a waymarker post which directs the walker inland for about 60 yards, after which the route turns left by an old lookout tower and flagpole. Pass a low building to reach a green MCT finger-post indicating that you have walked 5½ miles from Lossiemouth. Ahead is the MCT to Kingston (1½ miles) and Garmouth (2½ miles). To the right is the alternative forest route via Binn Hill (1 mile).

*Map continued on page 206*

Take the MCT ahead towards Kingston, now with the concrete defences on your left. The firing range is soon exited by another flagpole and lookout tower. You are now entering the Lein, a Scottish wildlife reserve and part of the larger Spey Bay Wildlife Reserve. The concrete defences finally merge with the shingle bank and disappear about ½ mile before Kingston. Follow the trail to a car parking area and the first metalled road since leaving Lossiemouth. Two information boards will be found at the edge of the car park, detailing the Lein and local walks. One of these walks is used by the MCT to go via Whinnyhaugh Farm and School Brae to Garmouth and on over the Spey Viaduct to join the Speyside Way.

> The Scottish Wildlife Trust manages the 1100-acre **Spey Bay Wildlife Reserve**. Kingston shingle spit, 7 miles long and up to 30ft deep, is the largest vegetated shingle complex in Scotland and in the UK second only to Dungeness in Kent. The reserve encompasses shingle beach, river estuary and young woodland. There are numerous ridges and hollows parallel to the current coast, each representing a former shoreline in the era of falling sea levels over 10,000 years ago. A variety of plants and insects, including butterflies, can be seen in spring and summer, and feeding ospreys make an exciting sight, whilst in the winter sea ducks and divers attract bird watchers. Stonechat can be observed in the scrub and the Small Blue, the UK's smallest butterfly, can be seen in the open grassy area of the reserve. Otters, grey seals and bottlenose dolphins are all residents in the waters of the area. Visitors are asked to avoid walking on the shingle spit during the tern-nesting season of May to August.

Walk ahead into the small village of Kingston-on-Spey (usually known simply as **Kingston**). After a football field on your left, turn right at a MCT signpost for Garmouth, ¾ mile. Follow the track between houses, then the path beyond to a small lane; bear right onto this, Burnside Road. Soon leave this where the road swings to the right, and walk ahead on a dirt track, signposted to Garmouth via School Brae. Take the path to the left, immediately in front of a building, and head over School Brae to sit on the first bench encountered since Lossiemouth. There are fine views from this vantage point, down to fields and out to sea.

Continue, soon passing a trig pillar, No. S7214, which is located at only 25m above sea level, surely one of the lowest in Scotland. Next comes Browlands Standing Stones and a restored tower and toposcope, identifying features in the surrounding landscape from this viewpoint. Descend from School Brae into **Garmouth**, turning right in front of Fyfe Cottage. In a few yards note the plaque on the wall that indicates the point where Charles II signed the Solemn League and Covenant in 1650, after he had sailed over from France and landed in Spey Bay, an important event in Scottish history.

## GARMOUTH AND KINGSTON-ON-SPEY

These two small, pretty villages are only ½ mile apart on the west side of the wide Spey estuary.

Garmouth, or Garmach as it was originally known, seems an unusual name for a port on the mouth of the Spey, but it is derived from 'gearr magh' in Gaelic, which means 'short or narrow plain'. The Maggie Fair, which received its charter in 1587, is still held on the last Saturday in June. Garmouth's heyday as a port was in the 18th century, when grain from farmlands and manganese ore brought by pack ponies from the mountains was exported from here, with coal and glass being imported. Although a natural harbour, it had a dangerous entry between the bars of shingle skirting the River Spey, and required the expert guidance of local pilots. A plaque in Garmouth commemorates the landing at Kingston of King Charles II on 23 June 1650 and his signing of the Covenant and the Solemn League in Garmouth soon after he came ashore. This document was intended to impose Scots-style presbyterianism on episcopalian England. On a hill to the north above Garmouth stand the Browlands Standing Stones, four large stones erected around 1500BC and believed to be the remains of a stone circle.

Perhaps surprisingly, Kingston's name does not commemorate the landing of Charles II here in the 17th century. The village was previously known as the Port of Garmouth, but was renamed by Mr Dodsworth of Kingston-upon-Hull and Mr Osbourne of York in 1784 in honour of their old home. They leased the extensive forest of Glenmore from the Duke of Gordon, felled the timber and floated rafts of these to export from Kingston to English shipyards. They then encouraged a shipwright, Thomas Hustwick, to establish a shipyard at the river mouth. Shipbuilding flourished from 1789 to around 1890, with some 80,000 tons of shipping launched from 19 different shipbuilding companies. The great floods known as the 'Muckle Spate' of 1829 altered the course of the Spey estuary, but it was not this that caused the eventual decline of the port, but rather the demise of wooden ships at the end of the 19th century.

**Facilities**: hotel and B&Bs. Post office and store (in Garmouth). Local bus service.

Follow MCT signs through the pretty village of Garmouth, past a small shop and post office, to turn left into Church Road and reach a disused railway line at the edge of the village. Descend steps to reach this, turning right, east, on it, following NCR 1 signposts to Portgordon, 5 miles. You will soon cross the mighty iron structure of the Spey Viaduct, from which there are very fine views out over the Spey estuary. On the far side of the river continue ahead on the cycle track, or footpath to its left, to reach a crossing track in about 400 yards. Turn left here, so joining the Speyside Way.

*The Spey estuary*

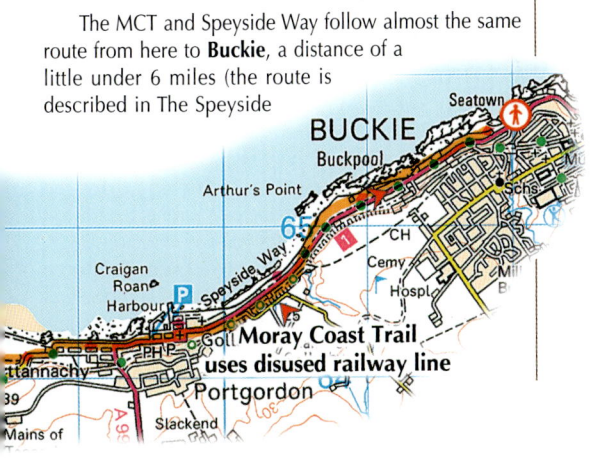

The original **Spey Viaduct** was designed by Joseph Mitchell for the Inverness and Aberdeen Junction Railway. The main span measured 230 feet in length, and each of the six approach spans was 30 feet. The line opened in August 1858, but the present lattice-girder structure replaced the original viaduct in 1906. It had to be a very wide bridge because of the force and constantly shifting nature of the Spey beneath it.

The MCT and Speyside Way follow almost the same route from here to **Buckie**, a distance of a little under 6 miles (the route is described in The Speyside

## THE SPEYSIDE WAY

Way, Stages 9 and 10, above). However, the two routes do part company in one short section – the Speyside Way takes a coastal route through Portgordon, whereas the MCT follows a disused railway line at the rear of the village. For those wishing to keep to the official route of the MCT through Portgordon the route is described below.

At the war memorial in **Portgordon**, the Speyside Way and MCT part company for a while. For the MCT turn right to reach the village hall, 20 yards after which turn left onto the MCT which shares its route with NCR 1, as both follow the line of a disused railway line. The route passes to the rear of Portgordon's houses at 'roof height', so offering a pleasant balcony trail. On reaching the distinctive National Cycle Trail Network metal signpost, indicating that Buckie is 1¼ miles ahead, turn sharp right to pass under **Bridge No 74** and so return to the coastal road and the route of the Speyside Way.

### STAGE 5
*Buckie to Findochty*

| | |
|---|---|
| **Distance** | 4¾ miles/7.6km |
| **Maps** | OS Landranger 28 (Elgin & Dufftown) |

*For more information about Buckie, see The Speyside Way, Stage 10.*

At Buckpool harbour you will see a green fingerpost which indicates that the MCT continues for ½ mile into the heart of Buckie. Keeping to the seaward side of the main road, walk from Buckpool harbour to **Buckie** harbour. From this working harbour keep to the pavement of the main coast road, heading for Portessie. Pass Buckie fish market. The commercial fishing area is hardly picturesque, but it is full of interest. Passing the shipyards you enter Gordonsburgh, followed shortly by Ianstown. Continue along Reidhaven Street and then, quite suddenly, the grime and bustle of a shipbuilding town gives way once more to an tranquil, relatively undeveloped rocky coastline, as the MCT begins its journey round Portessie Bay.

## Moray Coast Trail Stage 5 – Buckie to Findochty

Walk along the grassy foreshore, pass the houses of **Portessie**, and the Great Eastern Road Coastal Car Park, and walk above or along Strathlene Sands, heading for the Moray Firth Lookout Point in ¾ mile.

This fine headland at **Strathlene** was the site of an outdoor swimming pool and lido from 1932 until the 1970s. It was finally infilled in 2005, and an information board on the headland tells its full story – of popular venue to steady decline, as changing aspirations and holiday destinations altered the face of Scottish tourism during the 20th century. Today, there is an excellent 'all-abilities path' around Strathlene headland, so that all can now enjoy this magnificent coast, even wheelchair users.

Follow a metalled drive from 'The Lodge' out onto the grassy headland (picnic tables), passing old Strathlene House on the way. Take the smooth and clear trail ahead, and where this 'all-abilities path' comes to an end continue on a rougher, narrow and undulating trail around the rocky headland, passing the edge of golf links (beware flying golf balls). On rounding the headland, picturesque **Findochty** comes into view. Descend School Hill into the village.

*THE SPEYSIDE WAY*

*Looking across Portessie and tranquil Portessie Bay*

## FINDOCHTY

This very picturesque fishing village on the Moray coast is famous for its brightly painted old houses, particularly those around the harbour. Founded in 1598, its heyday was in the 19th century with the white fish and herring trade. The Hythe harbour dates back to 1880, but nowadays is mainly used by pleasure craft. On Long Head, a peninsula to the east of the village, is a church that used to act as a beacon for shipping. The cliffs around the village are an excellent place from which to scan the sea for cetaceans (whales, dolphins and porpoises).

**Facilities**: B&B, caravan/camping site. Bakery. Post office. Bus service.

## STAGE 6
*Findochty to Cullen*

| | |
|---|---|
| **Distance** | 4½ miles/7.1km |
| **Maps** | OS Landranger 28 (Elgin & Dufftown) and 29 (Banff & Huntly) |

Pass immediately to the right of **Findochty**'s sheltered marina/harbour and head up Sterlochy Street. Keep the bulk of the village on your right as you round the

## Moray Coast Trail Stage 6 – Findochty to Cullen

headland to reach Sandy Creek Beach. Climb the path on the far side of this small beach onto the coastal cliffs, now heading away from the village. Soon an excellent yard-wide surfaced path is encountered. Follow this eastwards along the coast, soon passing a viewpoint and information board. This fine trail, a specially constructed cycle track, part of the Moray Coast Cycle Route, is more used by walkers than cyclists. It leads over the tops of the cliffs, all the way to **Portknockie**.

> The **coast around Portknockie** is full of interest. The Green Castle, an 80ft-high promontory that protects Portknockie harbour, is thought to have been occupied from the Iron Age (1000BC) to when the Vikings were raiding this coast in AD1000, and remains at the site show similarities to the Pictish fort at Burghead. The Three Creeks shoreline by Portknockie village is one of windswept headlands, skerries, rock pools and shingle beds, all of which provide ideal habitat for sea birds. Herring and black-backed gulls, black shags, guillemots, kittiwakes, fulmars and oystercatchers are all commonly seen. Common eider ducks are found in the bay in early summer, and rock doves, turnstones, skylarks and yellow hammers can be observed in the area. Sparse vegetation of grass, heather, gorse and thrift, supported by thin acid soils, covers the top of the windswept coastal cliffs, below which lies heavily folded quartzite and slate, formed over 650 million years ago. Wave and wind erosion have created the numerous stacks, arches, ledges and caves that are such a feature of this magnificent stretch of coast.

Follow NCR 1 through the village, passing above Portknockie's picturesque harbour. Leaving the port area turn right along Patrol Road. Pass above the Three Creeks area and follow the sign to the Bow Fiddle Rock. Near the end of the village leave NCR 1, which heads to the right, and continue ahead onto the cliffs (MCT signpost). But before following the main trail, be sure to make the short detour on the signposted path on the left to **Bow Fiddle Rock**.

*The Speyside Way*

**Bow Fiddle Rock**, the best-known rock feature on the Portknockie coast, is one of Britain's most amazing sea rock arches and haunt of many sea birds. There is a seat provided, from which to enjoy this quite stupendous natural feature, a slender rock arch on a rocky islet, a few yards off the mainland. It originally started as a sea cave at the base of the headland, and was widened by wave action on its weaker rock strata until eventually the sea was able to flow through the naturally formed arch. In time this arch will collapse to leave yet another sea stack on the coast.

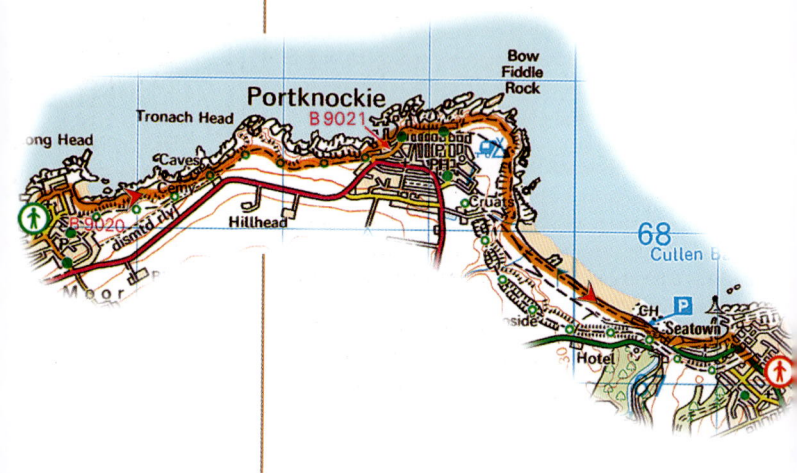

Passing Bow Fiddle Rock you round the headland and soon the village of Cullen comes into view, your final destination. Note the impressive railway viaduct, now disused. On reaching a waymarked path to Jenny's Well and Cullen, turn left on this down a flight of concrete steps towards the sea. Look to your left on this descent to see another rock arch, this one known as the Whale's Mouth, for reasons that will be readily apparent. The path leads down over rocks to arrive at the north-western end of Cullen Sands. ◀ Walk across the sands of **Cullen Bay**. At the far end of the beach, climb the steps to the

> This path may be slippery and dangerous in wet and windy weather. In that case, continue on the higher path which eventually leads to Cullen.

*Bow Fiddle Rock, Portknockie*

right of a huge boulder. Walk to the left of the massive eight-arched railway viaduct, cross a footbridge over the river and enter the village of **Cullen**. Walk to the harbour, where you will find a sign directing you to the right, to Town Square. Climb steeply to meet the main road. Turn left along this to pass through a railway arch, after which a further short climb leads to The Square (toilets) and the end of the MCT.

## CULLEN

Cullen is an old settlement, established in 1189. Until the herring boom of the 1800s its wealth came from textiles and threadmaking. The coastal village is built around the mouth of the Burn of Deskford and has two distinctive areas, the first close to the sea and the other inland and uphill. The fishing village area, known as Seatown, established in the 1820s, is a collection of small stone-built, brightly coloured fisherman's cottages. Cullen harbour is at the eastern end of Seatown, the original one having been built by Thomas Telford. The inland part of Cullen, where the shops, cafés and services are located, is reached from Seatown via a wide main street under the most easterly of three railway viaducts. The imposing Cullen Viaducts were built because the powerful Countess of Seafield, who owned the land hereabouts, would not allow the Great North of Scotland Railway to build its line across her land. Now disused, the line and the viaducts form part of Sustrans National Cycle Network. A form of smoked haddock, potato and onion soup called Cullen Skink is named after the village. It also boasts a famous homemade ice-cream shop.

**Facilities**: independent hostel, hotels, B&Bs, caravan/camping site. Cafés. Co-op food store and other shops. Bank and post office. Bus services.

Those who want to explore the coast further can follow the 1½-mile waymarked **Salmon Bothy Path** from the edge of Cullen eastwards to Portlong Hythe and return. Near here is the site of a former salmon bothy, but only the old launching ramp remains. On this walk it is possible to climb up to Nelson's Seat, a good viewpoint.

# APPENDIX A
*Route summary table*

| Stages | | Distance (miles/km) |
|---|---|---|
| **Prologue** | | |
| Stage 1 | Roybridge to Laggan | 28½/46 |
| Stage 1A | Spean Bridge to Laggan | 34½/55.4 |
| Side trip | Garva Bridge to Loch Spey return | 14/22 |
| Stage 1B | Fort Augustus to Laggan | 31/50 |
| Stage 2 | Laggan to Newtonmore via Glen Banchor | 10/16.2 |
| Stage 2A | Laggan to Newtonmore via the Military Road | 15/24.4 |
| **Badenoch Way and links** | | |
| Stage 1 | Newtonmore to Kingussie | 2¾/4.5 |
| Stage 2 | Kingussie to Dalraddy | 12½/20.1 |
| Stage 3 | Dalraddy to Aviemore | 3¾/6 |
| **Speyside Way** | | |
| Stage 1 | Aviemore to Boat of Garten | 6/9.7 |
| Stage 2 | Boat of Garten to Nethy Bridge | 4½/7.2 |
| Stage 3 | Nethy Bridge to Grantown-on-Spey | 6/9.7 |
| Stage 4 | Grantown-on-Spey to Cromdale | 3½/5.6 |
| Stage 5 | Cromdale to Ballindalloch station | 11/17.7 |
| Stage 6 | Ballindalloch station to Aberlour | 10/16.1 |
| Stage 7 | Aberlour to Craigellachie | 2/3.2 |
| Stage 8 | Craigellachie to Fochabers | 13/20.9 |
| Stage 9 | Fochabers to Spey Bay | 5/8 |
| Stage 10 | Spey Bay to Buckie | 5/8 |
| **Tomintoul Spur** | Tomintoul to Ballindalloch station | 15/24 |
| **Dufftown Loop** | Aberlour to Dufftown to Craigellachie | 9½/15.3 |

## THE SPEYSIDE WAY

| Stages | | Distance (miles/km) |
|---|---|---|
| **Dava Way** | | |
| Stage 1 | Grantown-on-Spey to Dava, including 'Viewpoint Walk' and Huntly's Cave detours | 8¾/14.2 |
| Stage 2 | Dava to Dunphail | 6½/10.5 |
| Stage 3 | Dunphail to Forres | 9½/15.3 |
| **Moray Coast Trail** | | |
| Stage 1 | Forres to Findhorn | 6/9.7 |
| Stage 2 | Findhorn to Burghead | 7¼/11.7 |
| Stage 3 | Burghead to Lossiemouth | 9¼/15 |
| Stage 4 | Lossiemouth to Buckie | 15¼/24.6 |
| Stage 5 | Buckie to Findochty | 4¾/7.6 |
| Stage 6 | Findochty to Cullen | 4½/7.1 |

# APPENDIX B
## *Useful contacts*

**Speyside Way Official Website**
www.speysideway.org
Excellent web resource maintained by Speyside Way staff. It includes details on route, accommodation and public transport in the area, and has useful web links.

**Speyside Way Ranger Service (Moray Section)**
Speyside Way Visitor Centre, Old Station Building, Aberlour, Banffshire, AB38 9QP
Tel: 01340 881266
Email: speyside.way@moray.gov.uk
An information pack on the Speyside Way can be requested from the Ranger's office. The visitor centre has informative displays and a DVD on the Speyside Way, plus other general tourist information for the area.

**Dava Way**
www.davaway.org.uk
Well-designed, informative site about the route, places of interest and useful web links.

**Moray Coast Trail**
www.morayways.org.uk/moray-coast-trail.asp
Good website containing maps and route description, plus a variety of links to Moray Council and Community Pages with accommodation; other sections have information on the Speyside Way and Dava Way.

**Moray Way**
www.morayways.org.uk

**Visit Scotland**
www.visitscotland.com
Email: info@visitscotland.com
National Information and Booking Line: 0845 22 55 121
The official site for Scotland's national tourism organisation. Includes information on Tourist Information Centres.
It operates a specialist website for walking:
www.walking.visitscotland.com

**Undiscovered Scotland**
www.undiscoveredscotland.co.uk
A one-stop site for information about towns, villages, tourist attractions, accommodation, food and history. Good selection of photographs.

**Gazetteer for Scotland**
www.geo.ed.ac.uk/scotgaz/gaztitle.html
The largest Scottish resource available on the internet – an immense collection.

**Whisky**
www.scotchwhisky.net
An informative site about Scottish whisky and distilleries in Scotland.

**Scottish Youth Hostel Association**
www.syha.org.uk
Book accommodation on line or by phone.
Tel: 0845 2937373

**Independent Hostels in Scotland**
www.hostel-scotland.co.uk
The Blue Guide of independent hostels in Scotland, available from TICs and numerous other outlets in Scotland.

## *The Speyside Way*

**Walking in Scotland**
www.walkscotland.com

**Scottish Outdoor Access Code**
www.outdooraccess-scotland.com
Information about the Access Code in Scotland.

**Hillphones**
www.snh.org.uk/hillphones
This website provides contact details for estates where stalking can affect access.

**Cairngorms National Park**
www.cairngorms.co.uk
The official website of the Cairngorms National Park.

**Moray Council Ranger Service**
www.moray.gov.uk
Tel: 01340 881266
Countryside Ranger Services throughout Moray.

**Long Distance Walkers Association**
www.ldwa.org.uk
Contains a directory of long distance paths in the UK, the largest and most comprehensive available. It also includes the Register of National Trail Walkers, with full details of the scheme.

**Mountain Bothies Association**
www.mountainbothies.org.uk
Maintains over 100 shelters in remote parts of the UK.

**Scottish Rights of Way and Access Society**
24 Annandale Street, Edinburgh EH47 4AN. Tel: 0131 558 1222
www.scotways.com
Email: info@scotways.com
It works to protect and develop access for all in the Scottish countryside.

**Traveline Scotland**
www.travelinescotland.com
Tel: 0871 2002233
Information on any public transport service in Scotland, covering rail, coach and bus services.

**National Rail Enquiries**
www.nationalrail.co.uk
Tel: 08457 484950
(from outside UK +44 20 72785240)
Timetables and fares for all UK rail companies.

**ScotRail**
www.scotrail.co.uk
Rail company in Scotland. For information on timetables contact National Rail Enquiries or Traveline Scotland (above).

**Scottish Citylink**
www.citylink.co.uk
Tel: 08705 505050
Coaches from Glasgow or Edinburgh to destinations including Aviemore and Fort William.

**Stagecoach/Bluebird**
www.stagecoachbus.com
Major bus services in Speyside region. For telephone information on timetables contact Traveline Scotland (see above).

**Strathspey Steam Railway**
www.strathspeyrailway.co.uk
Tel: 01479 810725
Timetables, fares and information on this popular tourist attraction.

**Baggage Transfer along the Speyside Way**
Ace Taxis can provide a daily baggage-transfer service.
Tel: 01343 820820
Email: acetaxismoray@tiscali.co.uk

# APPENDIX C
## Further reading

**Scottish Hill Tracks**. Published by the Scottish Rights of Way and Access Society and the Scottish Mountaineering Trust. 5th edn (rev), 2011. Definitive guide to over 300 hill tracks, old roads and rights of way throughout Scotland. Thoroughly recommended.

**UK Trailwalker's Handbook**. Published by Cicerone Press, 2009. www.cicerone.co.uk. A directory of long distance paths in England, Scotland, Wales and Northern Ireland compiled by the Long Distance Walkers Association. Information on 730 national trails, long distance paths and anytime challenges, including the trails featured in this book.

**The Speyside Way – the Complete Map**. Published by Footprint www.footprintmaps.co.uk. Email: footprint@stirlingsurveys.co.uk

**Long Distance Route – Speyside Way: XT40 Map**. Published by Harvey Maps www.harveymaps.co.uk. Email: sales@harveymaps.co.uk

**The Moray Way Map**. Published by The Moray Way Association. Available from shops and distilleries in the Moray region.

**The Spey – from Source to Sea** by Donald Barr and Brian Barr. Published by Luath Press, 2009. Informative text and excellent photographs, a good souvenir of walking along The Spey.

**The Speyside Way, an Aerial Odyssey**. DVD. 2007. Filmed along the Speyside Way with a soundtrack by Speyside fiddler James Alexander and Fochabers Fiddlers. Available from Speyside Rangers Office or Moray Council. Proceeds used for the management and maintenance of The Speyside Way.

**Malt Whisky** by Charles MacLean. Published by Mitchell Beazley. Reprinted 1997. A well-illustrated coffee-table guide.

**Whisky and Scotland by Neil Gunn.** Published by Souvenir Press Ltd. New edition 1998. New edition of a classic written in the 1930s.

**The Whisky River: Distilleries of Speyside** by Robin Laing and Bob Dewar. Published by Luath Press, 2007. Describes a journey to all the distilleries on Speyside.

**The Speyside Line** by Dick Jackson. Published by the Great North of Scotland Railway Association. The story of the railway that ran from Craigellachie to Boat of Garten.

**The Spey Viaduct** by John Ross. Published by the Great North of Scotland Railway Association. The story of the Great North of Scotland's viaduct over the mouth of the River Spey.

**Collins Bird Guide** by Mullarney, Svensson, Zetterstrom and Grant. Published by HarperCollins Publishers Ltd, 1999. Excellent text and drawings. Includes the birds that will be observed on the trails.

# APPENDIX D
## Whisky production and Speyside distilleries

### Whisky production

Malted barley, yeast and water are the three ingredients that are needed to produce malt whisky. Water is of the utmost importance, as the final flavour of the product depends critically on the provenance and qualities of the water. Indeed the availability of a pure, clean water source often determined the location of a distillery. Firstly barley is malted – soaked in water for a few days and then spread and frequently turned on a malting floor – a process that allows the barley to partially germinate, converting starch into sugars. The malted barley (or 'malt') is then dried to end this germination. Nowadays this process is seldom carried out at the distillery, which sources malted barley ready for the mashing process.

Mashing involves grinding the malt to a fine 'grist' and then dissolving this in hot water to produce a 'mash' in a vessel known as a 'mash tun'. It is the local water that accounts for much of the difference in flavour between different malt whiskies. The mash is heated to improve the solubility of the ingredients. The liquid is drained off and the process repeated twice to maximise extraction from the malt. This liquid, 'wort', is cooled so that yeast can be added to start fermentation, when it becomes known as 'wash'. This fermentation takes place in a vessel known as a 'washback'.

Once fermentation is complete, distillation can begin. The traditional copper stills used for distillation operate in pairs, the 'wash still' followed by the 'spirit still', so that the alcoholic vapours produced on heating the wash, once condensed, could be redistilled to raise the alcoholic content of the distillate. With an alcoholic content of about 70%, the young spirit is matured in oak casks for at least eight years to produce malt whisky. This maturation process loses about 2% of the spirit in the casks each year, this portion being known as 'the angel's share'. The alcohol will then usually be diluted to about 40% for bottling.

### Distilleries of the region

**Tamdhu** (Speyside Way, Stage 6)
The Tamdhu distillery was built in 1896, but like many distilleries it suffered during the Depression and war years and so was closed between 1927 and 1947. Its water is drawn from Tamdhu springs. Tamdhu is owned by Highland Distilleries, and much of its output forms a major component of the blended Famous Grouse. The single malt 'Tamdhu' was launched in 1976. It is the only distillery on Speyside to malt its own barley on site. It is not open to visitors.

**Knockando** (Speyside Way, Stage 6)
Knockando is from the Gaelic for 'little black hill'. The distillery was built in 1898 to take advantage of the clear water available from the southern slopes of Knock Hill; today the source is the Cardnach Spring. When production first started, the two huge pot stills of the distillery could produce 2500 gallons of spirit per week, and these remain in use today. Workers were housed in cottages built around the distillery, so creating a new community.

The site closed in 1983, but was bought by Inver House Distillers in 1988 and reopened. Its output is a major contributor to Haig's blends. It is not open to visitors.

**Cardhu** (Speyside Way, Stage 6)
Cardhu means 'black rock' in Gaelic. In 1824 John Cumming obtained a licence to distil whisky legally at his farm at Cardow in Upper Knockando, though he had been operating an illegal still since 1813! In 1884 a new distillery was erected next to the farm. The water is drawn from springs on Mannoch Hill and the Lyne Burn. The name of the distillery has changed several times, between Cardow and Cardhu. In 2002 Cardhu ceased to be a single malt, but a single malt was relaunched in 2005. It is currently owned by Diageo. A visitor centre was opened in 1988. Tours, for which there is an admission charge, are available on weekdays throughout the year and at weekends from July to September. The site is on the B9102 in Cardow, 1.5 miles north of the Speyside Way as it passes through Knockando.

**Dailuaine** (Speyside Way, Stage 6)
Dailuaine means 'green vale' in Gaelic. The distillery was founded in 1851 by William MacKenzie in a hollow next to the Carron Burn, and after 30 years was one of the largest distilleries in the Highlands. Like many distilleries it has had to be rebuilt after several fires. Its water source is the Ballieumullich Burn. It used the Spey Valley Railway to distribute its products and even had its own locomotives. This line closed in 1967, but the company preserved locomotive Dailuaine No 1, which today runs on the Strathspey Railway. It is a major component of Johnnie Walker blends, and since 1991 has bottled single malts. The company is owned by Diageo. It is not open to the public.

**Aberlour** (Speyside Way, Stage 7)
Aberlour in Gaelic means 'Mouth of the chattering burn'. James Fleming established his distillery in 1879, drawing its water from springs on the Corbett of Ben Rinnes. The distillery, which had to be rebuilt after a fire in 1898, has had many owners, the current being Chivas Brothers. A visitor centre was opened in 2001: a charge is made for visits, but this includes a two-hour tour and a tutored 'nosing and tasting'. Tours are available throughout the year.

**Glenallachie** (Speyside Way, Stage 7)
The distillery was built in 1967 by a division of Scottish and Newcastle Breweries. It is located at the foot of Ben Rinnes, and its water source is springs on this Corbett. The site is 1 mile south of Aberlour, on a minor road off the A95. It is owned by Campbell Distillers Ltd, does not produce single malt and is not open to the public.

**Craigellachie** (Speyside Way, Stage 8)
The distillery is situated on the hillside above the village of the same name. It was founded by Alexander Edward in 1891 and draws its water from Little Conval Hill. Under former ownership it was a major constituent of White Horse blended whisky. It is now owned by John Dewar and Sons Ltd. It is not open to the public.

**Macallan** (Speyside Way, Stage 8)
The distillery was built by Alexander Reid in 1824, with its water drawn from the Ringorm Burn. The stills are the smallest on Speyside. Unusually, all the whisky is matured in old oak

sherry casks, and although single malt was not bottled until the 1970s it is now acclaimed as one of the finest single malts produced. The distillery is owned by the Erdington Group and is situated 1 mile south-west of Craigellachie, south off the B9102. The visitor centre is open throughout the year, for which there is an admission charge.

**Glen Grant** (Speyside Way, Stage 8)
This distillery was founded in 1840 by John and James Grant. After the death of James, his son, Major James Grant, took over the distillery, a charismatic character who ran the company for 60 years. The water source is the Caperdonich Well. The distillery remained in the family until 1977 and is currently owned by Campari. Major Grant planted a renowned garden which has now been restored and, together with the distillery, is open to visitors throughout the year (there is a charge for entrance to both attractions).

**Glenfiddich** (Dufftown Loop, Stage 2)
Glen Fiddich, meaning 'valley of the deer' in Gaelic, is the home of arguably 'The World's Favourite Single Malt Whisky'. William Grant built his distillery with the help of his wife, nine children and a stonemason in 1886. The water is drawn from the Robbie Dubh, and the first spirit was produced on Christmas Day, 1887. Unlike many distilleries it is still family run, owned by descendants of William Grant. In 1963 this was the first distillery to market its single malt in the United Kingdom and overseas, while other distilleries at that time were still selling their single malts to blenders. The site uses unusually small copper pot stills and has traditional warehouses with earthen floors and stone walls. Excellent free one-hour Standard Tours of the distillery are available on weekdays all year around, with additional weekend visits from Easter to October (Monday to Saturday, 9.30am to 4.30pm and Sunday 12 noon to 4.30pm). A 'wee-dram' of standard 12-year old Glenfiddich single malt whisky is included. An in-depth 2½ hour Connoisseur's Tour can be booked, for which a fee is charged (including the possibility of sampling some of the older single malt whiskies). The site also has an artist's gallery, café and gift shop.

Descriptions of the following distilleries can be found in the text:
**Tormore** (page 123)
**Glenlivet** (page 148)
**Cragganmore** (page 151)
**Dallas Dhu** (page 179)
**Benromach** (page 186)

# CICERONE GUIDES TO THE BRITISH ISLES

**BRITISH ISLES CHALLENGES, COLLECTIONS AND ACTIVITIES**
The End to End Trail
The Mountains of England and Wales
  1 Wales
  2 England
The National Trails
The Relative Hills of Britain
The Ridges of England, Wales and Ireland
The UK Trailwalker's Handbook
Three Peaks, Ten Tors
**MOUNTAIN LITERATURE**
Unjustifiable Risk?
**UK CYCLING**
Border Country Cycle Routes
Lands End to John O'Groats
Rural Rides
  2 East Surrey
South Lakeland Cycle Rides
The Lancashire Cycleway
**SCOTLAND**
Backpacker's Britain
  Central and Southern Scottish Highlands
Northern Scotland
Ben Nevis and Glen Coe
Border Pubs and Inns
North to the Cape
Not the West Highland Way
World Mountain Ranges: Scotland
Scotland's Best Small Mountains
Scotland's Far West
Scotland's Mountain Ridges
Scrambles in Lochaber
The Border Country
The Central Highlands
The Great Glen Way
The Isle of Skye
The Pentland Hills: A Walker's Guide
The Scottish Glens
  2 The Atholl Glens
  3 The Glens of Rannoch
  4 The Glens of Trossach
  5 The Glens of Argyll
  6 The Great Glen
The Southern Upland Way
The Speyside Way
The West Highland Way
Walking in Scotland's Far North
Walking in the Cairngorms
Walking in the Hebrides
Walking in the Ochils, Campsie Fells and Lomond Hills
Walking in Torridon
Walking Loch Lomond and the Trossachs
Walking on Harris and Lewis
Walking on Jura, Islay and Colonsay
Walking on the Isle of Arran
Walking on the Orkney and Shetland Isles
Walking the Galloway Hills
Walking the Lowther Hills
Walking the Munros
  1 Southern, Central and Western Highlands
  2 Northern Highlands and the Cairngorms
Winter Climbs Ben Nevis and Glen Coe
Winter Climbs in the Cairngorms
**NORTHERN ENGLAND TRAILS**
A Northern Coast to Coast Walk
Backpacker's Britain
  Northern England
Hadrian's Wall Path
The Dales Way
The Pennine Way
The Spirit of Hadrian's Wall
**NORTH EAST ENGLAND, YORKSHIRE DALES AND PENNINES**
A Canoeist's Guide to the North East
Historic Walks in North Yorkshire
South Pennine Walks
The Cleveland Way and the Yorkshire Wolds Way
The North York Moors
The Reivers Way
The Teesdale Way
The Yorkshire Dales Angler's Guide
The Yorkshire Dales
  North and East
  South and West
Walking in County Durham
Walking in Northumberland
Walking in the North Pennines
Walking in the Wolds
Walks in Dales Country
Walks in the Yorkshire Dales
Walks on the North York Moors
  Books 1 & 2
**NORTH WEST ENGLAND AND THE ISLE OF MAN**
A Walker's Guide to the Lancaster Canal
Historic Walks in Cheshire
Isle of Man Coastal Path
The Isle of Man
The Ribble Way
Walking in Lancashire
Walking in the Forest of Bowland and Pendle
Walking on the West Pennine Moors
Walks in Lancashire Witch Country
Walks in Ribble Country
Walks in Silverdale and Arnside
Walks in the Forest of Bowland
**LAKE DISTRICT**
An Atlas of the English Lakes
Coniston Copper Mines
Great Mountain Days in the Lake District
Lake District Winter Climbs
Roads and Tracks of the Lake District
Rocky Rambler's Wild Walks
Scrambles in the Lake District
  North & South
Short Walks in Lakeland
  1 South Lakeland
  2 North Lakeland
  3 West Lakeland
The Central Fells
The Cumbria Coastal Way
The Cumbria Way and the Allerdale Ramble
The Lake District Anglers' Guide
The Mid-Western Fells
The Near Eastern Fells
The Southern Fells
The Tarns of Lakeland
  1 West & 2 East
Tour of the Lake District
**DERBYSHIRE, PEAK DISTRICT AND MIDLANDS**
High Peak Walks
The Star Family Walks
Walking in Derbyshire
White Peak Walks
  The Northern Dales
  The Southern Dales
**SOUTHERN ENGLAND**
A Walker's Guide to the Isle of Wight
London – The definitive walking Guide
The Cotswold Way
The Greater Ridgeway
The Lea Valley Walk
The North Downs Way
The South Downs Way
The South West Coast Path
The Thames Path
Walking in Bedfordshire
Walking in Berkshire
Walking in Buckinghamshire
Walking in Kent
Walking in Sussex
Walking in the Isles of Scilly
Walking in the Thames Valley
Walking on Dartmoor
**WALES AND WELSH BORDERS**
Backpacker's Britain: Wales
Glyndwr's Way
Great Mountain Days in Snowdonia
Hillwalking in Snowdonia
Hillwalking in Wales
  Vols 1 & 2
Offa's Dyke Path
Ridges of Snowdonia
Scrambles in Snowdonia
The Ascent of Snowdon
The Lleyn Peninsula Coastal Path
The Pembrokeshire Coastal Path
The Shropshire Hills
The Spirit Paths of Wales
Walking in Pembrokeshire
Walking on the Brecon Beacons
Welsh Winter Climbs

For full information on all our British and international guides, please visit our website: **www.cicerone.co.uk**.

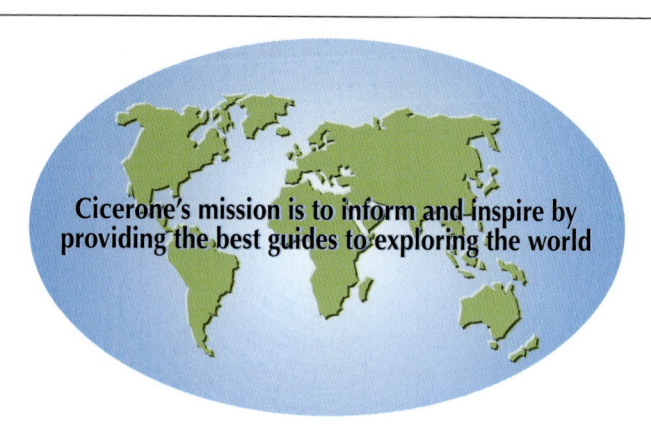

**Cicerone's mission is to inform and inspire by providing the best guides to exploring the world**

Since its foundation 40 years ago, Cicerone has specialised in publishing guidebooks and has built a reputation for quality and reliability. It now publishes nearly 300 guides to the major destinations for outdoor enthusiasts, including Europe, UK and the rest of the world.

Written by leading and committed specialists, Cicerone guides are recognised as the most authoritative. They are full of information, maps and illustrations so that the user can plan and complete a successful and safe trip or expedition – be it a long face climb, a walk over Lakeland fells, an alpine cycling tour, a Himalayan trek or a ramble in the countryside.

With a thorough introduction to assist planning, clear diagrams, maps and colour photographs to illustrate the terrain and route, and accurate and detailed text, Cicerone guides are designed for ease of use and access to the information.

If the facts on the ground change, or there is any aspect of a guide that you think we can improve, we are always delighted to hear from you.

**Cicerone Press**
2 Police Square  Milnthorpe  Cumbria  LA7 7PY
Tel: 015395 62069  Fax: 015395 63417
info@cicerone.co.uk  www.cicerone.co.uk

**CICERONE**